I AM NOT BIPOLAR

A Memoir

BRIAN TALARCZYK

Mountain Ash
Press

ISBN - Print - 978-1-965889-03-9

ISBN - Ebook - 978-1-965889-04-6

Published by Mountain Ash Press - https://mountainash.press

This is a true story.

However, the names of some people have been altered to protect their identities.

for Kim,
for helping me understand who I am

for my children,
for allowing me to become the father I always wanted to be

Introduction

Dear Reader:

This book was written, in large part, as a way for me to address my fears of telling my son and my daughter about my mental illness. Before publishing this memoir, my wife and I informed them I have bipolar disorder. However, since they are both presently in elementary school, we kept the conversation simple.

In a few years, if they so choose, they will have an opportunity to read this book and learn more about my bipolar history. As such I've left them a few notes along the way, but until then, I hope you find meaning and support in them, too.

Sincerely,

Brian

To be nobody but yourself in a world which is doing its best,
night and day, to make you everybody else, means to fight
the hardest battle which any human being can fight;
and never stop fighting.

e. e. cummings

PART I

Aversion

Friday, April 27th, 2001

I awake to the sound of my Motorola flip-phone vibrating on the nightstand beside the bed. I pick up the phone and see there are six messages, all from my sister Joy, all left in the middle of the night.

Something's wrong.

Something is very, very wrong.

Two messages means Joy has something important to tell me. Six messages in just a few short hours is a crisis.

I sit up and listen to the first.

"Beej, please call me as soon as you get this," she says in a state of utter panic. "Dad had a heart attack; he's in the hospital here in New Haven."

A wave of anxiety paralyzes me, and I drop the phone. Sarah, my girlfriend, rolls over from her deep sleep and puts her hand on my thigh. She can tell by the stunned look on my face that something is, indeed, wrong.

"Brian, are you okay?" she asks. "What happened?"

I don't know what to say to her. I don't want to believe it. I don't want to verbalize it and make it real.

I attempt to call Joy, but I can't get a cell phone signal in the rural town of Waterville Valley, New Hampshire, where Sarah and I are visiting my best friend from high school, Marcia, and her husband, Charlie. I had brought Sarah here to introduce her to Marcia for the first time – to show Sarah off like a trophy I had recently won. We had arrived just the night before, but now we must go. Immediately.

We pack our suitcases, frantically, then get on the highway, where I am finally able to reach Joy.

"How is he doing?" I ask, now in a state of full panic.

"It's not good, Beej," she says in a tearful voice. "His heart attack resulted in further complications in the middle of the night, and he slipped into a coma."

I begin to cry. Sarah grabs hold of my hand and steps on the gas.

"He's going to be okay, Brian," Sarah says.

Yes, he's going to be okay, I tell myself, over and over and over again.

He's going to be just fine.

The drive to the hospital in New Haven, Connecticut is a long one, made even longer by the early morning traffic. When we arrive, I leap out of the car and run ahead of Sarah, shaking and breathless. My watery eyes are blurry; my mind is spinning like a roulette wheel.

We stumble through an endless maze of dark hallways lined with wheelchairs and gurneys until we finally reach the ICU. I push open the heavy double-doors and see Joy standing in the waiting area next to Mom, Uncle Joe, Grandma, and the rest of our family. Joy runs to me. She hugs me and cries into my shoulder. I give her a moment to release, but my foreboding overcomes me.

"Joy, where's Dad?"

Joy leads me to the front desk, where she tells the on-duty nurse I'm her brother. The nurse nods, and we continue to Dad's room. When we reach it, Joy moves close to me, grabs hold of my arms, and stares deep into my eyes.

"They aren't sure if he's going to make it, Beej," she says, choking up.

I don't believe her. Dad's stronger than that. Dad's stronger than all of us.

"He'll pull through," I say. "Let me be with him."

I walk into the cool, dimly-lit room and close the door behind me. I gasp at the sight of Dad lying lifeless on the bed. An air tube is plugged into his nose, and electrodes are taped to his bare chest and fat belly. Wires extend from other parts of his body to bags of liquid that dangle above him like toys on a child's mobile.

I pull up a chair from the corner of the room and sit beside him, grabbing his hand with both of mine. It's warm and clammy, yet limp, absent. I examine his face, nested gently into the pillow. His lips are an off shade of violet, his cheeks flush white. His eyes remain closed. He seems unaware that I am here but appears to be at peace.

I want to say so many things, but I can barely get my thoughts past my stalled brain to my clenched throat. Finally, I mutter, "Hold on Dad."

Lord, God, I pray – please let him hold on.

I sit alone with him for a while, watching his torso move up and down in steady rhythm with the slow gurgle of the oxygen machine. I glance up at the heart monitor periodically and watch the green blips crawl slowly across the antiquated screen – tiny hints of life ticking like an analog clock.

I brush my hand along the side of his face and beg him to wake up, but I can tell we're beyond that now. He's beyond that. And when we both come to terms with that, I let go of his hand and walk over to the foot of his bed.

I stand as upright and strong as I can, taking deep breaths until I'm fully composed.

"Don't worry, Dad," I say. "I'll take care of Mom. I'll take care of everything. I promise."

I breathe in and calm myself further.

"I love you," I say, and just as I do, a steady buzz rings out and the green blips on the monitor go flat.

The word "journey" is often used to describe a series of events that take place throughout one's life that are difficult to deal with, such as "my journey with alcoholism," or "my journey with cancer," but I don't like that word. It makes alcoholism and cancer sound a lot more enjoyable than they are, as if the inflicted had thought about their struggles ahead of time, bought a plane ticket and some new hiking boots, loaded up a backpack with granola bars, and went on some glamorous excursion to explore them. Unfortunately, I don't have a better word which encompasses the breadth of my bipolar disorder experiences, and neither does thesaurus.com. Expedition, Pilgrimage, Odyssey, Adventure – none of them really cut it. Discovery is a bit closer, but doesn't pack as much of a punch as it probably should.

Whatever you want to call my "journey" with bipolar, it began in 2001. That was the year my father died, and his death was the trigger event that caused my illness to surface within me for the first time, even though it had been lurking inside my chromosomes since the day I was born. It was April 27th, 2001 to be exact, just three days before my 27th birthday, when I stood at the foot of my father's hospital bed and watched him die. He was 55 years old at the time, the same age I'll be turning in a few years. He was far too young to leave us; far too young to have a massive heart attack from which his body could not recover.

Even though my dad was not in the best health – 30 pounds over his ideal weight and smoking two packs of Marlboro Lights a day – losing him so suddenly confused us all. One day he was his jovial self, taking my mother to a Saturday movie matinee, driving down to Virginia to play in a golf tournament with me and my co-workers. The next, he was cheering on his racehorse at the *Off-Track Betting Center* in New Haven when he instantly began gasping for breath. Grabbing his chest, he fell to the ground and lay there unconscious for untold minutes.

In the weeks following his death, I missed him more and on deeper levels. The loving relationship we had shared had created a dependency I was not cognizant of. After the initial trauma faded, I drew inward. Instead of reaching out to Mom and Joy and burrowing into the love of our extended family in the greater New Haven area, I returned to my life in Alexandria, Virginia, where I was living at the time, and excluded them, refusing to allow myself to feel my cataclysmic loss.

I threw myself into the small software development business I had founded the year prior. Less than a week after the funeral, I was fully immersed in work, flying all around the country to visit clients, often without a reason. When working 40 hours a week wasn't enough to suppress the pain, I ramped up to 50. And when that still wasn't doing the trick, I pushed to 60. My colleagues and clients were amazed at my productivity, and I could feel myself soaring beyond my own wildest expectations for start-up success. I had morphed into a fast-talking, instant-thinking, hyper-vigilant super-creator. Rarely tired, always driven. By the time Thanksgiving rolled around, my consulting income was at an all-time high, but my emotional health was deep in the red, a condition I was in no way capable of confronting.

Since the funeral, I had allowed myself to be enticed home only twice. The first time was to attend the wedding of two close college friends, who asked me to sing and play acoustic guitar as they walked down the aisle. I played and sang terribly, drank myself into an incoherent stupor during the reception, and puked all over the hotel room. My second visit was to attend the first birthday party of my nephew, Josh. Joy and her husband, Greg, brought our entire family together for the celebration that August, a gathering that doubled as a chance for us to come together under happier circumstances after several months of lamenting my father's passing. But I did not stay long enough to engage in the inevitable rounds of tears and stories of all the things he did to make us laugh.

Mom and Joy had asked me to come home on multiple other occasions, to check up on me and make sure I was handling my dad's death in a healthy fashion, but I always had a good excuse. However, when Thanksgiving arrived, I had no choice in the matter. I was obliged to go to my Uncle Joe's house, where my father's family had gathered since I was a child. I had no excuses to save me, no way to block out the dissonant voices I knew I would have to endure.

By that time, of course, September 11th had turned the world upside-down. The attacks just a few months before were never far from anyone's mind. It was a very difficult time for our country, and for me, the tragedy furthered the grief and confusion I felt after losing my father. In the weeks that followed, I managed to conflate the sudden, horrific loss of life with my dad's death, forcing myself to stop thinking about either one. Somehow, in the dizzying fog of suppressed emotions, I believed that there was some mysterious connection between the two, and I promised myself I would get to the bottom of it one day, just as soon as I could take a break from work.

That would not, I firmly decided, be over Thanksgiving weekend. I was going to drive home to Connecticut, exchange superficial niceties with family and friends, then return to Virginia without so much as a moment of sentimentality. My goal for Thanksgiving dinner was to make an appearance at Uncle Joe's, smile and nod, then get out of there, emotionally unscathed.

It was delusional at best to have thought I could get through the gathering without incident. I had barely slept since my dad's death seven months before. Every nerve ending in my body was hypersensitive, and every breath I took was painful. Sure enough, from the moment I stepped into Uncle Joe's entryway, my plans went awry.

Barely in the front door, I felt the crush of Uncle Joe's beefy arms around me. I could smell the celebratory libations in his breath, and I felt his need to hold me fast. I could make no attempt to pry myself loose.

"We're gonna miss your father today," he said. "I'm gonna miss my big brother. These holidays will never be the same."

He broke down and wept into my captive chest. Over his shoulder, I watched everyone join him. My grandmother, who had glued herself to her parish priest's side since she laid my father in the ground, wailed as she had at the funeral. Joy, my normally sanguine sister, was tucked firmly into Greg's arms, sobbing gently. Even Nicky, my Aunt Louise's playful golden retriever, looked glum and listless.

The only person in the room who seemed to be holding it together was Mom, whose face betrayed none of the anguish she might have felt. She stood apart from the commotion, peacefully sipping her ginger ale, unperturbed by the sorrowful chorus. To look at her, one might have thought it was just another holiday at her in-laws. But I knew that deep inside, she must have been as dispirited as everyone else.

The manner in which Mom processed my father's passing was the polar opposite of mine. Though my dad was the center of her life for over 30 years, she had quickly adjusted to life without him, just like she quickly adjusts to pretty much anything. Each time I talked to her on the phone she was explaining her next coping mechanism to me. First, she joined a widows' support group assembled through her church, where she had found confederates from whom she could unabashedly derive comfort. Next, she took a new job as a librarian at the University of New Haven to support herself financially, where she became good friends with several of her co-workers. With additional support from Joy and Greg who live nearby, she pushed through the heart-wrenching loss of my father with poise and determination.

I forced myself to look away from Mom. I could feel a tug behind my eyes, and I was not about to fall prey to the communal outpouring of sadness that seemed to have turned the holiday into a reprise of Dad's wake and the gathering held after, right there in Uncle Joe's house.

I made a beeline for the dining room and poured myself an extra-large glass of red wine. As everyone filtered in for dinner, I made sure to sit at the opposite end of the table from Joy and Mom. I talked about the Yankees frustrating, postseason defeat with my cousins, but my mind had ventured far from the company of relatives. Inside my head, I had conversations with clients and colleagues and fretted because I wasn't actively working. *There is so much to be done*, I thought. My consulting work was eminently more important than Thanksgiving dinner. Uncle Joe was right. Our holidays would never be the same, but I would not engage in any moribund obsession with what a great guy Dad was. He was dead. I had responsibilities to take care of.

As we passed trays of antipasto around the table, seasoned with speculation over the Giants' prospects for reaching the Super-bowl, I remained aloof, concentrating on my inner monologue. Then, suddenly, all faded to an awkward silence as the inevitable awareness of 9/11 insinuated itself into our midst, snapping me out of my trance.

At first, the conversation around the dinner table was positive, upbeat, focused on the inspirational aftermaths of the tragedy: the bravery of the NYFD, NYPD, and first responders; how unified and supportive our nation had become as we bonded together to understand life in a post 9/11 world. Then, however, politics inserted its ugliness, and the conspiracy theories began to fly.

Since it was a long time ago, I don't recall everything that was discussed that day, but it went something like this:

"They give us colored threat codes to warn us about attacks – blue, green, yellow, orange – but they don't tell us what they really mean or how they'll protect us. . ."

"The government just needs an excuse to curtail our civil liberties. We'll be victims of the Patriot Act before any terrorists are caught. . ."

"No, that's not true. There are terrorists everywhere. Osama Bin Laden is trying to poison us all with anthrax. . ."

As the absurdity rambled on, I held my breath, wondering if someone was going to suggest that the terrorists had conspired to kill my dad as well before they destroyed the World Trade Center. It was an abstract notion, but it was an abstract day, at least for me. I shook my head to drive the bizarre thought out, but it bored more deeply into my cranium.

I needed to disengage, so I escaped to the adjacent kitchen, where I pretended to be engrossed in slicing Italian bread. Mom suddenly looked up. Our eyes connected and the lump that rose in my throat threatened to undo me. Her look asked the question I had so often heard over my lifetime. She needed no words to make me hear it.

"How are you doing?" her eyes implored.

I looked away. I could face neither her nor the answer she sought.

How am I doing?

Terrible. But I wasn't about to admit that to her. Or to myself.

My stomach tightened, and the taste of vomit formed in my mouth. Afraid I might hurl right there into the bread bowl, I darted down the hall to the bathroom, locked the door behind me, and sat on the cold, tiled floor next to the toilet, shaking. I could not speak or cry, and suddenly, everything I was holding inside heaved itself into the bowl. I was motionless. All I could do was kneel there, gripping the toilet seat like a sailor holding his ship's wheel as he steers through a perilous storm. When my body finally calmed, I studied the foul contents, examining each piece of myself.

I wanted to leave. Immediately. But I knew that wasn't an option, so I washed my face, straightened my clothing, and returned to my seat at the dinner table. Mom glanced down and cast another inquisitive look. I lowered my head so she could not see my eyes.

My muddled thoughts about my dad continued, and I was sure by this point everyone would be talking about him, extolling his virtues, tearfully reminding each other of his quirks and foibles: how much he loved sipping on his holiday 7-and-7s with Uncle Joe; his devotion to my grandmother's illustrious roasted red peppers. The kinds of things people talk about in the aftermath of a loved one's death. Instead, the heated discussion about 9/11 continued.

The heroism – no cowardice – of George Bush. He's a genius. No, a dictator.

Racial profiling.

People jumping out of buildings to escape the terrorists, or because they were terrorists?

Who's Al Qaeda? Are we safe?

What, I asked myself, does any of this have to do with my father? Was he there? No, he wasn't. Why aren't they talking about him?

I couldn't stand it anymore. My head began to spin again, and I needed to leave. As I was putting on my coat, Mom cornered me into a hug. I tried. I really did. But I couldn't let myself melt into her arms as I might have. As I wanted to. I had to get out of there.

"I'm beat, Mom," I said, gently easing myself away. "You know. . .

the drive up here, all the traffic, the wine. I'll be in bed when you get home."

Mom nodded, and I bolted.

Stumbling through the front door of our family home, the smell of my father's cigarettes engulfed me. I was afraid to inhale. Questions crowded me. *Are you here, Dad?* I didn't see any ashtrays, but I could still smell them. Nothing in our house had changed since he died. Mom hadn't moved a piece of furniture or a single wall hanging or photograph. Nothing. The curtains looked like they had never even been opened or closed. My father's extensive collection of *Eagles* vinyl records on the shelf below the television hadn't been touched.

When I opened the hallway closet to hang up my wool coat, my dad's beloved polyester Yankees jacket leapt out and slapped me across the face. *Maybe you are here.*

My bedroom was safer, I thought, and I bounded up the stairs. I skipped brushing my teeth, got undressed, climbed into my childhood bed, and pulled my old thin, raggedy comforter up to my chin to protect myself, to shield me from the Thanksgiving dinner deliberations that would not leave my mind. Uncle Joe's tearful embrace, suffocating me. Mom asking me questions I could not answer.

To distract myself, I turned my attention to the contents of my bedroom, which Mom had also preserved, even though I had left home over five years prior. My Don Mattingly and Dave Winfield Yankees posters taped to the wall; my high school baseball and cross-country trophies collecting dust atop my dresser. The distraction worked, temporarily, until I caught a glimpse of my Pez dispenser collection on my desk – a row of plastic figurines that my father brought home from the Pez warehouse where he worked. Donald Duck and Mickey Mouse and Frosty the

Snowman staring me down, like a military brigade armed with candy missiles, ready to attack.

The room spun around a few times, and I couldn't wipe the image of my dad out of my line of vision. He was looking at me through my dirty window, the glare of the moon shining on the glass lighting up his bristled brown hair, his chubby face, his bushy moustache and dimpled chin.

Why did you leave us, Dad?

I didn't leave you, Beej.

When will I see you again?

Soon. When the time is right.

The hours passed – 11:00 pm . . . 1:00 am . . . 3:00 am. . . – as I lay in bed staring at the ceiling, trying to let the disturbance go on without my engagement. I'll wake up in the morning, and I'll see this was all a dream, I told myself, over and over.

It was not a dream.

Dear Kids,

I've told you a lot about my father, John, over the years, and I've enjoyed answering all the questions that you've asked me about him:

What was his favorite dessert? Boston cream pie.

Which baseball position did he play? Catcher.

How did he become such a Yankees fanatic? That one, I still can't answer. But he was so obsessed with the Yankees, he once put a hole in the living room ceiling while jumping up in jubilation after one of Derek Jeter's postseason home runs. Grandma T. was simultaneously impressed and disgusted, just like Mom feels when I wear my faux-leather vest to Springsteen concerts. Actually, just like Mom feels about most things I do.

Telling you both about my father and keeping his memory alive is very important to me. It's part of a cycle that keeps me well, and I miss him as much today as I did then.

Love,

Dad

My father grew up in New Haven, Connecticut, in a section of the city called "The Village" – a tightly bonded Italian enclave flanked by Pepe's and Sally's world-famous Wooster Street pizza. He lived there with my grandmother, Jenny, and his brother Joe. Grandma Jenny was the proud owner of the J & J Dress Company, a clothing factory she named after her two boys, who both worked there when they were young.

My grandmother was born in Southern Italy and migrated to America with her parents through Ellis Island when she was a toddler alongside many Italians who all settled in The Village in New Haven. The tight-knit community built their lives around the Catholic church, and my father and Uncle Joe were raised Italian Catholic. Very Italian, and very Catholic. Their childhood was like a scene straight out of *The Godfather*. They went to Saint Michael Elementary School, where my father got his knuckles slapped with a ruler by the nuns every time he goofed off, which was often. They were altar boys at Saint Michael Church. They ate fish every Friday night, steak every Saturday night, and pasta every Sunday afternoon surrounded by all their grandparents and aunts and uncles and cousins, who all lived in The Village as well.

While my father's childhood was, on the surface, a joyous parade of stick ball games, street festivals, and extravagant holiday feasts, there was one person noticeably absent: his father, John Walter Talarczyk, or Walter as he was referred to, although that was rare.

I only heard my dad speak of his father once. When I was roughly ten years old, he and I were sitting in the barbershop waiting for our haircuts, casually chit-chatting with fellow patrons, when a gentleman recognized the last name "Talarczyk" and asked my dad about its origins.

"I don't know much," my dad replied. "One day when I was young, my father went out for eggs and milk and never came back."

That was the end of the conversation.

The casual chit-chatting turned to uncomfortable silence.

Walter's absence in my father's life is shrouded in obscurity. When I was very young, I learned from my older cousin that my grandmother and Walter divorced when my dad was around five years old. The impetus of their separation remains as much of a family mystery as Grandma Jenny's insistence that "John W. Talarczyk" be engraved on my father's headstone – the "W." standing for Walter, the father he never knew.

Though both Joy and I were born creatures of perpetual curiosity, neither of us ever asked my dad or Uncle Joe or any other relatives about Walter. It was an unwritten family decree that such inquiries were forbidden, that Walter's ghost was to never be summoned. I hoped one day my dad might share more details about his father with me, but that day never came, and he died before I could inquire further. There's a chance, I guess, that my dad had little information about his father himself, though I always suspected he knew more than he let on – more than Walter's trip to the grocery store for eggs and milk.

What I do know, what is clear to me now, is that the absence of a father in my own father's life was the driving force of the almighty Super-Dad he perpetually aspired to be, and particularly his omnipresence in every activity in which Joy and I participated as kids. Where many of our friends complained they rarely saw their dads because they were working, we could not evade ours. He was our baseball and softball coach, our tennis and golf and swimming instructor. He was the person in the audience cheering the loudest at Joy's dance recitals and my god-awful high school garage band gigs. A domesticated roustabout, he was ever ready to engage in a round of frisbee throwing or to lead a game of wiffle ball in the front yard.

"Big John," as his friends affectionately referred to him, smothered Joy and me with the love and attention he never received from his own father growing up. We were the beneficiaries of a big, gaping hole in my father's heart. and we readily welcomed all the love he offered us.

My father and I developed a close bond early on, one he codified with the family nickname he gave me – "Beej" , short for Brian John, my middle name. As the epithet implies, I became a direct extension of my dad from the start, relishing in his relentless disbursement of corny dad jokes and witty sarcasm. Our bond strengthened through my high school and college years, where his Super-Dad powers evolved as I navigated the murky teenage waters of dating and driving and choosing an academic path. He counseled me when I wanted him to, and kept quiet when I didn't. I cherished every golf tournament we competed in, every game we saw at Yankee Stadium, every guy's night out at Milford Jai Lai where we placed three dollar bets on teams that rarely won. He was my father, but as I grew older, he became my best friend.

Of course, the relationship my dad and I had wasn't perfectly perfect. No relationship ever can be. He and I had several blowouts over the years – our dueling stubbornness and Type-A personalities getting the best of us.

I'm embarrassed to say this now, and although they were rare, there were times when I didn't always like the irrepressible attention my father gave me, especially when I was in high school and started seeking independence. The best example of this was my father's interest in watching my baseball practices. In addition to each of my games, my dad attended every practice. While I've been known to exaggerate occasionally – it's in my Italian blood to do so – I'm not exaggerating here. My dad literally showed up to every single baseball practice I had throughout all four years of high school. Every day he'd sneak out of the Pez warehouse early, park his rusted Volkswagen beetle out by the left field foul pole, and watch me and my teammates take hours upon hours upon hours of batting and infield practice.

After a while, it pissed me off, and one day I confronted him about it.

"You're humiliating me, Dad," I yelled. "My teammates are making fun of me. Leave me alone and save your enthusiasm for the goddamn games!"

My dad let a couple days go by without showing up to my practices, but then there he was again, sitting in his car on the street adjacent to the right field foul pole instead of the left, trying to be discreet, as if I didn't know he was there.

What a jerk I was.

What a self-entitled, unsympathetic jerk.

If I could go back in time I'd apologize to him.

PART II

Mania

Saturday, April 28th, 2001

*J*oy's childhood mattress is so old that it caves into the center like a hot-dog bun, causing Sarah and me to sleep close enough to smell each other's exhales. I remove her arm wrapped around my waist, slide out of bed, tiptoe out of the room, and descend the rickety wooden stairs as quietly as I can.

In the kitchen, I make a pot of coffee and take out the half-and-half from the refrigerator. I read the expiration date on the container. It says "Best by May 23, 2001" – three weeks from now. Three weeks, I think to myself. The carton of creamer will outlive Dad by three weeks. I put the carton back into the refrigerator and shut the door.

I bring my coffee into the living room and sit in the recliner and turn on a lamp, which casts soft light into the dark room. I take slow sips, and the semi-sour taste awakens me after a night of limited sleep. Sarah seemed to sleep fine, even crunched next to me in the hot-dog bun mattress. I did not. I stared at the ceiling most of the night, struggling to contain my emotions so I wouldn't wake her up.

On the coffee table across from me is Dad's latest crossword puzzle book, his trusty thesaurus, a pencil, and an empty ashtray. I picture Dad there this early Saturday morning, leaning back on the couch, smoking cigarettes and working through a puzzle. I watch him balance the cigarette between his lips as he steadies the book on his lap and pencils in a word. I see him take the cigarette out of his mouth and smile, pleased with himself, then release the smoke through his nose.

Around the room, other memories of Dad creep out of the early morning shadows – disparate illusions buzzing around me like a swarm of angry wasps whose nest has just been destroyed.

At 7:00 am, I return to Joy's room to wake up Sarah. She's heading back to D.C. this morning, and I am jealous. She'll be there all week, back to the daily routine of her life, while I am here at home helping Mom and Joy plan the wake and funeral. I want to go with Sarah. I want to escape this prison of sadness in which I feel trapped. I want to run from the swarm of indignant wasps. But I know I can't.

Mom steps out of her room wearing a bathrobe over her cotton, snowflake-patterned pajamas. Sarah says goodbye to her and we walk outside to Sarah's car. Before she hops in, she gives me a kiss and a hug.

"I'll see you soon," she says. "Hang in there, Brian."

Hang in there. I'm unsure how to respond to that. Hanging in there is not something I do well. Screaming at the top of my lungs and crying my eyes out is more like it. But I tell her I'll try.

I walk to the middle of the street and wave goodbye to Sarah as she drives away. I turn around to look at our home – our tiny, one-bathroom, split-level ranch on Ezra Street. My childhood castle. My impervious fortress, now crumbling to the ground.

Mom steps out the door and calls over to me.

"Hey Beej, want to join me for some breakfast? I can make you some eggs if you'd like."

I am not hungry, even though I can't recall the last time I ate.

"No thanks, Mom."

Her invitation makes me quiver. I need to get out of here. The walls of our castle are closing in, and I need to be alone.

I walk up the street, stop at the first corner, and look up at the bright blue sign. It says "Saint John Street." How befitting, I think to myself. Big John lived his entire life just a stone's throw from Saint John Street, a correlation I've never previously made for some reason. How ironic and comical. Dad was far from a saint. His life bent more towards the Sinners side of the Saints and Sinners dichotomy.

I continue down the road past the houses of my childhood neighbors, many of whom still live here after all these years. My kind neighbors took such good care of me when I was growing up. They'll be there for Mom now, I tell myself. They'll watch out for her when I'm gone. There's nothing for me to worry about.

At the end of Ezra Street, I pause in front of the big red stop sign. I recall sitting here on my silver BMX bicycle, obeying Mom's strict instructions to never go beyond it when I was first learning to ride. I remember how badly I wanted to cross the threshold, but I couldn't. It's the same feeling I have now. I cannot move forward, held back by obligations. Life has, indeed, stopped. Time is standing still, and yet, somehow, it's moving faster than it ever has before.

U p until that year, 2001, my life was one long winning streak. Twenty-seven years of wins to be precise, sewn together with a ribbon of sunshine and a slew of good luck. Yes, I faced challenges along the way, as everyone does. Karma came around to bite me in the ass on occasion, and I probably deserved it. I failed my driver's license exam when I was sixteen, thanks to an overzealous DMV worker who deemed my parallel parking didn't meet "acceptable standards." That was embarrassing. I also fractured my wrist after a failed slam dunk attempt while show-boating in front of a group of girls. Even more embarrassing. But by and large, I won most of the games in which I played and managed to maintain a pretty good batting average along the way.

2001, on the other hand, was a year of losses. A lot of them. First, we lost my father. A sudden, shocking event that transformed me into an emotional zombie meandering through a haunted mansion. Then, despicable acts of terror carried out by a group of despicable men killed 3,000 innocent people on September 11th left our country in a state of confusion and mourning. That year, even the Yankees suffered a dismal playoff loss, following a series of come-from-behind wins that briefly lifted up the City of New York, then deflated everyone's spirits once again.

Just before the holidays, I had lost someone else that year. Or perhaps more accurately stated, I let her go. I let Sarah go.

Until I met Sarah, I had been a serial monogamist. I would meet a woman and fall instantly, totally in love after our first date. A few days or a week or a month later, my passion would cool. I would break up with this latest woman of my dreams and move on to the next one I met at happy hour.

With Sarah, things were different. We dated casually at first. I liked her, respected her. She was a talented artist, and I deeply admired her drawings and paintings. She was unlike other women I had dated previously. She had high self-esteem and cared little about material possessions. She found all the happiness she needed with a paint brush and a blank canvas. As time went on, instead of growing weary of Sarah's charms, I grew more committed to her promise. I soon realized that I loved her in a way I had never experienced before.

Though our commitment was largely unspoken for a while, Sarah and I solidified our status as a devoted couple by spending Christmas together in 2000 at home in North Haven, where she met my parents and Joy and Greg. They, too, were impressed by everything Sarah had to offer and even more so that I was settling down with a woman after a rather unimpressive dating history; a long trail of empty, fatuous affairs.

Our love for each other grew stronger that winter, and in late April, Sarah and I went on our fateful weekend getaway to Waterville Valley, New Hampshire. We had only been there briefly when my father had his heart attack.

For the weeks and months that followed my dad's death, Sarah was my tether. She nursed me through the initial wound, and then I let her down.

Everything changed for me when I lost my father. The shock, the trauma of the surprise of his death made me question every choice I had recently made, especially my relationship with Sarah. Even though Dad and I were very close, I regretted that I didn't know him better than I had, and from that disconnect, I had lost sight of who I might become. I was a confused, floundering boy, who thought he had long since grown up. Sarah was there for me, but I didn't know how to cling to her. It seemed more expedient to push her away.

Executing the separation was very difficult. She was good to me, and I needed her comfort, so throughout that summer, I selfishly continued to act as though I were fully committed to her. But in my heart, I was conflicted. Did I really want to be weighed down? Could I really trust myself to be with one person for the rest of my life? Returning to bachelorhood was easy and safe, as it always had been for me. I loved Sarah, but my love for her could not transcend my inability to process my grief.

I wish I had been more honest with Sarah, more willing to share my feelings, open up to her about my regrets. Instead, I was thoughtless. A few weeks before Thanksgiving, I simply stopped calling her, dismissed her from my life. When she finally pinned me down, I blurted that our relationship was over. There was no easing out of the affair, no gentle it's-not-you-it's-me speech. Nothing but a cold brush-off. I ran away, and I never looked back.

Breaking up with Sarah left me alone. . . very alone. . . heading into the holidays. . . Left me alone to get through the Thanksgiving Day massacre at Uncle Joe's house. . . Left me alone to fend off my father's ghost back home that evening. . . Left me alone to lie awake all night, thinking about the year of extensive losses I had endured. . .

The following morning, before my mom was even awake, I had already taken a shower, had some breakfast, and packed my duffel bag. My original plan was to stay home for at least one more day, to carry on our family's Black Friday tradition of avoiding all the crazy shoppers at the packed mall and take Mom to the movies. But I was in no condition to entertain the affliction any longer than I already had. I needed to get out of there.

"Mom, I've got a lot of work to do back in Virginia," I said, as soon as she came out of her bedroom. "I'll stay longer when I come home for Christmas in a few weeks."

I could tell by her crooked lips and heavy eyes that she had concerns, but I could not address them. I kissed her on the cheek and hopped into the car.

The sun was just peeking into my rearview mirror as I drove across the Tappan Zee Bridge in New York and headed toward the New

Jersey Turnpike. Light seeped over the skyline shadows of New York City to my left, and I nearly swerved into a guardrail when I turned to see the amputation – the void of the twin towers amid the smoky morning haze rising from Lower Manhattan. With little sleep to keep me focused, the confusion in my head started up again, this time with flashbacks to my own September 11th experience. . .

I was back on The Beltway in Northern Virginia, trapped in bumper-to-bumper traffic, attempting to return to my townhouse after a Marine Corps technology conference I was attending in Quantico was abruptly interrupted. The crowd on the highway was frantic, drivers pacing along the line of cars, cell phones pinned to their ears. My brain whirled, unable to make sense of the news screaming at me from my car radio. Planes crashed into the World Trade Center? Another slammed into the Pentagon? One more hijacked, aimed at Washington, DC, but diverted into a Pennsylvania field?

Details kept coming as I sat paralyzed in my car, asking myself questions that made little sense. Thousands dead. . . *Oh my god.* Is Mom okay? What about Joy and Greg and Josh? *And where's Dad?* I need to call him.

Hold on, this can't be real. . .

This isn't real. . .

It wasn't.

I looked around and suddenly did not recognize my surroundings.

Wait a minute. Where am I?

Oh, right. It's Thanksgiving weekend, and I'm driving back to Virginia, but I'm not where I'm supposed to be.

I stopped at a rest area, shook the cotton wool out of my head, and looked at a map. Only three miles off. Better than I had feared.

I turned the radio off and forced myself to concentrate on driving. I didn't lose my focus until I crossed over the 14th Street Bridge in D.C., when I was confronted by the army of cranes and bulldozers lined up beside the Pentagon where repairs from the Flight 77 fuselage explosion were still being made. The huge American flag waving above the construction site put me into another stupor. Then, I realized I had missed the King Street exit, the same one I used multiple times every day.

When I finally found myself in my own garage, I had no idea how I came to be there. I laid my head on the steering wheel and laughed aloud.

You're a jackass, Brian. Idiot!

I knew what I needed. After sitting in my car all morning, it was time for a run. A good long run. Then, I'd be rejuvenated and physically tired, and I could count on catching up on sleep that night.

I strapped my iPod to my arm and hit the pavement. My body complained a bit at first – sleep deprivation making my legs heavy – but after steering my mind toward the business calls I would have to make on Monday, my exhaustion depleted. My heart pounded louder with every stride. My skin was tingling, and my breathing settled into a slow, calm rhythm. Soon, my runner's high gave me tunnel vision. I ran on. And on. And on. My high getting higher, and higher, and higher with every passing mile.

I don't know exactly how long I ran that day, but based on the general route I recall taking along the Potomac River where I did marathon training, it was probably well over two-and-a-half hours. That excursion marked the beginning of my "hypomania" – the clinical term used to describe the onset of a bipolar manic episode, where mood is elevated, energy levels are increased, and contextual cues start to get blurred. Hypomania is the opposite of balanced. It's obsession, enlightenment. And soon after, if not caught in time, it evolves to full-on manic euphoria.

That night, I thought I'd sleep like a baby and rightfully so. After my long drive back to Virginia and my draining running excursion, I sensed how tired my body was. As I prepared dinner, I could feel the tightness in my legs and my eyes flickering. I put myself to bed earlier than normal, hoping to get a good night's rest. Then, I laid awake. All. Night. Long.

Again.

My mind would not leave me alone. My trip home had stirred up a hurricane of unbearable emotions. Seeing Mom and Joy and the rest of our family had dredged up fear and anger that would not leave my gut. Where it came from or how it got there was a mystery to me. I just knew it hurt. Too much.

Scenarios played in my head until I had to get out of bed and take Tylenol for the pain burning between my eyes. Back under my covers, I encountered ghosts of my Christmases past. . .

A happy memory – my dad giving me my first set of custom built golf clubs – led to an obsessive preoccupation. Where are those clubs now? In Mom's basement back home? Did I leave them behind when I moved from my last apartment? Did I give them away?

Then guilt. Why can't I remember? Why didn't I use them more often? Why did I buy new ones? They haven't helped me play any better.

Then, my dad's baseball cards, the ones he passed on to me. They must be worth a fortune. So many classic Yankees cards. Even a vintage Thurman Munson. Where are they? I should find them. I could make thousands.

Money thoughts led me to my business and the success I'd had that year working as insanely as I did. I was on my way, I thought, to being a mega millionaire. Famous. Popular. Living in Silicon Valley among the other dot-com technology startup CEOs. I made a mental list of well-known capital investment firms to whom I could pitch my company's value. Another list of Hollywood celebrities I would mingle with at philanthropic fundraisers. One more of media outlets I should contact to promote my thriving business.

When dawn began to bleed into my bedroom window, I realized I hadn't even tried to wrestle the racing thoughts away. I just let them play in my head like a protracted Grateful Dead song I could not stop singing to myself. It felt okay. I ceased being tired. I was ready for another day.

Who needs sleep anyway?

I got out of bed and thought I'd shower, but I got lost on my way to the bathroom and wound up outside, chipping ice off my front stoop, until my hands and feet felt frostbitten because I was still wearing pajamas. Back inside, I wanted to make coffee but couldn't remember why I was in the kitchen, so I went to make my bed and get ready for work. But it was still the weekend.

My heart was beating as fast as my mind was racing. I lost my breath and panicked, grabbing my chest and forcing myself to sit down. Then after settling, I'd jump right back up and dive headfirst into the next activity.

Without hydrating properly, dizzy spells became routine and wielded perpetual nausea. I could feel my stomach turning and my esophagus tightening as the room spun around. I was elevating from hypomanic to manic and quickly.

In the days that followed, my attention span grew shorter as my tortuous disorientation continued. My behavior became further and further erratic, punctuated by extended periods of overzealous exercise and work, nights of tossing and turning, my jackhammer heartbeat keeping me wide awake.

Incomprehensibly, my physical energy was limitless. I worked feverishly around the clock in my home office. I could not stop, as I never quite accomplished what I set out to do. I'd rewrite simple programming sequences over and over, frustrated by how disorganized everything was but unable to fix it. System functions that would normally be indented and notated properly rambled across the screen in a single line as if the return key had been removed from the keyboard.

All social constructs began to crumble. I confused my work relationships with my personal ones and addressed co-workers in inappropriate ways. I sent one colleague an email laden with heavy, private information, including the sadness I felt from my father's loss. Other communications contained subject lines that were as long and as incoherent as my computer code, asking odd, and often unseemly questions.

"How are things with your husband and family?"

"Next time I'm in town, do you want to see that movie?"

As out of control as I was, I did recognize my cognitive miscues and even tried to nap occasionally throughout the day to refresh myself. But my mind refused to shut down. On the rare occasions that my body won the sleep battle, I'd doze off briefly then spring up, every neuron firing simultaneously, excited for the next task at hand.

Despite my ongoing nausea, every day I clocked in mile after mile of endless long-distance running, winding my way through the streets and parks and trailways of Alexandria and Arlington. I'd finish a run then forget that I ran. So I'd run again a few hours later. I was never sure how far I'd gone, and I had trouble making myself stop. I was so lost in my thought loops that I forgot to watch where I was going or to beware of oncoming traffic.

On one run, my inattention nearly killed me. With so many scrambled ideas racing through my brain, I missed a left turn on the sidewalk in front of T.C. Williams High School and ran straight into a routinely busy intersection. In my peripheral vision, I spotted a car coming and stopped dead in my tracks. Luckily the driver saw me, slammed on his horn, and swerved around me just in time, nearly hitting another car parked on the opposite side of the road. In a state of shock, I scurried back to the sidewalk, dropped to my knees, and shoved my heart back into my chest.

I was lucky to be alive, but still clueless.

Euphorically, narcissistically clueless.

There is no doubt I must have been miserable during this time. Keeping Mom and Joy at a safe distance, pushing myself beyond my natural limits, daring death to claim me. But I thought I was invincible. After all, my business was flourishing. I was impressing the world with my brilliance and charm. There was nothing I could not do. Nowhere in my conscious mind was there a glimmer of doubt that I was by far the most gifted software developer on the planet. The fastest runner. The most talented guitarist. My bipolar mania blinded me from my misery and gave me a new sense of purpose, a new lease on life. A glorious, disillusioned life.

At night, my mania continued to taunt me. Some nights, I'd give up on trying to fall asleep all together and seek out activities to keep me busy, like learning new piano songs and playing solitaire. Other nights, I'd fall into waking dreams that played like noir films preventing me from sinking into real sleep. I'd grope for the off switch and find none. I'd bury myself beneath the covers, shaking my head to expel the ghosts. They refused to leave.

Time after time, audio flashbacks would revive hallucinatory visions I had about my father. I'd revisit the phone message I received from Joy after his heart attack – *"Beej, please call me as soon as you can!"* – and the desperation in her voice drove me to relive my dad's death as I pictured it then: raising his fist in the air when the racehorse he bet on crossed the finish line in first place, then dropping to the ground, struggling for breath, in agonizing pain. Over and over, I saw Sarah and me speeding to the hospital, me sitting beside him in the ICU, holding his limp hand and staring at his fat, bare belly; sleepwalking through the process of letting him go.

Scenes of my father's wake and funeral were intermingled with horrific images of 9/11: the fiery explosion of the planes crashing into the Twin Towers; men and women jumping out of windows and plummeting to the ground; the gigantic skyscrapers crumbling in mere seconds; the mushroom cloud of smoke.

I would emerge into each morning more exhausted yet paradoxically more indomitable than I had been the day before – my mania lusting for any imbalanced emotion it could latch on to. Happiness, pain, sorrow – whatever my subconscious chose to stir up from whatever external cue it received. My mental illness, which had been hiding in the crevices of my cerebrum all my life, was making itself known to me for the first time. Of course, I did not recognize it as dysfunction. I embraced the oddity of it and encouraged it to blossom. As it entwined itself with my neurotransmitters, I needed to feel it ever more and more thoroughly.

The behaviors took over every aspect of my life and my work got sloppier with each passing day. My client communications became increasingly incoherent. Eventually, my mania took over my work persona in utterly humiliating ways.

The week before Christmas, I received a phone call from my biggest customer in Florida who made an unexpected request.

"Brian, we'd like you to fly down and provide a status of your BFT work," he said. "I know the holiday is approaching, but the Army's demanding a meeting before releasing the next tranche of funding. Can you make it happen?"

Can I make it happen? Can I make it happen??? You bet your ass I can...

"Yes, of course, I'll book a flight right now!"

BFT stood for "Blue Force Tracker," a new Army telecom platform that was in early stages of development. My client, a defense contractor, was responsible for producing the training software to be used in military school houses, and I was leading the programming effort. The multi-year project represented over 50% of my business's annual revenue, and I needed the meeting to go flawlessly.

Without surprise, it would not.

Working overtime on my laptop to create the presentation, I spent days assembling what I believed was the perfect showcase for my client. On my screen, in varying colors, intermingled with one another like preschool scribbles, were circles, squares, rectangles, left arrows, right arrows, up arrows, down arrows, hexagons, octagons, and stars. One page featured web art pictures of Army tanks and helicopters. Another had machine guns and ammunition. Fragmented corporate lingo – terms like "teamwork," "synergy," and "turnkey operations" flittered around the clipart like flies hovering around a pile of dog crap.

On the flight to Florida, I was so excited to show off my presentation that I shared it with the passengers lucky enough to be seated next to me. I stood in the aisle, held up one page at a time, and practiced the speech I would deliver when I unveiled it. The bewildered look on their faces confused me. Everything couldn't be more clear. Why weren't they understanding this?

A blonde, attractive flight attendant who had previously administered the safety briefing came scurrying down the aisle. My sexually heightened senses rose to attention. Maybe she'll ask me for my number?

"Do you want to participate in our discussion?" I asked slyly, as if I were Tom Cruise flirting with a female co-star.

"Not at the moment, sir" she replied, in a sexy Southern drawl. "But how 'bout you sit back down in your seat right here and leave these other kind passengers alone?"

"Sure! Want to join me?"

"Maybe later, sweetie."

When I arrived at my client's office, I assembled the entire executive team in the conference room. Each received a copy of the slides I had created, and as they sat looking at them, dumbfounded, I was pleased. They seemed enthralled.

"Let me explain the pattern here," I ventured. "My idea is that the military theater is within reach of the general population, and the blue squares here represent the transponders they'll be doling out. . ."

"Brian, are you –"

I cut my questioner off.

"The colored circles are the codes we give them, and. . ."

At this point, the meeting attendees burst into gales of laughter. I stared at them disapprovingly, and they abruptly stopped, astonishingly perplexed.

"Oh," said the head account representative for the BFT program. "You're serious."

I was.

To this day, I have no idea why my colleagues didn't stop me right then and there, but, at the time, I was blissfully unaware why they might find me funny. I was on a roll, I thought, at an all-time professional high. Everything I did that day seemed amazing to me. Inspirational. Authentic. I would be in Silicon Valley soon.

Before leaving, I stopped by the company vice president's office to give him a chance to congratulate me. A retired Navy captain and leader of the division, he had been present at my illustrious performance.

"Hey, Captain," I greeted him as I stuck my head inside his doorway. "I'm heading out to the airport – just wanted to say goodbye."

Though he was busy working with his assistant, the captain came into the hallway to talk with me.

"Hey Brian. Glad you came by. Is everything okay with you?"

I took a step back, stood up straight, and saluted him.

"Okay? Not just okay, sir. Fantastic, sir! Couldn't be happier, sir!"

He did not reply.

There was not much left to say.

I had spun myself into a state of quasi-catatonia, and as I walked out of the chilly, air-conditioned office into the boiling-hot Florida sun, a dizzy spell nearly dropped me to the ground. I collected myself, then hailed a cab and returned to the airport. It was several hours before my plane's departure, so I scrunched my jacket into a makeshift pillow, sprawled across a row of chairs outside my gate, and closed my eyes. Somehow, I managed to fall asleep but was woken shortly after by a gentle tap on my shoulder, followed by a surprisingly familiar voice.

"Brian? Are you alright?"

"Ben! So nice to see you!" I said, leaping up.

Ben was one of the co-owners of the company I was consulting with. A stern, yet warm and approachable leader, he lived near me in Virginia and had flown down to Florida to meet with a new client. Unbeknownst to me, he had chatted with the captain before leaving my client's office, and I could hardly know at that moment how deeply mortifying it was to be, by chance, on the same flight with him back to Virginia. At the time, I was delighted to see him.

Ben and I boarded the plane together, and after I persuaded the passenger sitting next to him to switch seats with me, I climbed over Ben's long legs and we began talking. I delved immediately into work topics, but Ben quickly steered the conversation far away from anything having to do with work.

"Where will you be spending the holidays?" he asked.

His avoidance confused me. Then, it angered me. I was at the top of my career. I could make both his company and mine millions of dollars. Why would he not want to discuss that?

I didn't want to be rude, so I made a show of my fatigue, turned my head toward the window, and took in the magnificent evening view of the sun falling below the horizon – the soft orange and blue hues blending into the puffy white clouds floating across the sky like rolling hills. I imagined myself walking on top of the clouds. I also imagined my father, further above – his celestial incarnation looking down on me, watching over me, guiding me.

Dad, can you see me?

Have you been watching my business grow?

Are you still proud of me?

Before I knew it, I burst into tears. Ben, dear empath that he was, put his strong hand on my back and asked me what was wrong. His touch brought me back to reality temporarily.

"My dad died earlier this year," I said. "This will be our first Christmas without him."

Ben had met my father once before at a company golf tournament. My dad had driven down from Connecticut to play in my foursome and I had introduced him to Ben at the dinner held afterward. That memory triggered more tears, and the next thing I knew I was bawling into Ben's shoulder, telling him all the details of my father's passing.

By the time the plane landed, I had dissolved into an impassioned puddle of grief, but as Ben and I waited for our luggage at the baggage claim, he showed no signs of wanting to escape. He offered only concern for my general well-being.

"You're clearly off-kilter, Brian," he said. "Are you going to be all right getting home by yourself?"

My soaring energy instantly returned.

"Yes. Of course!" I replied as I gave him an exuberant handshake and hopped on the parking garage shuttle bus.

That was the last time I ever saw Ben and the last day I ever worked with his company.

Dear Kids,

As scared and vulnerable as I am to tell you about my bipolar disorder struggles, to explain my darker experiences and the mayhem that ensued, these are things you need to know. When I was growing up, the topic of mental illness was forbidden to discuss. The big bipolar elephant was pushed deep into the back of our family's closet, locked away for anybody to see or touch or feel. But that is one family tradition we will not be carrying forward.

Love,

Dad

There's a stigma attached to bipolar disorder, one that remains as prevalent today as it was when I was first diagnosed. My illness isn't looked upon favorably, but that's largely because it's misunderstood. I didn't understand it myself for quite some time. Like many people who are diagnosed with bipolar, I just knew I didn't want to be associated with it. That is, until my wife came along and helped me approach my relationship with my illness differently, helped me garner a more practical view on its significance, helped me see that bipolar disorder isn't some monster to fear or identity to be ashamed of. As she once phrased it, my illness falls squarely into the bucket of "it is what it is," and I couldn't agree more.

So what is bipolar disorder?

If you break the illness down to its most basic elements, bipolar disorder is a biological condition that allows one's moods to drastically fluctuate between over joyous and materially depressed. As this happens, energy levels can rise and fall at accelerated rates, making someone feel super-human in one instant and nearly immobile in another, as if they were running repeated wind-sprints on a track with limited breaks in between. When not under control, this continuously imbalanced physical and emotional state can wreak havoc on a person's life – destroying relationships, breaking up families, and causing debilitating sadness.

One important element of bipolar disorder is that it is a hereditary illness, genetically passed down from one generation to the next. Sometimes, it skips generations. Sometimes, it doesn't. For me, obviously it didn't. In my family, the illness doesn't stem from the Talarczyk side of the family tree, from my father's side. It comes from the Scecinas, my mother's family.

There's a lightness to the Scecinas, an aura of humility and simple living. It stems from my grandparents, Mema and Papa as we lovingly called them, who migrated to the United States from what is now eastern Slovakia with little money but a rich supply of humble virtues: compassion, respect, honesty. Mema and Papa taught us all what really matters – helping others whenever there is a need or opportunity, working hard but not at the expense of missing time with one's family, never taking oneself too seriously. These altruistic values were passed down to each of my aunts and uncles and cousins who are all as kindhearted as my mother.

My mom was the third of Mema and Papa's four children. By the time she was born, they had a small farm in Shelton, CT – a sleepy town on the outskirts of New Haven County. Each of the siblings developed a distinctive personality early on, and my mother was the quiet one in the family, the sweet girl, whose shyness can delude others into thinking she is weak, which she decidedly is not.

Mom says that she felt somewhat obscured growing up in Shelton. Her oldest brother, my Uncle Tom, was a scholar and an athlete, popular and well-known in the community. Her younger sister, my Aunt Diane, was the creative, outspoken town hippie. But the most distinguished sibling was my Uncle Danny, who was closest to my mom in age but furthest away in personality. He was a hard one to handle.

Danny's behavior was erratic, his moods mercurial. He could be attentive and loving in one instant, then suddenly turn sullen, withdrawn, angry. No one ever knew from one moment to the next which Danny would present himself. Mema was always aware that at any time the phone could ring, and the school would demand she come and take him home. He was never cruel, never violent, but he was unpredictable.

As a teenager, Danny had bouts of hyperactivity that dissolved into total withdrawals. He often said and did things that were socially inappropriate, even downright belligerent, and he took risks, with limited impulse control. Sometimes he seemed drunk to the family, and he did drink excessively on occasion, but no one was sure how many of his antics were alcohol-induced and how many were just Danny being Danny. He was an enigma.

A few years after Danny's high school graduation, the family shared a collective sigh of relief when he got a steady job in New Jersey. He moved there and seemed to be adjusted well enough, appeared to be handling his life with grace and maturity . . . until one Easter Sunday, about a year after he left home.

The family was just sitting down for their holiday dinner when the doorbell rang. My mother answered and found a woman they did not know standing on the front porch cradling a baby.

"Is this Danny Scecina's house?" she asked.

"Well, yes, but he doesn't live here now," my mom replied.

"Where is he?"

"He's away. Working. Can I help you?"

"I just wanted to tell him he's a father," the woman said, holding the baby up to my mother's face. "This is his."

Mom politely promised to give Danny the message. Then, she shut the door and returned to the dinner table to tell Mema and Papa. They were not nearly as placid as she. Danny had never spoken about a girlfriend, but, in fact, they all knew he had many casual relationships with women. He was attractive to them, and he easily fell into their beds. But he was also entirely noncommittal.

The following week Mema made a trip to New Jersey to confront Danny about the woman's allegations. Danny was adamant that he wasn't the baby's father, and even if he were, the thought of having any responsibility for raising a child scared him. He needed to run.

Around that time, Uncle Tom took a teaching job in San Diego, and Danny followed him there. Tom was an apt anchor, but

Danny was Danny after all. His erratic behavior and mood swings convinced Uncle Tom to get Danny into therapy. He was reluctant to go but appeased his older brother whom he looked up to. The psychiatrist diagnosed Danny as "manic depressive," an earlier name for bipolar disorder before it got a public relations facelift by the National Alliance on Mental Illness (NAMI), and he was prescribed appropriate medications. Danny's day-to-day conduct stabilized enough that after a couple of years, Uncle Tom returned to Connecticut to marry his girlfriend, my Aunt Marge. Danny stayed in California.

Fearing Danny's instability would reanimate, Mema and Papa sold their farm in Shelton and moved to San Diego to be close to him. When they arrived, they were delighted to find Danny as balanced as Uncle Tom had reported. Smart and innovative, Danny managed to make a good living manufacturing and renting Halloween costumes. His relationships with people remained fragmented, but he seemed happy. However, with time his stability changed – rapid cycles of mania and depression overtook his life, and he found himself in the hospital repeatedly. In the wake of each episode, Uncle Tom, Aunt Diane, and Mom took turns visiting San Diego, helping Mema and Papa get Danny back on his feet.

For a long time, Danny was romantically involved with a divorced woman who he wanted to marry, a choice which Mema and Papa discouraged. They needn't have worried. When the woman finally grew tired of Danny's precariousness, she left him. Then he got sick. Pancreatic cancer. Mom and her siblings took turns traveling to California to help care for Uncle Danny, but it did not take long for the disease to spread throughout his body. He died at age 62.

Until my own diagnosis, I hardly remember Danny's illness being named. I think I recall hearing that Danny was "manic depressive" once or twice, but for all I know I could be superimposing a memory I have actually fabricated. However, one thing is crystal clear about my knowledge of Uncle Danny: we never talked directly about his illness.

Never.

The mental health struggles Uncle Danny had were tucked away, hidden from everyone except those who took care of him each time he fell from grace. Mema and Papa, Mom, her siblings, and the rest of the extended family ignored the enfeebling elephant in the room at all costs. My father, my sister, and I each followed suit.

I cherish all the fond memories I have of the Scecina clan, the lightness they continue to carry forth. I look forward to every "bring your own pierogi" party and the other Slovak traditions we've forged together over the years. I remain enamored by the lives Mema and Papa led and the values they passed on to all of us. But talking more openly about Uncle Danny's mental illness is something that I wish the Scecinas approached differently. We all would have benefited from that shared experience, just like we all benefit from the uncompromising love that we still have for each other today.

PART III

Psychosis

Sunday, April 29th, 2001

As we walk towards the entrance of the North Haven Funeral Home, Mom stops to admire a row of pink tulips lining the sidewalk. A subdued smile forms on her face as she takes hold of one of the flowers, closes her eyes, and sniffs its succulent spring aroma. She seems at peace, although i do not understand how she can be. None of this is peaceful. None of it at all.

"It's nice to meet you," the funeral director says after we step inside. "Let's tour the facility before we sit down and discuss what pack-ages we offer."

The director has a pleasant enough rapport, but his words frustrate me. There are "packages" to choose from? What options can there possibly be? I feel like we're about to buy a car from a used car salesman, one who is very good at his job.

"This is the Sitting Room," the director says. "This is where people will first gather and view any pictures of John you'd like to display."

I cringe at the thought of flipping through old family photo albums with Mom and Joy, reminiscing about Dad. I do not have the resolve needed to complete the homework we're being given. Maybe I can get out of it. Maybe I can pawn the photo-flipping onto them and bake cookies or something else for the Sitting Room.

We move on to the Viewing Room, where Dad's casket will be placed.

"You'll all be over there," the director says, pointing to a row of padded folding chairs against the wall. "You'll stand and greet everyone as they move past the casket."

I wonder how many people will come. i wonder how many hands we'll have to shake, and how many hugs we'll have to give. I wonder *if Mom will be able to sit down in those chairs if her legs tire from standing too long. I wonder if our guests will find that disrespectful. I think about what I'll tell them if they do.*

We follow the director to his office, and he hands us each a pamphlet which outlines the "packages" he referred to, the features of the car we're about to purchase. They are ranked by price, from high to low. As he talks us through each of them, I pretend to listen. I don't care what package we will choose. I don't care how many flower baskets will be scattered throughout the room or how ornate Dad's casket might be. None of this matters. Why doesn't everyone understand that?

Mom chooses a middle-tier package, then we follow the director into a dimly lit room where various models of caskets rest atop tables. He describes the attributes of each to us: the materials each is constructed from; the overall weight which the pallbearers will bear. He leaves us alone, and we slowly walk around the showroom examining them.

"I like this one," Mom eventually says.

"So do I," Joy agrees.

"Me too," I reply, not wanting to think about this any further than I've already had to.

Mom hands the director a check for the down-payment, then we walk outside to the parking lot. Mom pauses again to admire the tulips.

"Pink," she says. "Pink tulips. I'd like to make sure we have some of them at the funeral."

"We'll make sure of that, Mom," Joy replies.

Anything you want, Mom, you will get, I think to myself. Anything at all.

Before we leave, Joy asks me a question: "Beej, Mom and I were chatting earlier, and we were wondering if you would be willing to give the eulogy at the church?"

"Of course," I respond confidently without even thinking about it, without envisioning myself standing in front of the entire congregation, without assessing what I might even say, or how difficult it will be to get through the speech without crying.

"I'd be happy to, Sis."

E ven though much time has passed since all of these events occurred, many of the vivid details of my manic escapades are still sharp in my memory. That is one of bipolar mania's efficacies, at least for me. On the surface, it may seem like I was acting crazy, my thoughts disconnected from my actions, and my memory displaced because of it. But that could not be further from the truth. During this manic period, my senses were so heightened that these experiences burned deep into the corners of my brain like an array of mental tattoos, and I can still recall many of them like scenes from the latest *Seinfeld* reruns I binge watched, albeit much less humorous.

Where I have gaps in my memory from these events – scenes where only half of the actors appear or the dialogue is fragmented, or I can remember what I did but not where or when I did it – I've been fortunate to have other actors who played a role in my abstract film shed some light on what transpired. Mom, Joy, Greg, and a few close friends and co-workers have all helped me reconstruct these scenes, helped me contextualize my scattered thoughts and better understand their significance. These conversations didn't happen right away, of course. Like Uncle Danny's bipolar experiences, mine would be imprisoned in the ruinous dungeon of my family's history for many years to come. But I'll tell you more about that later.

The vice that has been the most beneficial to recounting the particulars of incidents which occurred over two decades ago now is a personal journal I started keeping in the aftermath of my first bipolar episode – a cerebral chronology of everything I encountered along my rocky, mentally ill road. My journal would ultimately become the most critical element of dealing with the post-traumatic stress induced by these experiences, and I'll tell you more about that later, too.

My trip to Florida in the middle of December, where I thoroughly embarrassed myself in front of my biggest client, is one of the most vivid memories I have from my first bout with mania. I can still picture the army tank and machine gun clipart in my Blue Force Tracker slideshow. I can recall the details of the conversation that I had with the flight attendant, the gloss of her cherry-red lipstick, and the thin, double-knotted polyester scarf that hung around her neck. I remember the bewildered look on the captain's face when I took several steps back and saluted him like a freakin' moron just before leaving his office.

In the days following my Florida excursion, my insatiable hunger for adrenalin-laced activities continued, and so did my desire to connect with my father's ghost. My imaginary conversations with my dad as I sat next to Ben on the airplane, drifting in and out of the puffy white clouds, had a profound spiritual impact on me, as if I had strolled through Heaven's gate and briefly reunited with him. During my continued long runs, I went back to that cosmic place, seeking further discourse and assurances that he was still with me. During my sleepless nights, I told him stories of my life that I had never shared with anyone – intimate moments and, in some cases, shameful acts, following which I repented for my sins.

Dad, please forgive me.

I shifted my relentless focus on work to reconstructing my relationship with my father. With the same exuberance I had used to create my presentation, I assembled a collage on the floor of my bedroom dedicated to his memory – a celebration of his life supplanting my grief over his death. Sprawled across the carpet, I placed every photo of him that I could find in the house and several others I printed out; golf balls and tees; *The Eagles* CD covers. I framed the outer edge of the collage with Santa Claus and Snow-Man Pez dispensers I had placed around my townhouse for the holidays, and by the time I finished, I was suddenly, inexplicably ecstatic at the idea of going home for Christmas break.

I called Mom to share my enthusiasm and provided her with a list of all the things I wanted to do during my visit.

"Let's have Italian ice at Zapelli's."

"I'd like to meet up with my high school English teacher if I have time."

Most of these activities were senseless and confused Mom. For example, Zapelli's had closed when we were kids. And I hadn't been in contact with any of my high school teachers since graduating over 10 years before.

I also called Joy and had an extensive talk with both her and Greg about work, including the prospective acquisition of my business that I had entirely fabricated.

"Sis, do you know if a C-Corporation can buy a Limited Liability Company without the approval of Federal regulators?"

"Greg, once this deal goes through, I'm buying both of us brand new Taylor guitars!"

I rambled on and on about everything and nothing, barely giving either of them a chance to speak – sentences spewing from my lips at lightning speed as if I was an auctioneer at an art auction.

Joy and Greg remember my inquiries being somewhat odd, but at the time, they didn't question them. They just thought I was excited about my latest professional endeavors. Perhaps a bit too excited, they say in retrospect. But there was nothing about our discussion that caused them immediate concern. Of course, today, they both wished they recognized what was happening, wished they could have somehow prevented the madness that was about to ensue. Unfortunately, they weren't there to stop it. Nobody was there, except me and my increasingly befuddled mind.

In preparation for my visit home, I needed to buy spectacular Christmas gifts, and that necessitated a trip to the mall for a lavish shopping spree. As I raced through each store, I was Santa in the flesh, but Santa with no elves to do his work. I bought gifts for Mom, Joy, Greg, Uncle Joe, Aunt Louise, my nephew Josh, each of my friends, co-workers, neighbors, local bartenders, my mail-man, and even the dog down the street. I wanted everyone in my general orbit to have a merry Christmas on me, and cost would not be a factor in my largesse.

"Are you sure you want to buy 50 gift certificates?" the check-out woman at a computer electronics store asked. "That's five-thousand dollars, Sir."

"Absolutely!"

I filled my bags with sapphire pendants and chocolate truffles in gold-plated boxes, a $200 leather wallet with a gold chain, a $300 pair of dress shoes, anything that caught my eye. By the time I was finished, I had spent close to $10,000 on a huge pile of crap that my family and friends would never even receive. While I recall what I bought, my memory draws a blank on where it went. With exception of a few presents, like the titanium watch that I gave to a gentleman washing tables at the local McDonald's, and the gift certificates that I used to buy computer equipment in the years that followed, somewhere in my travels my Christmas bounty vanished. In the end, the only thing that remained was a very large balance on my credit card.

Like gasoline being poured on an already raging fire, my spending frenzy thrust my manic euphoria even higher, and that, coupled with continued dizzy spells and proliferating sleep deprivation, sent me drifting away from reality. My fantasy had started to become my truth.

Enter psychosis, stage right.

The next phase of my episode was a doozy – a grandiose, wildly fascinating, and very dangerous doozy. "Psychosis," as it is clinically referred to, is much less common for people with bipolar disorder, but it does occur, particularly when someone is experiencing extended mania as I had been. It is more common for people with schizophrenia – a more acute, and often more destructive, mental illness. Regardless of the clinical designation, what's important is that under the right environmental conditions my personal genetic makeup is hard-wired to create alternate psychotic realities, and at this point in my episode, my mind was eager to take my mental super-powers on their first test-drive.

One morning, as I was having coffee in my favorite local bistro, I sensed a middle-aged man in a business suit staring at me. While it seemed a bit strange at first, I ignored him. But after a while, he was staring so intently that I figured I must know him, it was just a question of how – a subconscious inquiry my imbalanced brain was eager to answer.

Does he play in my softball league?

Did I meet him at that big technology conference in Philly last fall?

I stared back at him, unable to turn my eyes away. But as hard as I tried, I couldn't place where I knew him from, probably because I had never seen him before in my life. But I found that strange. Why would he be looking at me if he did not know me?

At the time I had no awareness that he was probably staring at me for no other reason than I was staring at him, my discombobulated mind experiencing some intense *déjà vu* as I tried to convince myself that I had seen or met or talked to him somewhere before. The mystery intrigued me, but the mystery was not solvable. I thought about it and thought about it and thought about it some more until finally I simply created my own reality, tying it back to my father.

Oh my god, that's Dad's friend Jim from the golf course! I haven't seen him in years!!! What's he doing in Virginia???

I walked over to "Jim" and spread my arms wide, inviting him in for a bear hug.

"What the hell is your problem, dude?" he bellowed, pushing past me and bolting out the door.

How rude, I thought, confused. *Jim had always been so nice.*

While that encounter was relatively harmless, the next one, which occurred that afternoon, turned darker.

For reasons I cannot recall, I was shopping at a local Home Depot when I became aware that a man was following me. He had a menacing look about him – a scruffy beard, unkempt grey hair, and a basketball belly. He was wearing paint-soiled carpenter pants with a grungy white t-shirt covered by a tattered flannel button-down. Everything about him was creepy, especially since he seemed to be staring at me, just like my good buddy Jim.

What does he want from me?

Is he stalking me? And if so, why?

I was immediately frightened. I ducked down a service aisle to evade him, but he followed right behind. I darted over to the appliances section, crouched behind a display of stackable kitchenware, and hid there for several minutes, hoping he had left. But when I stood up, he was walking right toward me.

I sprinted to the front of the store, where I grabbed a check-out clerk's arm and pleaded, "There's a strange man following me in there!"

The clerk didn't move.

I shouted, "Can you PLEASE escort me outside???"

The clerk still didn't move.

"What the hell, man!"

I tore out of the store, scrambled into my car, and peeled out of the parking lot. I sped across town, hardly braking for traffic lights or stop signs along the way. As soon as I was inside my townhouse, I ran around closing all the curtains and ensuring all the doors and windows were locked tight.

What is this about? Who is after me?

I turned on the television, tried my best to relax by watching an *NYPD Blue* episode, but before the opening credits even rolled I heard a faint knock at the front door.

Tap. Tap. Tap.

I leaped off the couch, ran over to the window, ripped open the shade.

Nobody there.

What the hell?

I muted the television and stood in the middle of the living room, straining to hear something, anything, but all I heard was my own pounding heartbeat. Then, another knock. This time loud.

BANG! BANG! BANG!

Now terrified, I raced upstairs to my walk-in closet and hid behind a row of my well-pressed suits. I ducked down, trembling in the dark, ominous silence, listening for signs of an intruder. Then I heard noises, one after the next, bouncing back and forth between my ear drums.

Who's doing this to me?

I retraced all my activities from the day, trying to figure out who it could be. Suddenly I recalled an image of Jim smiling slyly at me in the coffee shop.

Is that Jim again? Why would he be here?

Wait, it can't be Jim. He doesn't know where I live. It must be that man from Home Depot. He must have followed me home.

Then, it hit me. . .

Suddenly, I was cloaked in sweat. There was no question about it. I was the target of some secret government operation. And the operatives were using the Blue Force Tracker software I had developed for the Army to keep me under surveillance.

Everything started to make sense. Or did it?

Wait a minute. Why would they want to hurt me? My software code is only valuable if I'm around to decipher it. I bet they're not trying to hurt me at all.

I calmed down, briefly. Then, I jumped out of the closet.

Damn! They want to recruit me!

Well, if that's what they want, they can have me. I am ready for any challenge they might offer.

Bring it on!

I needed to reveal my willingness to comply, but I also needed information. What did they already know about me? What exactly did they want from me? What devices might they have planted to spy on me? What persona were they creating for me, what cover identity? *If I'm going to be a secret agent,* I thought, *I'll need a clearly defined character to play.*

I had to find whatever clues might be hidden in the house, clues that would perhaps guide me toward my first mission. I dashed through every room, opening drawers, emptying boxes, turning over furniture. In the kitchen, I took everything out of the refrigerator, looked inside a ketchup bottle and a jar of mayonnaise. In the pantry, I emptied a box of Cheerios on the floor and examined a large stack of paper plates, one-by-one.

Nothing.

A flash of brilliance came to me and convinced me that the most important clue would likely be hidden in a profound literary passage, so I pulled one book after another off my bookshelf, flipping furiously through the pages but found nothing. Then, my copy of *Catch-22* by Joseph Heller fell to the floor and opened itself to a highlighted paragraph. I don't recall the exact passage that I read, but I do remember it involved a sarcastic association to military ranks.

Eureka!

Military hierarchies made sense. I assumed the captain and Ben were involved, naturally. Maybe they were evaluating my skills in Florida during my visit. *Maybe they are secret agents, too!*

I read the extensive margin notes throughout the book, encrypted messages cleverly penned for me by the agents and in my own high school handwriting no less. *So smart*, I thought, *that they chose a story about the military to disclose the secrets I'll need for my expected work with the government. The FBI. The CIA. Or perhaps to build off the work I've already done for the Army.*

It was a perfect first clue, and now, I just needed to decipher its meaning.

I read and re-read the scribbles, but they were nonsense. What was I supposed to do next? Something must be missing.

Wait.

Emails! All those emails from my military clients. I bet there are more clues hidden in those. I recalled a colleague making a Catch-22 joke one day; *maybe I can find it.*

I grabbed my laptop and sifted through the countless missives stored on my hard drive, trying to uncover any encrypted notes the agents could have planted, the ones that would explain what I should do next.

Boo-yah! I got it. A message from a prospective client I had recently met. *Maybe he's one of the agents?*

The search drew me outside, where I ran around my neighborhood, lurking in the shadows, hiding from the prying eyes of government officials wearing dark sunglasses and driving around in non-descript vehicles. In the stillness of the cold December evening, I became captivated by the patterns emanating from the blinking Christmas lights draped across shrubs and trees. I studied the timing, memorized the alternating intervals, analyzed the varying color schemes, attempting to understand their connotation.

Red, Orange, Green, White – check. Just like the terrorism threat codes I keep reading about in the newspaper.

My search somehow led me back to my car, and eventually I found myself in downtown Washington, D.C. in the middle of the night, following the path around the reflecting pool in front of the Washington Monument. Then, I meandered through the Vietnam Memorial, discovering significant letter patterns among the names inscribed in the marble wall, juxtaposing them with characters from *Catch-22*, work colleagues, and other figments of my imagination. I never found *Yossarian* or *Major Major Major Major*, but it wasn't from a lack of trying.

Finally, I wound my way to the Lincoln Memorial. I stood there, looking up, feeling the light of Honest Abe's wisdom raining down on me from the marble thrown upon which he sat. Over and over, I read the inscription above his head: "In this temple as in the hearts of the people for whom he saved the Union. . ."

The words engraved into the monument seemed more important than any other clue, but no matter how many times I reread them, I could not decipher their meaning.

Standing in Lincoln's shadow, I lost my sense of time. I found myself reliving a family vacation to Washington, D.C. we took when I was in fifth grade. I could feel Joy, Mom and my father standing next to me. I pictured the finite details of my newly purchased "ET Phone Home" t-shirt that I was wearing, ET pointing his glowing red finger at the White House. I heard parental voices reading. First Mom's – strong, clear, comforting: "Now we are engaged in a great Civil War. . ." Hers blended into my dad's sonorous baritone picking up where she left off: ". . . this Nation under God shall have a new birth of freedom. . . of the people, by the people, for the people. . . ."

Wait. People. What people?

Suddenly, I had another stroke of genius.

Oh my god. It's been right in front of me the whole time.

Could it be? No. It must be.

It's the only way any of this makes sense!

Dad's short stint in the Army. No wonder he never talked about it. He obviously couldn't talk about the confidential jobs they gave him. He had to keep it hidden from us.

My father was a secret agent!

The evidence was always there. How else could he have learned the survival skills he taught me during our Boy Scout camping trips? The computer programming he showed me when PCs first came out? Wow. How did I miss it? Why didn't I know sooner?

I stood staring at Lincoln, who was staring back at me. Directly at me. What were his eyes trying to make me see? Why was he so stern? What was I supposed to know?

Finally, I understood.

Oh my God.

Dad's not dead. . . *he's very much alive!*

He never died. It was staged. It was all a hoax!

They knew exactly how to do it. The doctors and nurses in the ICU were pros, and they tricked all of us. Joy, Mom, me. . . every single one of us.

They needed him. The war on terror needed him. Now the world needed him.

It was time. They had called him back to active duty. *And now he's CALLING ME!!!*

Of course, my dad wasn't actually "calling" me. . .

Nobody was calling me. . . Or talking to me, or chasing me, or asking me to join the war on terror – including, and especially, my father, who had died seven months prior. But at that time, that's exactly what I believed.

Before I had my first psychotic episode, I had a different perception of what psychosis entails. Very different. My perspective was largely driven by movies and television shows that portray psychosis, where people talk to house plants that have suddenly come to life or envision cars becoming possessed by some cosmic power and flying through the air. That might be how psychosis plays out for other people who are genetically predisposed to it, but that's not what happened to me. My experience was much more *human*. More personal and relatable. More logical. Each scene of the absurd movie reel unfolded slowly and deliberately, one deeper level of abstraction building on the next – my mind picking up a long trail of deranged cognitive breadcrumbs, eventually shepherding me to lunacy.

I also assumed psychosis was a phenomena that only "crazy" people experienced – those committed to long-term psychiatric facilities. People locked up in loony bins like Randall McMurphy, Jack Nicholson's character in *One Flew Over the Cuckoo's Nest*. I never in a million years would have thought that someone like me – a middle-class software engineer driving around in a Mazda Miata – could one day experience psychosis without taking some kind of illegal substance like LSD or mushrooms. Never, ever.

Of course, how would I have ever known? Up until that point, I had never met anyone who experienced psychosis. Or even if I had, would they have told me about it? That's not exactly something someone blurts out in casual conversation: "Nice to see you again. Did I ever tell you about the time I thought my father's death was a gigantic conspiracy and he was really a government agent summoning me to join him on a top-secret mission?"

Not really the best ice-breaker.

Nevertheless, as I stood in front of the Lincoln Memorial on that bitter cold December evening, my abstract epiphany opened a secret doorway, a new way in. Another psychotic portal to enter. .
.

I had to share this with Joy. It couldn't wait.

Her answering machine picked up.

"Sis – You're not going to believe it! I can't tell you anything yet, but don't worry. I will. As soon as I can. I promise. . ."

"It's happening. That's all you need to know. It's really happening. . ."

"Dad loves you so much, Sis. . . And he knows how much you love him, but I'll tell him again anyhow. . ."

I could see it clearly. My father had been whisked away to fight the ultimate fight, to serve the country he loved and to protect the threatened freedoms of our nation. After the 9/11 attacks, he had convinced his superiors to have me join him in that battle. Well, I was ready. . . and willing. . . to serve my country. . . to be all that I could be. To see him, to be with him once again.

The next thing, then, was to find him.

Shortly after I left Joy that voice message, I began to feel vibrations from deep within my chest cavity, and I heard a high-pitched ringing inside my inner ear. Then, a quiet voice. It spoke to me, instructed me, moved me forward. This wasn't some magical house plant standing in front of me, telling me what to do. It was a subtle, internal message, and it was from my father.

Pack your things, Beej. There's no time to waste.

I did not question my dad's instructions. I understood that I was property of the United States government now, and I must follow blindly wherever I was led, so I raced back to my townhouse to gather what I might need for the mission. Into my car, I loaded enough non-perishable food, water, and other survival provisions to last for several weeks, should I need them for that long. In addition, I stocked the passenger's seat with caffeinated soda and running endurance Gu packs to help keep me awake as my eyes continued to flicker from exhaustion.

The inner voice continued and got louder, compelling me to follow orders, to stop thinking, to move mechanically. Each message began as a sharp pain in my stomach that occasionally forced me to my knees, then turned into an electrical impulse – the sensation of something crawling up my backbone, one vertebra at a time. It would briefly come to rest at the base of my neck before bursting upward and knocking back and forth inside my brain.

My father's voice got deeper and began barking short, specific demands.

Start the car. Get on the highway. Go to the hospital.

I sighed, thinking, *What a relief. Now I know where I'm going. To the hospital in New Haven, where they staged my dad's death. I've got my orders. I'll talk to the doctors, nurses, and other staff members, the ones who are in on the operation. They'll guide me to him from there.*

I was halfway up the Baltimore/Washington Parkway when I received my next message.

Follow the van, Beej. Follow the flags!

Directly in front of me, a white panel-van with a large American Flag decal on the back door was shifting gears, crawling up an incline. When I first saw the truck, the flag seemed insignificant, merely an image. After all, 9/11 was only three months behind us. Flags were ubiquitous at the time, appearing on restaurant menus and bridge overpasses and the lapels of every suit jacket. However, this one was not like those. It was three-dimensional. It gave the van gravitas. *There must be government agents inside*, I thought. Agents on a mission somehow associated with mine.

I could tell the driver knew I was right behind him, and I was relieved. These agents were clearly going to escort me all the way to the hospital, so I switched lanes and tailed the van. Soon after, a second white vehicle with another American Flag went by, and, sure that the escorts were tag-teaming, I switched and followed them. Then a third van came by. . . then a fourth and fifth and sixth. . .

The agents continued leading me north on Interstate-95, but in the middle of the Delaware Memorial Bridge, my instructions changed. I pulled over to the breakdown lane and stepped out of the car as my father's voice spoke to me again – this time distraught and loud, carrying high above the vehicles whizzing by me so fast that I could feel the breeze emitting from their tailwinds.

The enemy can see you. You need to switch cars!

How was that possible? Surely, I had been careful enough.

I was skeptical, but I trusted my father. He had not steered me wrong yet. He was taking me exactly where I needed to be, where my heart had been trying to go for so long.

I deduced that my own car was too well-known now. I had to steal another one. I got off the highway and drove through a maze of dark-shadowed streets leading to a 24-hour convenience store, where I parked, climbed into the back seat, and waited for another vehicle to arrive. Finally, a sporty coupe parked a few spots over from me, and a woman stepped out. As soon as she walked into the store, I sneaked over to the driver's side of her car and squatted down. Her door was open. Good. No alarm.

Through the store window, I watched the woman peruse the beverage refrigerator and understood I needed to hurry. I positioned myself underneath the steering column and fiddled with what felt like loose wiring, planning to hot-wire the ignition and drive away undetected. Unfortunately, hot-wiring was not within my automotive skill set. I could barely add my own oil.

Suddenly, the woman was standing in front of her car, looking straight at me, screaming.

"OH MY GOD! What the hell are you doing?? Help!!!"

As I leapt out of her car and sprinted back to mine, she ran back inside, shrieking at the clerk. Petrified, I punched the gas pedal and fish-tailed out of the parking lot, nearly flying off the road. I drove as fast as my car would allow, keeping my eyes on my rear-view mirror to see if I was being followed. Luckily, I was not.

I lost 'em, Dad.

I needed to hide, and I also needed to rest. By this point, I was so exhausted, even chugging the caffeinated drinks I brought on my mission had little effect. Several towns over, I found an inconspic-uous street in the middle of a colonial style sub-division where I could park without being noticed. I turned the motor off and reclined my seat all the way down. I didn't even know I had fallen asleep until I was awakened by my ringing cell phone. I saw who it was and flipped the receiver open.

"Joy!!!"

"Beej, what's going on? Greg and I got your voicemail from a few hours ago, but it didn't make sense. I left you five messages. It's nearly midnight now. Where are you?"

"Joy, I'm close. I'm very close."

"What do you mean you're close? Close to what?"

"I can't tell you yet, but you'll know soon."

"Beej, what are you talking about?? You're scaring me! WHERE THE HELL ARE YOU???"

"I can't tell you that either, but I'll call you soon. I promise!"

Afraid that in my excitement I might tell Joy about my conspiracy theory revelations and blow my cover, I hung up abruptly, just in time to receive my next command.

Find the mansion, Beej.

Huh, the mansion? What mansion?

Wait... I know what that means. The President's Mansion!

Yes, I thought I was being summoned to Camp David to meet George Bush, the President of the United States at the time. It makes sense though, doesn't it? After all, that's where you go if you need to be in a well-secured location to plan out classified counter-terrorism operations. I mean, where else would you do it, especially when you're in the Mid-Atlantic region of the East Coast?

Even though I was in a displaced, psychotic time-warp, I knew my adventure had taken me somewhere near the border between Maryland and Pennsylvania, so I figured I was close. I turned down one winding country road after another, each time reaching a dead end. I waited for my father's voice to provide me directions, but none came. Then, suddenly, my gas light was blinking red, and my car refused to accelerate. I drifted to a halt in the middle of the road.

Bewildered, I just sat there, unable to do anything but drop my head on the steering wheel and moan. I had no idea what I was supposed to do, but before I had much time to consider my options, the bright red and blue lights of a police car flashed behind me.

Aha! Finally. This was it.

No more clues to follow. No more instructions to decipher.

I'll see you soon, Dad.

I rolled down my window.

"Good evening, Officer. I sure am glad to see you."

"Good evening. What seems to be the problem?"

"Oh, no. No problem at all. At least not anymore, now that you're here."

"Sir, have you been drinking this evening?"

"Me? No! You can bet I will be soon, though. As soon as I get there. I'll be hoisting a glass with my father."

"Where are you headed, sir?"

"C'mon, Officer. You don't have to be secretive with me. I know you're here to get me there. Right?"

"Sir, please step out of the car."

"No problem. Are you going to drive? My car seems programmed to stop on its own, and I –"

"I'd like you to look at me, sir. Right at me. That's it. . ."

The officer held a pen in front of my eyes and moved it slowly back and forth from right to left. As my head followed its path, I kept talking.

"Hey, isn't this wasting time? Can't we just get going?"

"Sir, I'd like you to stand facing straight ahead. Put your left foot, facing forward, right here. That's it. And your right foot behind it facing the same way. When I say go, I want you to walk in a straight line till I say stop. . ."

I did what he said but continued my stream of subconscious babble. "Are you gonna need to blindfold me before you take me to Camp David?"

"Okay, now I want you to breathe into this little machine I'm holding. . ."

I was impatient, but I did everything the officer asked me to do, and I didn't resist when he told me to get into the backseat of his police cruiser. I was surprised when he pulled into a rural police station instead of the President's mansion, but once inside, the sound of police scanners resonating from behind the main desk made me confident that the officer was just awaiting clearance to drive me there.

I'm coming, Dad.

There was nothing to do but sit down on a bench and close my eyes.

When I talk about my childhood, I tell people that I was lucky to be raised by three-and-a-half parents: my mother, my father, and Joy are the three. Greg, who started dating my sister when she was in college and quickly became a role model for me, is the half. They were each a critical part of my upbringing, and to understand my relationship with my mental illness, you need to know more about my relationship with each of them.

There's a photo collage hanging on the bedroom wall of my mom's apartment filled with pictures that encapsulate my childhood. It used to reside in the foyer of our home on Ezra Street where Mom lived for over 50 years until older age made it difficult for her to climb stairs. It's a telling album, a multi-image portrait of me and the family who raised me. We appear in scenes from our collective life: me scooting around on my plastic three-wheeler one Christmas morning as my father chases me; loyal fans sitting in the upper deck at Yankee stadium, eating bologna and cheese sandwiches Mom snuck into the park; a family of tourists standing in front of Plymouth Rock learning about our nation's origins.

The most revealing photo of my childhood sits at the center. The four of us are standing on the front porch of our home the year Joy graduated from high school. She, in cap and gown, occupies the middle of the picture, with my mother and my father flanking her. I am about twelve, and the camera captures me grinning at a silly joke my dad has most likely just told. Joy's hands are on my shoulders, holding onto me, clearly intent on making me stay put and insisting that I take this moment earnestly. Someone had to. My dad was guiltier than me in that department, and my mom had her hands full.

My father was the "cool dad" and also the "funny dad," perennially on the lookout for an opportunity to make others laugh. While I learned the valuable lesson of not taking oneself too seriously all the time from both of my parents, my father took that to a whole new level. When I was a kid, there were many things he took a little less seriously than he probably should have like bedtime and teeth-brushing and not eating an entire box of animal crackers in one sitting. This drove my mom absolutely bananas, which was, perhaps, his objective.

In one of my earliest childhood memories, I was roughly seven years old when Mom and Joy went out of town for the weekend, leaving my dad alone to babysit me. I can still recall the stern instructions Mom gave my dad before she left. Actually, these were instructions she gave him often when I was a kid.

"You're in charge, John. Don't be an idiot."

My dad took that to heart – in the wrong way, of course – and shortly after Mom and Joy departed, he brought me to North Haven Bowling Alley where Uncle Joe and the rest of his teammates were drinking beer, smoking cigars, and telling inappropriate stories. We were there until about 11:00 p.m.; then, we went over to the local Knights of Columbus hall, where I drank a gallon of soda as I watched my dad hustle everyone on the pool table. That lasted until about 1:00 a.m., and then, he took me to the Athena Diner for a very late dinner/early breakfast before we finally returned home.

As he tucked me into bed, he made me an accomplice to his parental shortcomings – a role Joy and me played often when Mom wasn't around.

"Beej, don't tell your mother where we went tonight," he said. "It will be our little secret, okay?"

"Sure, Dad."

After Mom returned from her trip, somehow she found out about our little secret and read my dad the riot act. Since he was the father of her two children, she couldn't completely revoke his babysitting privileges. But from that point forward, Joy was "in charge" whenever Mom was out of town, even though my sister was only in 6th grade at the time.

Nevertheless, when it came to Joy and me, my mom and my dad formed a healthy, nurturing partnership. They collectively instilled a high-level of confidence in both of us, although they did so in very different ways. Mom led by example, teaching us resilience and ambition through her actions rather than words. Dad, on the other hand, employed the "do as I say, not as I do" parenting technique. He verbally provoked us to be strong in our convictions and to set and pursue goals. He did this, ironically, by denigrating himself, by challenging us to make different life choices than he made, particularly in our professions.

"I want you both to go to college and use that knowledge to build a career," he told us around the time Joy was just entering high school. "Don't do what I did. You're both smarter and more driven than me."

The reference to "what he did" was to skip his classes at Wilbur Cross High School regularly, barely graduate, and convince himself he was not intelligent enough to attend college nor skilled enough to learn a trade. Throughout his life, he bounced from one job to the next, taking any work that was available to him. He was a trucking dispatcher, an auto parts inventory stocker, a power equipment salesman, and eventually a warehouse manager for the Pez Candy Company. From my perspective, these were all worthy pursuits. They put food on the table and allowed him to spend more time with us rather than being bogged down by some high-stress, white-collar office job. But he never looked at it that way, or at least that's not how he presented it to us.

Mom and I had a very different relationship than the one my dad and I cultivated. I was as close to her as I was to him but in a contrasting way. While my dad pampered and indulged me as he figured out how to be a father, I was never my mom's "little boy." Even though I was the youngest, coddling me was not in her parental playbook, and by the time I had any awareness of my surroundings, I was an independent entity. Mom encouraged me to work as soon as work was feasible, to be financially independent. I was always solvent enough that when my dad was short on money to buy cigarettes or to place a surreptitious bet on a football game, he would come to me for a loan. Mom knew, and she trusted me to be my best self.

When I was growing up, Mom was, as she remains, a stalwart supporter of every endeavor that I undertook. She accepted any version of myself that I presented as customary and well-adjusted, no matter what, and from a very early age, she gave me as much autonomy as I requested. When I told her, out of the blue one day, that I didn't want to be a Boy Scout anymore because I found it boring, she didn't try to steer me back to it. She simply said, "Sounds good," picked up the phone, and called the Scout Master. When I wanted to skip a day of high school to take the train to New York with some friends to see the Yankees home opener, she said "Enjoy," and off I went to the Bronx. When I convinced myself I should use all my savings to buy my first middle-school, puppy-love girlfriend three dozen red roses and an enormous teddy bear for Valentine's Day, she did cast me an inquisitive look, but then she said, "That's sweet, Beej. . . what a nice gesture," and drove me to the flower shop.

In between Big John's humorous, often clueless fatherly antics and Mom's belief that I should choose my own adventure regardless of the circumstances or risks my decisions imposed, there was a large parental void, and before I was even old enough to watch a PG-rated movie, Joy stepped right in to fill it.

Although she is just four and a half years older than me, in my formative years, it seemed like Joy was twenty. Well before she was a teenager, she had a parental maturity about her that commanded my attention, and if she ever asked for my help, I was always eager to please. Whether that was cleaning the basement when Mom asked her to, baking a cake for my dad's birthday, or feeding Sunshine, our yellow parakeet, I wandered around the house fulfilling Joy's requests like a faithful employee kissing his boss's butt. Joy never took advantage of my willingness to comply. That was neither her intent nor her interest. But even if it were, I would have blindly appeased her.

In addition to supporting Joy around the house, I also mimicked the goals she set for herself as well as how she achieved them. When she was younger, she worked hard to become a strong tennis player and bowler, so I worked hard to become a strong tennis player and bowler. She studied extensively and got straight A's in school, so I got straight A's. After graduating *summa cum laude* from Clark University with a B.A. in psychology, she went to law school and soon became a successful attorney, driven to raise a family that was more financially stable than ours was growing up. After I graduated from the University of Connecticut, I chose a professional path that provided the same.

As for Greg, I was just starting high school when Joy and he first met each other. They were a committed couple soon after, and Greg nestled himself into our close family dynamic right from the get-go. Because Greg is a devout Yankees fan, it was easy for him to fall into my father's good graces; it never took much more than that for anyone to dance their way into Big John's heart. Mom, too, was impressed by Greg's kind, respectful demeanor, and Joy's adoration of his confidence and compassion. I, on the other hand, was skeptical of Greg at first. I didn't like anyone dating my older sister/third parent. I felt as if I was losing Joy in a divorce, concerned I would no longer get the attention she always gave me, and I wasn't happy about it. But it didn't take long for Greg to win me over, especially when he offered to teach me how to play guitar and to give me a ride on his Harley Davidson Roadster.

With every new song Greg showed me how to play, every discussion we had about women, every White Snake and Steve Miller concert he took me to at New Haven Coliseum, Greg quickly elevated his family status from the older brother I never had to a father figure who taught me all the "fatherly things" that my dad knew nothing about. There were a lot of them. A dump truck full, such as how to change the oil of a car, how to wire a basic electrical socket, how to properly swing a hammer. Well, how to properly use any tool, really, since the only tool my father owned was the telephone to call a repairman whenever something was broken. Of course, once my dad found out how handy Greg was, Greg became the repairman.

By the time I left for college, my three-and-a-half parents had provided me with a warm blanket of security and a plethora of self-awareness. They had collectively given me all the tools that I required to succeed on my own, including their phone number to call them anytime if something went wrong. Even after I graduated and moved to Virginia, I felt protected by them as if I were still living in the cozy comfort of our tiny castle on Ezra Street. No matter what might happen, they would be there for me, for whatever I needed.

As it turned out, I would need a lot.

More than I could have ever imagined.

PART IV

Denial

Monday, April 30th, 2001

I stumble into the kitchen, sleepy-eyed, exhausted from another night of tossing and turning. Mom sits at the kitchen table, drinking a cup of herbal tea with fresh lemon. She is stirring bananas and raisins into her oatmeal but stops and smiles when she sees me.

"Happy Birthday, Beej."

Happy Birthday.

What can possibly be happy about this birthday, I think to myself. This is the unhappiest birthday I've ever had, and I cringe at the thought of every single birthday to come. Every birthday that will now have a cloud of thick, black smoke overshadowing it – horrific memories of this grisly week home.

"I talked to Joy earlier," Mom tells me. "She said the party starts at 5:00 p.m., but we can come over whenever we want."

Right. The damn birthday party. The gathering I've been dreading ever since Joy mentioned it to me. I want no part of the attention I will receive, the attention that should be on Dad, not me, regardless of my birthday. But Joy insists that we celebrate. She wants to lift the thick cloud of black smoke that is hovering, even if only briefly.

To distract myself, I do yard work throughout the day. I mow the grass, trim the hedges, clean the gutters; all the tasks Dad is no longer around to do. Then, we leave for Joy's, where my distressing birthday party awaits.

As we enter, Joy welcomes me with a big hug.

"Happy Birthday little brother," she says. "Can I get you a beer or some wine?"

"Both, please," I reply.

Joy chuckles and hands me an Amstel Light.

"I'm not ready for this," I tell her.

"It will be fine, Beej. It's your birthday! Go relax. Everyone will be here shortly."

I sit alone on the couch in the living room and admire the thoughtful decorations Joy has scattered: a happy birthday sign dangling across the fireplace mantel; several balloons hovering about. From behind the love seat, Josh comes crawling in, holding onto the string of a red balloon and cooing, as if he has just discovered the greatest toy on earth. I pick him up and sit him on my lap.

"Hey little buddy. . . what do we have here?" I ask him.

"Baa-leen" he says, letting the string go and watching the balloon float up to the ceiling. I reach up to grab the string and hand it back to him. He lets go again and giggles. I hand it back to him and giggle myself. We do this several more times, and the giggling relaxes me for the first time in as long as I can remember.

The birthday party guests trickle in. They are largely family members and mostly the Scecinas since Uncle Joe and Grandma and the rest of the Talarczyks are preoccupied with other funeral arrangements, including picking out the gravestone and prepping for the post-wake gathering that will be held at Uncle Joe's house. I cringe at the thought of another party, but at least that one will be in honor of Dad, as it should be.

When it's time to eat, we gather around the kitchen island and bow our heads as Greg gives thanks for the feast in which we are about to partake: Joy's homemade lasagna, eggplant parmesan, broccoli salad, and several other side dishes. Joy has been cooking for two days now, Mom told me earlier. Like all of my yardwork, this is her way of distracting herself, I assume. Her way of dealing with her heartache by nourishing all of us with some of Dad's favorite comfort foods.

I open presents, kind gestures from my family who went out of their way to cheer me up. When we're done, Joy brings out the birthday cake. I call Josh over and prop him up on my lap again. The top of the cake reads "Happy Birthday Uncle Beej!" and as Joy lights several candles, the party guests sing the familiar tune. When they are finished, Josh and I blow out the candles, and everyone claps. Josh claps too, excitedly, enjoying all the attention that I am trying to deflect.

Joy places Josh in his high chair beside me, and I watch him dive head first into his piece of cake with both of his hands. As chocolate frosting smears across his lips and cheeks and nose and chin, I cannot stop staring at him. His innocence melts my heart. He has no idea what has transpired. He has been told "Poppy" will no longer visit him, but he doesn't understand what that means. His life is carrying on without the confusion we all share, the pain that we all feel.

I wish it were that simple.

Dear Kids,

Mom and I both believe that spirituality is a personal journey, and while we felt it was our responsibility to introduce you to various religions when you were younger, we've never tried to steer you in one direction or another since. But as I go further into my experiences with bipolar disorder, it's important that we go deeper into my own feelings on spirituality, because in many ways, it's my mental illness that has solidified my beliefs.

Love,

Dad

Although I attended a Christian church when I was growing up, sitting in a pew between my mother and sister at West Woods Bible Chapel in Hamden every Sunday morning, my spiritual beliefs today aren't aligned to Christianity, per se, or any other formal religion. I am not an atheist – I don't disbelieve a higher power may exist. That's a bit bold in my opinion. I just don't believe anyone knows for certain, and I don't attach myself to any religious ideology that does. I guess you can consider me agnostic in that regard, although even that sounds a bit righteous. What I do believe is that "everything happens for a reason," so they say – that some cosmic force in the universe presides over us. Something must be out there, I feel, particularly when the randomness of life seems a lot less random.

On the night I had embarked on my psychotic journey to be reunited with my father whom I believed was still alive, I have no doubt that cosmic force paid my family and me a visit.

As I was packing my car in Alexandria with everything I would need for my secret agent training, Jcy and Greg were sitting at their kitchen table listening to my nonsensical voicemail over and over and over again, and they were confused and worried sick. They could tell something was wrong but had no idea what that might be. It made them both frantic, and they didn't know what to do. Should they call the police? No, they didn't know what they would say to them. Should they call Mom? That was another hard no as they didn't want to worry her about something they hoped would resolve itself.

Without any other good options, they did what they always do as devout Christians when difficult events are beyond their control: they prayed, hoping God would guide them in the right direction.

A few minutes later, the phone rang, and their prayers were answered.

"Hey Greg, it's Tyrone. What's going on man?"

Tyrone was an old friend from the church that Joy and Greg still attend today, and at the time, the three had not been in communication for quite a while. There was a reason for that: Tyrone was immersed in his quest to become a psychiatrist at the Yale School of Medicine. He was also the only person with any mental illness experience that either Joy or Greg knew back then.

Thank you, Dad.

"Hi Tyrone. Well, there's a lot going on. . ." Greg replied, then proceeded to tell him about my voice message and their concern.

Joy and Greg didn't know what to do next, but they both felt that sitting around and waiting for another phone call from me probably wasn't the best approach, an opinion Tyrone also shared given what had been relayed.

"Well, how do you feel about taking a drive?" Greg asked Tyrone.

"Where will we go?" he replied.

"I don't know, but I can't stay here and wait around for Brian to contact us again."

"Sure, come get me."

Greg guessed that I was somewhere between Virginia and Connecticut, so he and Tyrone drove south on I-95, hoping at some point they would find out where I was located. Along the way, Tyrone solicited information about my potential state of mind from Greg, including if I was acting strange the last time that he or Joy saw me, but there wasn't much that Greg could offer. Thanksgiving was several weeks prior, and neither he nor Joy had noticed anything out of the ordinary while I was home visiting. The same was true during our phone conversation in mid-December about the fictional sale of my business, although in hindsight, that discussion now seemed somewhat peculiar.

By the time Greg and Tyrone were in Southern New Jersey, the police officer who brought me back to his station had contacted Joy. I don't recall how the officer got Joy's number, but luckily he did. Joy was relieved that she at least knew where I was and that I was in the safety of authorities. She gave Greg my location, and shortly after, my rescuers arrived to find me asleep on a bench in the waiting area of the police station.

I was awakened by Greg's strong hand on my forearm, shaking me. I leapt off the bench, backed away, and put up my fists, ready to fight. Then I realized it was Greg and my demeanor instantly softened.

"Greg! It's so good to see you man!!! How are you???"

"It's nice to see you too, Beej."

I ran to Greg and smothered him in a gigantic hug. I was genuinely excited to see him, but I was also suddenly confused.

Why is he here?

Is he part of the mission somehow?

Tyrone was standing behind Greg with his hands tucked into the pockets of his jeans. He remained still as he watched Greg and me embrace.

"Beej, this is Tyrone," Greg explained. "He's a friend from church."

"Hi Tyrone," I said, shaking his hand, aggressively. "It's nice to meet you."

"It's nice to meet you too, Brian."

When Tyrone saw how physically run-down I looked after several manic weeks, and after I answered a few basic questions he asked me about my mental state, it did not take him long to diagnose my condition, and he pulled Greg aside to tell him.

"Listen, Brian's fully manic, maybe even psychotic," he said. "We need to get him to the hospital as quickly as possible."

Greg didn't know exactly what that meant, but he trusted Tyrone. They put a plan together to get me back home and admitted to Yale New Haven Psychiatric Hospital. Tyrone would drive my car as I rode with Greg, as it was obvious I was in no condition to do much of anything, especially operate a motor vehicle.

It didn't take long for my delusional brain to introduce both Greg and Tyrone as new characters of my abstract, psychotic movie. I just assumed they had both been part of the mission all along, and everything was unfolding exactly as it should have been.

Maybe Tyrone will be my drill sergeant during my next round of training exercises?

Perhaps Greg is one of the people who helped fake my father's death?

I kept these revelations to myself, however. After all, while I was hopeful, I could not be sure either of them were part of the mission, and I was clearly sworn to secrecy by the government until I was told otherwise. I would not break protocol, even for Greg. Still, clearly I was getting close.

"Beej, how about you take a ride with us?" Greg said, gently guiding me out of the police station.

"That would be great!" I replied. "Wait, where are we going?"

"We're going home to see your Mom and Joy. Are you okay with that?"

"Yes! Lead the way my friend. . ."

It wouldn't be until many years later when I learned just how scared Greg was on our drive back to Connecticut that night. Both of us were experiencing something we had never experienced before, and while I was psychotically elated, he was frozen in fear, keeping two hands on the wheel at all times in case I suddenly turned belligerent. He didn't know what "mania" or "psychosis" entailed. There wasn't time for Tyrone to provide him further guidance. He just knew he needed to get me to the hospital as quickly as he could, and he prayed he would make it there without incident.

As we drove, the voices inside my head quieted down, but I still rambled on about random numbers, color combinations, and other clues I had found. I did not speak of secret agents, of our pending war on terror, or of anything about my father. Greg listened quietly to my steady stream of nonsense and tried to remain calm. At one point, I managed to fall asleep briefly in the car, but I awoke just before we reached New York City. Ahead in the distance, the Big Apple skyline was growing ever larger, and as I watched the new morning light creep up behind the tall buildings, I felt as though the universe were opening its arms to me. Then, I saw it. The amputation.

All of a sudden, I was compelled to weep. Inconsolably, uncontrollably. I contracted my body into a tight ball and huddled against the passenger side window. Greg put his hand on my shoulder and gently rubbed it. Eventually I calmed down, but the minute we pulled off the highway in New Haven and turned into the parking lot of Yale New Haven Hospital, I jumped to the edge of my seat and grabbed hold of the dashboard with both of my hands as if a bolt of lightning had struck the car. I tried to keep my cool, to not break my secret agent cover, but it was futile by that point. We had arrived! We had finally arrived at the place to which I was instructed to go from the very beginning! At the place where it all began.

I'm coming, Dad.

I leapt from the SUV and ran into the hospital, looking for signs to the "I.C.U." – where I had last seen my father. Greg caught up to me and helped me get through security then led me to a seating area in a separate wing of the hospital – the psychiatry ward, where Mom and Joy had been waiting.

It was finally time to release everything my brain had been holding in. The emotional strain was too much to bear any longer. I had to share the secret with the two people who needed to hear it the most.

I wrapped my arms around Joy and whispered in her ear. "I made it, Sis. I'm ready. Take me to Dad. . ."

Joy had absolutely no idea what I was talking about, but her confusion and exhaustion from being awake all night brought tears to her eyes – tears which reassured me that my secret agent initiation was nearly complete and the celebration would soon begin.

Mom approached and embraced me, too, although no emotions emanated from her inviolable resolve. She took my hand and led me to a table in the corner of the room where a mountain of paperwork had been placed.

"Brian, you'll need to sign all these documents before they let you in," she said sternly.

Easy. I was accustomed to government bureaucracy after working for years with the Department of Defense. After all, I was about to join an elite fighting force of finely-tuned military machinery, and I was more than ready to sign my life over to my country.

After we finished all the paperwork, Mom walked beside me as I followed a woman, who I didn't recognize to be a nurse, into an examination room. She corralled me into a chair and strapped a blood-pressure cuff tight around my bicep. As she pumped the pressure gauge, I became confused and frustrated.

"Excuse me, ma'am, what are we waiting for? It should all be done now. I'm ready to move ahead."

Mom interjected before the nurse had a chance to reply.

"Let's be patient and do what they tell us, Brian. Just relax and be patient."

Patience was impossible in my state of high agitation, and though Mom and the nurse tried to calm me, I was too excited, too full of questions.

"Does my father still look the same?" I asked the nurse "Will I be going out into the field with him right away?"

"That's something you'll be talking to your doctor about, Brian."

The nurse left briefly, and her departure frustrated me. I stood up and walked around the room to keep myself busy – examining the oxygen machine, picking through the Q-tip jar, opening several drawers and cabinets, searching for evermore clues. I also weighed myself on the scale in the corner of the room.

"160 pounds," I said to Mom. "That can't be right. This scale must be broken."

It was right. My three weeks of limited, sporadic food intake, drinking a fraction of the water that I normally would, and guzzling gallons of coffee and soda to keep myself awake had resulted in 20 pounds of weight loss. In addition, my heart rate was so high that the medical staff was shocked and immediately concerned. Their first priority was to lower it, which they did with several pills the nurse handed me upon her return.

The drugs kicked in right away, and the room became hazy, my eyes droopy. Within minutes, I collapsed onto the examination table. I was drowsy but still awake. Mom stood beside me, holding my hand as I lay there nearly unconscious. I looked deep into her gentle eyes, and suddenly I was brought back to the last moment I sat beside my father in the hospital the morning he died. I was holding *his* hand, staring at his torso raise and lower, watching the green blips crawl slowly across the heart-monitor screen.

Through the drug-induced fog, everything became clear. They were staging my death, just like his! And in the same hospital no less.

I'm ready, Dad. Let's do this!

Splayed across the metal table, I burst into tears, as did Mom.

"Don't worry, Mom. I can do this. I'll make you both proud."

"I'm sure you will, Brian."

The world faded to black.

W hile I was sleeping that day, Mom and Joy and Greg went home to get some rest themselves, although for Joy that was difficult. Unbeknownst to me, she was in her first month of pregnancy with my second nephew, Jason. She had recently been experiencing terrible morning sickness, and the stress of the previous twelve hours had only made things worse. Joy had planned on surprising me with the exciting news when I was home for Christmas break. Now I was home, but there was no break. Far from it. There was confusion, and anxiety, and physical and emotional exhaustion. While I was in a drug-induced haze, sleeping like a baby, she was curled up in her bed with her hand wrapped around a plastic bowl trying to keep her dinner from regurgitating.

When I awoke, roughly twelve hours later, I was alone in a blinding fog, my cheek itching under crusted drool. I could tell by the crack of moonlight drizzling in through the half-closed metal blinds that it was the middle of the night, but as for where I was, or even what day it was, I had no idea at first.

Physically, I felt refreshed. Twelve hours' sleep was a gift my body had forgotten how to wish for after several weeks of sleep-deprived ecstasy. Mentally, however, I was still entangled, and excited that my mission to be reunited with my father would continue to unfold.

A different nurse than the one who had given me my medication when I first arrived at the hospital entered and re-took my vitals.

"Good evening, Brian, and Merry Christmas Eve," she said with a pleasant smile. "How are you feeling?"

"Great! Couldn't be better," I replied, my hyper-energy re-igniting. "Can I see him now? Can I see my father?"

"Well, the first person you'll be seeing is your doctor, but that won't be until the morning. For now, how 'bout I take you to your room where you'll be staying."

Thank goodness, I thought. *We're getting somewhere now. Leadership will certify me fit for service, and they'll sign off on my security clearance so I can get to work.*

"That sounds lovely, Ma'am."

As we walked through the psych ward, its décor reminded me of my freshman dorm at UConn. There was a common area with a small galley kitchen and tables arranged so residents could mingle. Adjacent to that was a makeshift living room decorated with old, worn sofas, a plush leather recliner, and a television embedded in a scratched wooden console. On top of the coffee table there were board games, crossword puzzles, and coloring books for adults. A Christmas tree with a few dull-colored bulbs and some scattered tinsel stood in the corner. Everything about the space seemed like perfect cover for a super-secret operation.

The nurse led me down a long corridor and into a small, private room. Against the wall there was a pine-wood bed draped with threadbare blankets and sheets. On the opposite side was a press-board dresser and an older desk with a legal pad and several pens resting on top.

"You'll be staying in here," the nurse said. "Why don't you get some more rest before your appointment in the morning?"

"No thanks," I replied. "Do you know when I'll be getting my equipment?"

"Let's worry about that later. If you're not tired, how about I give you a quick tour of the facilities?"

Our next stop was the recreation area, where we reviewed the "Rules of the Ward" and the daily activity schedule posted on the large corkboard beside the front desk. Breakfast, lunch, and dinner were served in the cafeteria. Between meals, residents were encouraged to participate in several small group social activities. There were scheduled arts & crafts, card games, writing workshops, and light exercise assemblies. All of that was optional, but patients must attend both group and individual therapy sessions, where they would work with doctors to develop personal "Wellness Plans."

Wellness plans. Interesting. Must be affiliated with my upcoming assignment.

When we finished the tour, it was time for more medication, and I gladly consumed it but not for reasons you might expect. I believed the pills would give me extra-human abilities to augment my natural talents as I worked beside my father to complete the next round of secret agent recruitment exercises. My psychotic convictions were amplified by my detainment, and I assumed everyone in the hospital was affiliated with the government somehow. Doctors and nurses were the commanding officers and trainers. Patients that occupied the other rooms were my fellow recruits. Group therapy was where the covert operations planning would be done. I was in boot camp, eager to move on to my real job at the end of this indoctrination period.

Shortly after, the medication began to make me drowsy, and I retired to my room. I quickly fell asleep but only briefly. I was suddenly awoken by a blaring ambulance siren echoing from the entrance to the hospital's Emergency Room below, and I leapt out of bed as if I had just rolled over onto a cactus. I tried to fall back asleep, but my intense anxiety prevented me from doing so and my psychotic excursion continued unfettered.

Since there was no formal curfew imposed on the ward, I was free to roam at will as long as I respected the established rules, so I migrated to the main "conference room" as it was referred to during my tour. I sat atop the long table, folded my legs under me, and stared at a large, empty whiteboard that stretched the entire length of the back wall. It was there where I decided to show the government everything I had accomplished since the agents first planted clues around my townhouse in Virginia – a "self-debriefing" of sorts, to show them just how successful I had been.

Using markers of various colors, I documented all my travels from D.C. to Maryland to Pennsylvania to New Jersey. I drew depictions of American flags, scribbled literary passages and lyrics from *Eagles* songs, interwove images of Christmas lights and panel vans throughout. I added a long list of names down the right side, including as many politicians and terrorists from the news I could think of: Osama Bin Laden, Saddam Hussein, George Bush, Dick Cheney. Beside that I jotted down several of my favorite actors and movie titles, including Kevin Costner and *Field of Dreams* – films my father and I had watched together and bonded over through the years. I even added Oprah Winfrey to my chronicles. Why? I have no idea.

By the time I finished, I had filled up every square inch of the whiteboard with a map of my mind's journey over the previous few weeks, which I entitled "RECRUITMENT" in big bold letters at the top. After I returned to my room, one of the night nurses snapped pictures of my work, and the following morning when I met with my doctor for the first time, he questioned me about what everything meant.

"Brian, can you explain all this to me?"

"Sure!"

While my responses made less sense than the diagram itself, it did clue him into the severity of my psychosis and just how long it might take for me to fully return to reality, a prognosis he shared with Mom and Joy when they arrived around lunchtime.

"Brian is highly psychotic," he said. "Drugs and sleep will help expedite his return to reality, but that isn't going to happen overnight. And we can't properly diagnose what's going on until he's stable."

The news further saddened and frustrated Joy and Mom. While neither of them were expecting the doctor to determine a finite diagnosis given the short time I had been in the hospital, they were hoping he would provide them with some tangible sign of progress, such as "Our next step is to monitor X. . ." or "I'm starting to understand Y. . ." or even something as basic as "We're going to give Brian new drug Z to see if that helps. . ." Instead, they were told that I was still flying as high as a kite and nobody was exactly sure when the turbulent cerebral winds fueling my ascent would stop blowing.

To make things even worse for Mom and Joy, I was so lost in the latest scene of my psychotic movie that I paid little attention to them during their visit. Since it was Christmas Day, Joy cooked our traditional holiday meal and brought the food into the hospital along with several presents they had gotten me, hoping that exposure to a normal routine might aid my navigation back to sanity. Across the conference room table, they spread out Joy's famous beef tenderloin with homemade horseradish cream sauce, buttery mashed potatoes, string bean casserole, and freshly baked crescent rolls. In front of each seat, they placed green napkins and plastic cups filled with grape juice instead of wine, as if we were sitting in Joy's dining room.

It was a kind, sincere gesture, intended to introduce some normalcy into a grossly abnormal and stressful series of events. And what did I do in return? I walked into the conference room, looked at the vast spread of food, ignored their thoughtful holiday cheer, walked right out, and went back to my room without even saying goodbye. There they sat in front of the delicious feast, sipping on grape juice, dumbfounded and heartbroken, while I was doing push-ups and jumping jacks, preparing for the next training exercise.

Merry Christmas, everyone.

Dear Kids,

Although many years have now passed since all of this occurred, it still makes me sad to think about how difficult my bipolar episode was for Grandma T., Auntie Joy, and Uncle Greg. That Christmas was our first without my dad, and that was difficult enough. My sudden hospitalization only made things worse.

At the same time, I'm inspired by how courageously they each pushed through their confusion and fear to guide me through the hospital treatment I desperately needed. While genetics predisposed me to the insanity I experienced, it was their unmitigated love which dictated the outcome.

Love,

Dad

Over the course of the next few days, my continued medication made it possible for me to rest, truly rest after weeks of unprecedented insomnia, and little by little, reality reasserted itself. I became aware of my hospital surroundings, and I stopped obsessing about secret agent recruitment exercises and what job I would be given after I completed my training. With every visit from Mom and Joy and Greg and even Josh who came to the ward one day and graced me with his toddler snuggles, I returned to being the son, brother, uncle I once was, and the reality I had long since forgotten began to enlighten me. However, as well and normal as I felt, one indelible fantasy persisted. I firmly expected that, at any moment, the real reason I was in the hospital would unveil itself: my father would walk into the ward and take me into his arms.

I miss you, Dad. God, do I miss you.

With the help of my doctors, nurses, and daily visits with my family, all the fuzz and mist and blur had mostly cleared by the end of my first week in the hospital. As the psychosis diminished, so did my narcissism, and I became increasingly aware that I had previously seen, heard, and felt things nobody else had perceived. I recognized that I had trouble organizing my thoughts and connecting them logically. But as I shed my paranoia, I was overcome with confusion. It was hard to understand why everything had happened.

Part of me did not want to let go of the euphoria I had wandered into. The way a cocaine addict confined to a rehab center misses the soaring energy and golden-lit moment of the high, I missed the elation of being a chosen man. The mental detoxification was excruciating. Letting go of the belief that my father was still alive was traumatizing. I latched on to that mirage as long as I possibly could. But with each passing day, the truth became clearer, and I realized that I had been holding onto an impossibly grandiose illusion.

Once I was firmly anchored in reality, my doctor sat me down to spell out my future. I was already bristling a bit before he got to the punch line.

"So, Brian, I've had a chance to go through all the basic tests we've administered. The good news is we've ruled out any kind of tumor or brain injury, any stroke or earlier brain bleed."

Funny. I had never considered any of those.

"We've also ruled out any deficiencies or abnormalities in your blood or vitals."

Yeah. So?

"What we have concluded is that you have Type I Bipolar Disorder. It's a mental illness. Not curable, but fully manageable."

His words were a gut punch. Mental illness?

"I don't know what that is. What does that mean?" I asked, defensively.

"Well, Brian, you have a mood disorder, and we're going to teach you how to keep it in check, how to modify your lifestyle so you can live with it. We're also going to –"

Now I was angry. Very angry.

"Excuse me? What are you talking about? What the hell is – what'd you call it? Bipolar Disorder? And what does Type I mean?"

At the time, I honestly didn't comprehend. In those days, the more common name for my mental illness remained "manic depression," at least in my orbit. I had only heard the term "bipolar" once in my entire life. In college, a friend had mentioned to me one drunken evening that he took medication for bipolar disorder, but I was no longer in touch with him. Neither had I ever heard Mom refer to my Uncle Danny as bipolar. So, I was doubly surprised when she interjected herself into my discussion with the doctor, which was quickly escalating.

"Beej, do you remember all the health issues Uncle Danny had? All the times I flew out to San Diego to help with his recovery? Well, Uncle Danny had bipolar disorder."

I rejected her insinuation. I was nothing like Uncle Danny. No way. Not even close. If Danny had bipolar disorder, it could only mean one thing: crazy. I was not crazy.

The doctor tried to reassure me, to explain that all my behaviors from the past few weeks were attributable to a flavor of bipolar disorder that was prone to psychosis. With treatment and medication, I could return to Virginia and continue living the life I had created for myself. But I was not having it. Did they really think I was going to equate myself with Uncle Danny? To an unstable, social outcast? A loner? No way.

I shook my head vigorously as my blood began to boil.

"Look," I said. "I'm totally sane. Usually happy, socially popular. A truly stable guy. . ."

"No, Brian. This is a conclusive diagnosis, and –"

"How do I know I can trust you?" I screamed. "You know what I think? I think you're the one who's crazy. Maybe you just want me to be sick so you can keep sending me medical bills."

I stormed out of his office and returned to my room, slamming the door behind me. I sat on my bed and punched my pillow several times as hard as I could.

Bipolar? What a joke.

I am not bipolar.

In the days that followed, I attempted to rationalize everything the doctor had said, but I only confused myself further and became more angry. I shut down and refused to participate in my follow-on therapy sessions, in the small group activities, in anything prescribed by the hospital staff. I was appalled. The doctor's assessment was complete bullshit. How dare they call me "bipolar"? It just didn't make sense.

I contemplated possible alternatives. Maybe I accidentally consumed a hallucinogenic hidden in one of the many McDonald's cheeseburgers I had eaten in the previous few weeks? Maybe the passenger sitting next to me on the plane ride to Florida slipped something into my glass of bourbon? Maybe, maybe, maybe. . . anything but what the doctors were telling me.

Above all, however, I wanted out of the hospital. My confinement made me feel like a lab rat scurrying through an endless maze in search of an exit I would never find. Driven by the objective to extricate myself from the ward as soon as possible, I became obsessed with how bad my quality of life had become. The bland cafeteria food that hadn't really bothered me previously, now appalled me. My inability to breathe in fresh air, to feel the sun's warm rays penetrate my skin became utterly dispiriting. The blaring sirens of ambulances pulling into the hospital were perhaps the worst, waking me up in the middle of the night, displaced and terrified. I needed to get out of there.

I pleaded with my doctor, but he refused to let me leave.

"I'm doing better now, Doc," I said. "And I signed myself into the unit, can't I just sign myself out?"

"That's not how this works, Brian."

"Well that's how it should freakin' work. . ."

Asshole.

Although I was furious, I quickly realized that the only path to liberation was to make a show of acquiescence. I had to pretend to accept my diagnosis and work through my "Wellness Plan" in order to earn my release. Cooperation was my ticket to freedom, and I knew that I needed to shut up and start making everyone around me believe I was on my path to recovery.

So I lied.

From that point forward, I began blatantly lying to everyone, including Mom and Joy. I was intent on accommodating the "crazy" label. It was a small price to pay for my freedom, I reasoned.

It worked.

After a week of "impeccable behavior" as the head nurse described it, I was able to voluntarily release myself from the hospital. The doctors did stipulate, however, that given the severity of my episode, my release came with several non-negotiable conditions, all codified within another stack of legal paperwork and my signature a dozen times.

"Brian, you are required to remain under your mother's direct supervision for the next two weeks," my doctor decreed. "You must adhere to that, do you understand?"

"Yes."

"In addition, you must continue taking your medication, and you must attend outpatient therapy in both individual and group forums."

Great. More therapy. Just what I was hoping for.

"Do you agree to that?"

"Yes."

Do I have a choice?

I was disappointed I couldn't return to Virginia and get back to work and the rest of my normal, happy life right away, but I was in no position to challenge the arrangement. My sought-after release back into the work of my small business, back to my happy hours and pick-up basketball games with friends, would come soon enough.

At home, I mostly sat on the couch and watched TV. Mom welcomed me back to childhood and attended to her motherly duties. She washed my clothes and cooked all my favorite comfort foods, treating me as if I were home from school, sick with the flu. We didn't talk much about the hospital or my psychosis or anything else related to my episode. In the middle of one Scrabble game we played, she casually tried to coax me to open up a bit, but I wanted nothing to do with such nonsense and brushed her inquiry aside.

Following the doctor's, and my mother's, stern orders, I continued taking my prescribed medication – a cocktail of anti-psychotics and anti-depressants and anti-a-few-other-things I had never heard of before. I despised them. At first, they had only given me an occasional stomachache and curbed my appetite. But after several weeks, they made me perpetually lethargic and disori-ented. I wanted no part of them, but I followed the strict instruc-tions I was given in fear of delaying my release from the prison sentence I had been handed.

I was reluctant to attend all my outpatient therapy sessions, but I adhered to that directive, too. My one-on-one meetings with my psychiatrist were relatively painless, and after a while, lying about accepting my illness became an easy routine. Group therapy, however, was a completely different story.

If there was one thing that made me defiantly skeptical about having a mental illness, it was group therapy. Attending each session was the emotional equivalent of lying in a dentist's chair undergoing a root canal without anesthesia. There I was, forced to socialize with a dozen strangers pacing endlessly and chattering to themselves, chain-smoking cigarettes during the breaks, weeping through individual sob stories.

"I can't get myself out of bed in the morning," one woman said before she broke down in tears in front of everyone.

"My boss fired me, and I don't know how I'm going to pay my rent," said another man, attempting to play on everyone's heart-strings, as if he hoped we would all pull out our wallets and hand him some cash.

What a bunch of losers, I thought to myself.

In my full state of denial about my illness, the very idea of sharing anything about myself with anyone, especially complete strangers, repulsed me. The snob in me rejected the notion I could be anything like any of them. First off, except for me and the psychiatrist leading the session, there wasn't a single white-collar professional in the room. How could any of them possibly understand what I experienced? Second, many of them were recovering drug addicts being treated for withdrawal afflictions alongside their mental health issues. How was that remotely like my situation? I didn't do drugs, and I was nowhere near depressed.

Given the severity of my psychotic episode, coupled with decades of bipolar clinical statistics, my outpatient psychiatrist cautioned me on the potential for heavy depression I might experience during my recovery period.

"You should prepare yourself for distress, Brian," she said. "I know you feel good now, but that may very well change."

Of course, I was dubious. Never in my twenty-seven years on earth had I experienced depression. I was happy. I had always been happy. I was successful and confident. Why should that change? *Depression is weakness*, I thought at the time. No matter what life had dished out, I had never suffered from depression, and I was determined I never would.

I nodded my head to acknowledge her hypothesis, hoping she would move on to another topic. But she didn't.

"Bipolar episodes are like roller coaster rides," she continued. "The higher you go on the ride, the lower you descend, and your ride was higher than most."

Her analogy alone disgusted me. I despise roller coasters. How anyone can find enjoyment from feeling like they're going to fall hundreds of feet to their bloody death is beyond me. But I wasn't going to challenge her and continued my appeasement.

"I'll keep that in mind, thanks for the warning."

Looking back, I'm sure each of my doctors knew I was lying to them, at least to some degree. When they probed for more information about my feelings towards my diagnosis, I didn't give them anything noteworthy. I kept my answers short and sweet, nodded and smiled to shield my denial and anger. But clinicians know better. They can see through duplicity, and I doubt I fooled anyone as much as I thought I was doing.

The two people I know I didn't fool were Mom and Joy. While they didn't approach me directly about their skepticism in fear that any confrontation would disrupt the progress I seemed to be making, they had an inkling that I wasn't being truthful – my sudden, about-face acceptance of my illness in the hospital being the leading indicator. They, too, have regrets about how they responded to all these events, including not probing deeper and challenging me where appropriate. But hindsight indeed has 20/20 vision, and nobody except Marty McFly from *Back to the Future* gets to travel back in time to change history. We just have to learn from our mistakes and try not to repeat them.

Easier said than done, of course.

As my strength returned, being consigned to the home I grew up in became a source of anxiety just as it had been on Thanksgiving. The constant reminder of my father's absence, and in particular, the suffocating cigarette smoke odor baked into the carpet and furniture, was strangling. Trapped in a cage from which I could not break free, I did everything I could to make the required two weeks go by as quickly as possible, spending as much of the day outside the house as I could. I ran a lot, albeit short distances. I temporarily joined a local gym to lift weights. I went to the local coffee shop and bantered with the other patrons. I even pushed through and successfully endured my therapy sessions, as challenging as that was to do without losing my mind. Again.

In truth, though, despite all the progress I thought I was making, everything I had run away from the previous year after my father died was still there. While my delusional search for him had come to an end, my grief over his absence endured. But I pushed it aside, refused to confront it. It was easier just to escape.

At last, my two weeks of detainment concluded. I was released and allowed to return to Virginia. Where I belonged. As I was getting in the car, Mom made me promise her one more time that I would continue taking my medication and also that I would meet regularly with my psychiatrist in Alexandria, an arrangement the hospital had coordinated.

"I promise, Mom," I said.

But it was a promise I had no intention of keeping.

I had gone into the psych ward of Yale New Haven Hospital searching for my father's ghost, and I left being chased by another familial one: my Uncle Danny. From that point forward, my life began to resemble a not-so-fun game of Ms. Pac Man. There I was, scrambling through a complex labyrinth, where exits were entrances, power pellets were scarce, and the harrowing spirits now out-numbered me.

My bipolar diagnosis marked the beginning of my identity conflict – a gory three-way battle between my illness, the man I used to be, and the one I always thought I'd become. And at the center of the battlefield stood a dead uncle, the black sheep of the Scecina family, wielding a razor-sharp machete and choreographing each enemy attack.

Growing up, Uncle Danny was somewhat of a mystery to both Joy and me. He lived on the West Coast, and we only saw him on the rare occasions he visited us in Connecticut, usually around the holidays. Our feelings towards him were contradictory. On one hand, he was flighty, sporadic, traveling at a whim to various places for no apparent reason. His recurring hospitalizations were burdensome, causing fights between my mom and my dad who lacked the financial means to fly out to California and support him whenever he fell off the mental health wagon, which was often. On the other hand, he was funny, kind, and childlike in his willingness to shower Joy and me in ever-affectionate love whenever he visited us.

Since my relationship with Uncle Danny was distant, I had largely forgotten about him until Mom mentioned his name during that meeting with my doctor in the hospital. Then, I couldn't get him out of my mind.

After being anointed with the same "Scarlet B" as Uncle Danny, I began drawing comparisons of his life to mine in ways that I had never thought of before. Things like. . . we both left home right after college, excited to explore the world beyond the comforts of our families and childhood friends. . . and we both became entrepreneurs, driven to work for nobody but ourselves. . . and we both travelled randomly, and often alone – Danny to Costa Rica and Mexico and Hawaii and me to Los Angeles and the Bahamas and Detroit one time for no other reason but to see the Yankees battle the Tigers for playoff contention and return right after the game.

We both, we both, we both. . .

At the same time, my ego was dismissing the notion that I was anything like Uncle Danny. From the outcast image of him which Mom and the rest of our family routinely painted, my uncle appeared perpetually unstable, and his confidence seemed to ebb and flow. My confidence did not ebb and flow. Although I was timid and bashful in my younger years, by the time I reached high school I was self-assured, optimistic, proud, and occasionally a cocky son of a bitch — a persona that I carried into adulthood.

In addition to comparing myself to Uncle Danny, my identity crisis was exasperated by my extreme confusion over what the hell had just transpired. Everything I had experienced since Thanksgiving didn't make sense to me. Mania? Psychosis? How was that possible? Prior to my episode, there wasn't a single sign pointing to me having a mental illness, at least none that I was cognizant of. My life up until that point was successful, safe, secure, content, and generally well-balanced. Suddenly being told my brain functioned abnormally was like a hard ground ball coming out of nowhere and hitting me square in the nuts. Yet, even though I was knocked straight to the ground and required immediate medical attention, I still didn't want to believe it. I couldn't believe it. There had to be some other rationale.

However, what tormented me the most was the sudden emergence of Mom, Joy, and Greg as my health caretakers, and to some extent, the way they pampered me while they did so. Amongst my three-and-a-half parents, my father was the only coddler, not them. My mother and sister protected me but never once indulged or babied me when challenges were presented. That was, in part, because those challenges were never severe. Sure, I had fallen down a couple times and needed their help. But I had never gotten run over by a truck and desperately needed their utmost care. Now, suddenly, I had. The truck had come out of nowhere, and it had come fast. In its wake, I didn't just need their support; I needed to be *rescued* – picked up at a police station in the middle of the night and brought to a hospital. Guided back to reality then guarded like a convict upon my release.

The mania and psychosis I experienced perplexed me at the time, but it doesn't now. In fact, it makes perfect sense, especially since mental illness exists in my family's hereditary line. The brain is a powerful machine, and bipolar disorder is like a high octane fuel that gets pumped into its gas tank. When that machine is running at peak manic performance, it doesn't know how to shut itself down, and unless someone else is around to recognize the dysfunction and intervene, the engine will continue to roar.

Now that much time has passed, I have a better understanding of the similarities, and clear differences, between my Uncle Danny and me. Like me, Uncle Danny was very confident. Way too confident in certain situations is perhaps a better way to describe it. I didn't know this about Uncle Danny when I was growing up because we rarely talked about him, and when we did, his mental health struggles overshadowed the successful life he led when he was healthy. But in retrospect, this makes sense, too. Also like me, Uncle Danny was a "loner" who fought relationship commitment at every turn, just like I did for a long time. Whether or not he enjoyed living a life of virtual solitude for as long as he did, I don't know for certain. But I can assume that, like me, he both did and didn't.

For all the similarities between Uncle Danny and me, there is one which undoubtedly stands out the most: we both ran away from our problems and not just bipolar disorder. Uncle Danny began his long, treacherous marathon when he neglected to accept his responsibilities as a father. I began mine after suddenly losing my own.

PART V

Depression

Tuesday, May 1st, 2001

The drive to All Saints Cemetery is a short one, just a few miles up the road from Ezra Street. I am glad we have chosen this cemetery, so Dad can rest peacefully knowing Mom and Joy and Uncle Joe and Grandma are all close by. It will be an easier transition for everyone this way. Well, everyone but me, who will be hundreds of miles away.

When we arrive at the cemetery, the funeral director is talking with the head caretaker, coordinating this Saturday's events. The director had annoyed me at the funeral home, but now I am glad he is here. It's a relief to be guided through this arduous process, to have someone tell us where to go and what to do and who will be doing it. Without his assistance, we'd all be sitting around staring at each other like a herd of deer dazed by the lights of an oncoming car.

After Uncle Joe and Aunt Louise and Grandma arrive, we stroll through the cemetery looking at various plots where Dad could be buried. Scattered across the rolling hills are a small army of tall stone statues, each depicting one of the New Testament Apostles – the guardians of All Saints Cemetery who watch over the dead like sheepherders tending to their spiritual flock.

I wonder if Dad will like it here, I ask myself. I wonder if the Saints will put him at ease, or if he'd prefer to be buried elsewhere, or if he would have wanted to be cremated? I assume if it were his choice, he'd request to be buried 6 feet under home plate at Yankee Stadium instead. But I doubt that's an option now.

We stop at a patch of open ground at the bottom of a small hill overlooking the center of North Haven.

"There are four plots here," the caretaker says.

I suddenly recall an earlier conversation between Mom and Uncle Joe – one that I had tuned out, like so many others. We are in search of four plots, not just one, allowing Uncle Joe to be buried next to his older brother when his time comes, with Mom and Aunt Louise on either side of them. A thoughtful gesture, I think to myself. A place where their souls can be reunited, and we can come pay our respects all at once.

My heartwarming sentiments are blindsided by logistical questions for the caretaker:

"How close will we be placed next to each other?" Mom asks.

"How much do all four plots cost?" Uncle Joe follows. "And what assurance do we receive that these will never be taken by someone else?"

Their questions snap me out of my temporary trance. Now frustrated, I want to sarcastically ask if we can get a fifth plot free with the multi-plot purchase, a joke Dad might have made if he were here. But I keep my inappropriate comment to myself.

When my brain can no longer handle the group's administrative discourse, I step away and walk to the crest of the slope just in front of us. I close my eyes and take a deep breath. The robins and blue jays chirping at each other in the nearby trees settle the chaos in my mind. The hot afternoon sun cleanses me. Everything is going to be okay, I repeat to myself. We're all going to be okay.

I look over to my left and notice Joy has separated herself from the group as well. She sees me and calls me over.

"Beej, check this out," she says, pointing to the base of the statue that's just a few steps from the cemetery plot I am now guessing we will choose. Below the Apostle's feet, the inscription reads "Saint John."

"Well, I guess this was meant to be," I say, and we both smile.

Joy puts her arm around me.

"I believe so, Beej."

I step away from Joy to examine Saint John's broad shoulders and flowing robes; his woven-down hair and chiseled face; his commiserating eyes observing me. He holds a scroll in his right hand and a chalice in his left. From the center of the cup, a slithering snake protrudes like some mythical serpent rising out of the water. I return to Joy and put her arm back around me to protect me from the serpent, to usher me through my fear.

My diagnosis left me in a state of stunned denial. I had no idea what I was up against, but I believed that the sooner I got back to Virginia, back to my own life, the sooner I could put the whole thing behind me. Bipolar disorder, therapy, doctors, drugs, wellness plans. Everything. I could dismiss all of it and return unscathed to the sanctuary of my work and friends and weekly poker games with my buddies.

I was wrong. So wrong.

Returning that January was much more difficult than I anticipated.

To begin with, as far as my social life there was concerned, I had simply disappeared. None of my friends had any idea where I'd gone, why I had been out of touch for so long. I had skipped all the traditional Christmas and New Year's parties and had dodged phone calls from everyone I knew. When people saw me, they were befuddled because I told nonsensical, inconsistent lies, and I looked terrible. While I had recouped some strength before departing North Haven, my weight loss was still salient.

I was not myself, and I could not remedy the disconnect. There was no way I was going to tell anyone that I had been locked up in an insane asylum. I would never portray myself as a Donnie Darko, a mentally ill movie character from a psychological thriller that me and some friends had seen together several months prior. Donnie was crazy. I was not, and so long as I could help it, the truth would never escape.

My professional life was just as challenging to manage. Despite my concerted efforts, I was incapable of affecting damage control with my clients and particularly my biggest one in Florida whom I had humiliated myself in front of during my manic rampage.

"Hey Captain, I've been trying to reach you. Can you please give me a call back when you get a chance?"

He did not call.

Other clients, angered by my extended non-responsiveness, fell away. I tried to save face by invoking the standard "pressing family issues" excuse, the professional way of saying "it's none of your damned business," but that didn't work. My mysterious absence had caused significant disruption and left my colleagues holding the bag.

Thanks to my unhealthy work ethic in the wake of my father's death, I had accumulated plenty of savings to cover my expenses. But I wanted to work, to keep myself busy, to suppress everything that had happened to me. My answer was to seek out alternate clientele, and I contacted everyone in my network I could think of. I was obsessed with starting the new year with new clients, new responsibilities, new innovations to develop – anything that led me toward reconciling myself to a diagnosis I persistently rejected.

Mom and Joy called me often to check in on me.

"How ya doing, Beej?" Mom asked. "Are you taking things slow and easing back into work?"

I lied, assured her that was exactly what I was doing.

"You back to playing basketball at the YMCA with your friends?" Joy inquired.

I lied again. There was no time for basketball until I found a new revenue stream for my business.

Greg contacted me regularly as well and made several attempts to help me rebuild my confidence in any clever way he could surmise.

"Check out this archived Stevie Ray Vaughn song, Beej," he wrote in an email. "My fingers are too slow to play that intro riff, but I bet you can figure it out."

I had little interest in picking up my guitar, let alone trying to mimic the fretboard mastery of a legend. But I assured Greg I'd work on it and get back to him.

Deceiving each of them was easy. After all, they were over 300 miles away. It was also kind, or so I convinced myself. Why not let them think I was heeding their guidance and all was perfectly well? It would protect them, and it wouldn't hurt me. A win-win for everyone.

Disregarding the promise I had made to Mom, I also lied about my medications. I had stopped taking them, tossed them all in the trash alongside my prescriptions. I had grown tired of the listlessness they induced, and the daily reminder of an abstract illness I did not have. *Only sick people need drugs*, I told myself, *and I am not sick*. There wasn't a chance in hell I would put another psychotropic drug into my system. I did not need them.

When I stopped taking lithium and the other medications I was prescribed, I had an initial burst of physical energy. Running felt better than ever. But only for a little while. Then, suddenly, inexplicably, I began to feel drained. My focus ebbed, my breath faltered, and I was unable to find a comfortable pace. Eventually my endurance collapsed, and my body no longer wanted to run.

I stopped running altogether, which deflated me. After that, everything I loved became boring. I lost interest in all my favorite hobbies and pastimes: going to the movies, hosting parties, maintaining the visual appeal of my home, reading novels. I didn't see the point in any of them. All I wanted to do was lie on the couch and binge-watch reruns of *Gilligan's Island* and *The Love Boat*.

My disinterest eventually extended to my business. I could not fathom writing a single line of code, and I stopped trying to find new work. Then, I realized that with no clients I would eventually have to take a job working for someone else, which meant giving up my autonomy, my professional identity – everything I had worked so hard to establish. But I couldn't make myself care.

No matter how hard I tried, I was unable to process all this sudden, unbearable distress. I was stuck on a baffling ferris wheel without the strength or experience to exit the ride, a miserable place that was completely foreign to me. I felt like a total failure, and I hated who I had become.

I inevitably sank into the deeper depression my psychiatrist at Yale had warned me about, the same wretched place my fellow group therapy attendees had described which I had sharply ridiculed. Even then, I rejected my diagnosis. Instead, I rationalized that I was depressed because of what the hospital had put me through. It was the doctors' and nurses' fault – restricting me from breathing fresh air, shoving medication cocktails down my throat – and now I was paying the price of their mistreatment. If they had just let me leave when I wanted, none of this would have happened.

As the depression tightened its grip, I became an automaton, mechanically going through the routines of my day: Sleep. Wake. Eat. Watch soap operas and game shows. Eat. Watch. Eat. Sleep. I only left the house to buy groceries or fast food. After a while, even trips to Safeway and Burger King ceased. It was too much trouble to go anywhere, so I resorted to having pizza and Chinese food delivered in large quantities providing me with plenty of leftovers.

My apathy turned to abject fear as flashbacks of my psychotic exploits began to infiltrate. My demons preferred the darkness, and I'd wake up in the middle of the night, trembling, reliving scenes of the madness I experienced in vivid detail: driving my car at top speeds as I chased government agents; standing in front of the Lincoln Memorial listening to my parents speak; hearing tortuous voices dictate commands. Interspersed in between were snapshots of all the "clues" my adventure revealed: blinking

Christmas lights, book passages, ketchup bottles, client emails, American flags, panel vans, the New York City skyline. I buried my head underneath my pillow to fight off the terrifying images overtaking my mind.

In that dark, demoralizing place, I began thinking there had to be something in the information my doctors and Mom had imparted. Maybe they were both right about my medication? Maybe if I started taking my pills again, I could head this thing off and emerge from this misery? I hated the idea of putting more drugs into my system, but I was desperate.

My psychiatrist at Yale had recommended Marty, a practitioner near me in Virginia, whom she had contacted on my behalf at the end of my therapy sessions. I called him, apologizing first.

"Hi Marty. Sorry for the delay in contacting you. It took a while to get settled," I said. "Listen, I'm running out of medication, and I'd like to make an appointment to see you."

It felt good to contact Marty. I could stop lying to Mom, who remained under the impression that I was taking my meds and dutifully going to therapy. The move was another win-win. No more lying, no more guilt, no more faking it, and with a little luck, no more depression.

Marty saw through me the instant I walked into his office.

I was put off at first. His physical appearance alone repulsed me. The guy didn't look like any doctor I had ever seen. He was whacky and scatter-brained, lanky and loose-limbed, resembling a Christopher Lloyd doppelganger. His long, unkempt gray hair kept getting in his eyes, and with pen in hand, he swiped it away, occasionally knocking his crooked reading glasses off his nose and on to his desk. While we spoke, he sat in his perpetually swiveling chair, never really looking at me, shuffling through stacks of patient files and scraps of loose paper scattered across his desk.

As distressed as I was, my initial assessment was that I would never be able to trust this poseur of a doctor, wearing wrinkled, casual clothing and walking around his office in his dirty white athletic socks. Everything about Marty made me even more anxious, vulnerable, and depressed than I already was. If I had not needed those drugs, I would have bolted.

As Marty questioned me, I felt like a lab rat again. Even though he had a copy of my detailed Yale record, his inquiries were like general hospital intake questions that he should have already had the answers to.

Then, he shifted gears. No more benign eccentric. He turned invasive.

"Tell me what it felt like when you were experiencing your psychosis."

"Talk about your Uncle Danny. What did you know about him and his illness? What kind of a guy was he? Did you relate to him?"

The interrogation escalated.

"How did your father die? How did you handle his death? Do you think it was his passing that triggered your illness?"

My illness. Again with this illness bullshit. "Go fuck yourself, Marty," I wanted to scream at him, but I refrained.

I hated every question that spewed from Marty's mouth. I also hated my predicament, that the only way I felt I could tunnel out of my stultifying depression was with the help of the drugs I needed this nut job to prescribe. Why couldn't we just cut to the chase? Give me what I came for and release me from this hell.

I tried to relax, but Marty and his weirdness made that impossible. I got testy.

"Can you please just finish your questions and write me a prescription?"

He, too, became noticeably frustrated.

"Look," he said. "You're pretty defensive, even downright aggressive. I'll give you the meds, but only for one week. You want more? You have to come back next week to get them."

I snorted, angrily, but refrained from darting out the door until he was finished.

"If you don't want to come back here, I can give you names of colleagues. You can see anyone you like, but given your condition, you have to see someone."

I shrugged and left the office, pissed off. All this guy managed to do was make me feel worse. Thank God he gave me the prescription, but how could it possibly help to be coming back to this lunatic every week?

Even the initial gratitude for the medication was short-lived. The only effect it had on me was to make me so drowsy that I could barely get out of bed in the morning. My fear and self-loathing deepened, and I fell further into depression. My anxiety elevated to having panic attacks, feeling my heart palpitate, occasionally losing my ability to breathe. I had lost all self-confidence, and it felt as if there would never be a remedy to my despair.

As disgusted as I was by the thought of seeing Marty again, I called his office and made another appointment. By the time it arrived, I was shaking with fear.

The second time around, I approached Marty with an entirely different mindset. I needed help, and I was ready to shed my defenses, to drop my aggressive refusal of his professional care. The minute I entered, I burst into tears.

"Nothing's normal, Marty," I sobbed. "I'm losing it, and my world is caving in around me."

Marty's stance changed too. He came out from the shelter of his desk, placed his swivel chair beside me, and stopped swiveling. He pressed his boney, yet steady hand on my shoulder and nodded encouragingly.

"Cry it out, Brian. It's okay. You will feel better. Maybe not today. And maybe not for a while. But you will feel better. I promise."

We only talked briefly that day, and afterward, Marty wrote me another prescription. Before I left, he locked me into another appointment just a couple of days later. I filled my prescription, went home, took the pills, and fell onto the couch, fairly paralyzed with drowsiness once again.

My mental state only got worse from there.

———

Dear Kids,

Before we go any further, I want you to know that my acute depression is what has, perhaps, positively impacted my life the most. I know that may seem strange given the severity of the circumstances, but it's true. Enduring this torment has made me the person I am today, the father that you know.

It's a time-weathered, overused cliché, but it couldn't be more accurate: the things that hurt us the most, are, indeed, the things that make us stronger. It just never feels like that in the moment.

Love,

Dad

As the brutal cold of winter emerged that February, I had deteriorated into a world of perpetual blackness. Television no longer distracted me. My mind was too dazed to follow the dramas well, and heroes made me feel even more inadequate than I had perceived myself to be. The comedies were even worse, reminding me I had not smiled in weeks, which now seemed like eons.

Every day became a scratched record slowly spinning, the needle stuck in one perseverating groove. Nothing brought relief. Nothing moved the music forward. I would wake up depressed and take my meds, which did nothing to alter my lackluster state of mind and further depleted my energy. I'd doze on and off throughout the day, then go back to sleep for ten – twelve – fourteen hours. Every. Single. Night.

Some mornings when I awoke, I felt briefly rested, at peace. But the peace was an illusion, the product of that dreamy half-consciousness that comes after a long slumber. In that moment, the hopelessness would temporarily recede. Then, without any warning, I was adrift again, my mind obsessed with how much of a failure I had become, unable to remember what that inner peace had even felt like just a few minutes before.

I devolved into a vile-smelling zombie. Incapable of showering or donning clean clothes or brushing my teeth, I was rotting in my own filth. I hid under my unwashed sheets and comforter in a perpetual fetal position, nauseated by the smell of my unchanged pajamas but without the strength to do anything about it.

Even wrapped in all my winter blankets, I could not get warm. Blood ran ice-cold through my veins, as if I were standing naked in the chilly winter air outside. When the shivering became uncontrollable, I would drag my bedding to my carpeted floor, open a curtain enough to let in a ribbon of sunlight, and curl back up in its rays like a cat lying around the house waiting for its owner to return. As the sun shifted throughout the day, I would creep along with it to feel the warmth on my skin, resituating my covers, desperate to thaw my frigid body.

Too ashamed to share my despair with anyone, especially Mom and Joy, the two people I felt I had failed the most, I clung to Marty, fearful and disgusted with myself. At one point, he asked to see me every day, even on the weekends, given how worried he was about my well-being. I complied although my depression hurt so deeply that over time I barely had the strength to drive to his office. If I couldn't, he said he would pick me up himself. As heartwarming of a gesture as that was, it made me feel ever more inadequate and ashamed.

Marty kept altering my medication to see what might help, but nothing changed. After a while, it seemed like even he knew there would be no near-term resolution, no matter what chemical stabilizers we tried. He never verbalized that, but he seemed as discouraged as me that drugs were having limited, if any, effects on my state of mind. Regardless, he remained positive, ensured me that in time I would feel better. But I was incapable of believing him.

Eventually, total wretchedness settled in. I asked myself over and over why was I even alive? What was the point? What difference did anything make? I began to view everything – world politics, love, the mail service, even the Yankees – in the same way I viewed potato chips or M & Ms. No nutritional value, no redeeming qualities. The only emotion I experienced was deep sadness, and I just lay on the couch dejected, weeping.

I contemplated suicide. Often. Although I was conflicted about carrying it through. Yes, I had ceased to be alive, but I wasn't entirely ready to be dead either. I was also afraid I'd fail. Incomplete suicide would just add another failure to my long litany of self-defeats.

While I didn't have the fortitude to kill myself, the suicidal ideations, the morose preoccupations were no less prevalent, and I wondered how long it would be before the impulse to end the suffering would win.

Joy and Mom kept me alive. Indirectly. Their phone calls were always in my preconscious reasoning, and the concern in their voice messages kept my suicidal thoughts at bay.

"Beej. Why won't you call me back?" Joy pled. "I just want to know you're okay. Mom is worried She doesn't say much, but I can tell. Call us."

Mom was more forceful and out-of-character for her Zen self.

"Brian, I know you want your privacy. I respect that. But I'm your mother, and I do want to know that everything is okay with you. Please call me."

I could not return their messages. It wasn't that I wanted to hurt them. I was just unable to touch or be touched by them. I could not feel the emotions I needed to feel. I was numb. I couldn't feel anything. How could I face the people who loved me when I could not return their affection? How could I expose my lifeless condition? How could I interrupt their lives any more than I already had? It wasn't because of them I could not be a happy and healthy and independently functioning adult. I did not want to hurt them any further.

I had become Uncle Danny, the family burden, the black sheep, and there was absolutely nothing I could do about it.

Finally, I came to a juncture where I had to choose. There were only two possible ways this miserable state could end. I could live, or I could die. That was it, and the thought obsessed me. On what side of this sharp binary equation was I to stand? If I thought I could go back to the way I was, I would have known exactly what to choose. But my former life seemed beyond my reach. I was no longer any kind of me I recognized. I had morphed into a defunct alien. No one – not friends, not family, not work colleagues – would ever understand, and I wanted it all to end.

Standing at the edge of a cliff, poised to eventually jump, a blinding white light filled the void. In the middle, floating over the abyss, was my father. He extended his hand, and I took hold of it.

Take me home, Dad.

Bring me peace.

———

J ust as my psychotic experiences altered my understanding of what it means to be "crazy," my bipolar depression altered my beliefs on what it means to be, well, "depressed." Prior to my first bipolar episode, I had never experienced depression directly, and I oversimplified the impact it had on people who did. I equated it to being generally sad, feeling run-down a little longer than normal, lacking energy one would typically have. While depression embodies those traits, if you simplify it that way, it becomes a dangerous, misguided, colloquial trope which denigrates those who suffer.

People talk about feeling "depressed" and going for a walk to clear their heads. Perhaps they fail a test of some kind, stumble over some new obstacle in life, face rejection of some sort and find themselves drinking or eating too much, unable to engage in the things that usually make them happy. That state is serious, but it is temporary. I mean no diminution when I say that it can pass after some time with friends or self-meditation. Sufferers emerge from it and pick up where they left off. But acute bipolar depression, as it burrowed into my mentally ill mind and frail body, was something else altogether. Something I never could have imagined. It was all-encompassing and debilitating. It engulfed my soul, and it nearly took my life.

But it didn't.

What it took to recover was *time*. A lot of it. Nearly six months in total, to be more precise. And it also took my willingness to accept support from my family and friends, just as Marty had advised.

I did not have the strength to do much of anything, but I did continue my frequent visits with Marty, who guided me through the darkness with kind listening and constant encouragement. He reminded me that the simple act of leaving my house and driving to his office was substantial progress. So was taking my medication, which I did without question, still hoping it would soon magically cure me, even though he told me it wouldn't.

I was too depressed to fully grasp all of Marty's assurances at the time, but my trust in him expanded with each appointment, and slowly I began to accept my illness, to understand its power and control. That was a very difficult hurdle to get over. I fervently didn't want to be associated with my diagnosis, with anything equating me with Uncle Danny. When I caught a glimpse of my reflection anywhere, I saw *BIPOLAR* scrawled across my forehead, and I was sure Mom, Joy, Greg, and everyone else would look on me with pity forever after. Even if the drugs would help me, nothing would alleviate that.

At the end of each visit, as I was putting on my jacket to leave, Marty asked the same question: "Do you think you're ready to call your mother or sister?"

The answer remained "No" for a while. I wasn't ready to confront the web of shameful, humiliating lies I had spun. But with his relentless advocacy, I eventually drummed up the courage.

I talked with Joy first. It was difficult to get any words out, and I spoke very little as she asked me why I had been out of touch for as long as I had, even though she had already assumed the reason. The concern in her voice broke me down, and I cried uncontrollably. Joy cried too. Through my tears, I managed to share some of my suffering, but I could not bring myself to tell her how severe it had become.

"I'm worried about you, Beej," she said. "Why don't I come down and visit you?"

I wanted that. I needed that. Desperately. But I was too ashamed of everything I had already put her through, and too afraid to confront my own emotions on the matter if we met face-to-face.

"No, Sis, I'll be okay. You've got a lot on your plate with little Josh and being pregnant and everything else. Just take care of yourself."

Mom and I spoke as well, and I told her the same half-truths: my bipolar episode had caught up to me; I was struggling, lacking some confidence, but nothing further.

"I'm okay, Mom, really," I said, attempting to sound convincing. "This too shall pass, just like you always used to tell us as kids."

Mom consoled me without judgment and assured me I was not alone in my struggles.

"We're here for you, Beej. Whatever you need, it's yours," she said. "If that's privacy, we'll give it to you. If you want to come home, I'll fly down and bring you back myself."

In my heart, I wanted to go home, but my ruptured spirit demanded seclusion – a complicated, enfeebling paradox. I was comforted to know Mom and Joy were there for me. But at the same time, my shame was pushing their love and support further and further away.

Each conversation with Joy and Mom yielded a tinge of hope, but I still did not have the fortitude to share my depression with anyone else, not even with my most intimate friends. By this time, many of them – particularly those who lived near me – were worried about me. I continued to ignore their phone calls and emails, and I had ceased making appearances at our regularly scheduled movie nights and birthday parties. They had all stopped believing my standard work excuse that I was "busy wrapping up a very large project." I had been wrapping up that project for months by that point, but not the project I was fabricating. I had been trying to tie a pretty little bow around my psychosis and depression and put it all behind me. A futile endeavor, to be sure. But at the time, I had no direct context to draw from. I only knew that I was afraid.

It's here where my closest, life-long friends stepped in to help me get back on my feet, and without their support I'm not sure I ever could have. We are all still as inseparable today as we were when we first met in our early 20's – the type of friends that you don't see for months or even years, yet remain as close as if you had coffee with them several times a week. My "circle of trust" as Marty and I began to refer to them after I accepted their refuge and they helped me dredge through my despair.

It was my friend Steve who was the first person to step into my bipolar trust circle, and from that point forward, he appointed himself my guardian angel.

Steve and I met shortly after I graduated from UConn and moved to Virginia to begin an internship with an engineering company. A recent graduate of the U.S. Naval Academy, Steve was attending the Marine Corps' Officer Candidate School (OCS) in Quantico at the time, just a short drive from me in Alexandria. On the weekends, he would visit my roommates and me. We drank beer and watched football during the day and strolled through the bars in Georgetown at night, shooting pool and flirting with any woman who wasn't put off by our banal jokes and childish antics.

Steve and I quickly realized we had many interests in common, including running, which we did often together. He had also grown up in Connecticut, but he didn't meander into independence. He left to attend an elite military academy, where physical and mental toughness were pre-requisites. Moreover, he was preparing to be an officer, a leader of his fellow Marines. He was impressive in his commitment to his profession and in his strong moral and ethical convictions, and at a time when I was unsure if my departure from home was the right decision, Steve quelled my apprehension. He quickly became a dependable friend.

After OCS, even though Steve's military deployments took him far away from Washington, D.C. – to the Middle East and Asia and many other places around the globe – our friendship expanded. A few years later, the Marine Corps stationed Steve back in our Nation's capital, and I was ecstatic to have him close by again. Now, in the aftermath of my bipolar episode, I needed him more than ever.

At the time, Steve's day-to-day routine was exhausting. He worked at the Marine Corps barracks downtown during the day, and he was taking on-campus classes for his MBA at the University of Maryland in the evenings. He would arrive at work around 6:00 a.m. and be there until 4:00 p.m.. He had 90 minutes to himself until he had to drive to College Park, MD. After returning from class later in the evening, he'd stay up well past midnight to study and write papers before waking up a few hours later and doing it all over again.

As soon as he discovered my condition, Steve began to use his brief break between work and school to visit me. Daily. He sat with me for as long as he could, keeping mostly to himself at first, but eventually engaging me and helping me recuperate, one day at a time. While I was nervous of him seeing me in such a wretched state, his regular presence became a welcome reprieve from my self-induced isolation.

Although he never verbalized it, at least to me, Steve approached my recovery using the same methodology he did for marathon training. While not a trained psychiatrist, his edict was not far from Marty's.

"You need a plan, Talarczyk," he said. "Incremental goals to reach as you get back on your feet."

From Steve's perspective, my first milestone was eating regular, balanced meals. No more fast food and stale cereal. A healthy diet to aid my rehabilitation. Knowing I didn't have the strength to shop or cook myself, Steve brought groceries to my house and prepared meals for me. He coaxed me into eating at least some of the food, and out of respect for his efforts, I reluctantly complied.

The next goal was to shave and shower on a routine basis, which

Steve approached more aggressively after I began to follow his directive, as if I were an enlisted Marine under his command.

"You smell like shit dude; take a freakin' shower."

Achieving that was much more difficult. By that point, lounging on the couch in my pajamas was a self-preserving ritual, and one I had no interest in adjusting. Even on the days I visited Marty, I would change into a sweatshirt and jeans but neglect to shower. This led to several arguments with Steve. A return to basic human hygiene was essential to the plan. Eventually, I gave in to his pleas, but with limited energy, it wasn't easy.

The next hurdle was going outside and walking around the neighborhood to force myself back out into the world. If I could accomplish that, he thought, I might regain an interest in running again. That was his end goal. He felt that if I could run again, I could rebuild my confidence, one quarter-mile at a time. But I just couldn't do it.

Steve was disturbed, yet he remained patient with me. However, he knew his patience would only go so far, so he solicited some help from someone he knew would have a much gentler rapport with me than he had.

Sarah.

One afternoon, the ringing of my doorbell interrupted my daily television binge. Reluctantly, I opened the door, and there stood Sarah, smiling at me as though we were still dating and I was expecting her.

"Hey you," she greeted me.

"Hey," I replied, confused.

Was I smiling back? I could not tell. I felt no movement in my face, but she never averted her eyes, never changed her pleasant expression.

"Good to see you, Brian," she said, taking my hand.

I didn't know what to say to Sarah. I was bewildered. I had treated her like shit. The last words I had spoken to her were malicious, and I had assumed we would never speak again. Is she here to reconcile our relationship? Or maybe she's here to punish me? It would be so easy to kick me while I was down.

My thoughts must have been telegraphing from my brain directly to hers because she looked me in the eye and put my mind at ease.

"Listen, I know we haven't spoken in some time, but Steve called me. He's worried about you," she said. "Seeing you now, I am too. You look like you could use a friend."

Before I could refuse her, before I could slam the door and return to my faithful couch, Sarah stepped inside and took control.

"C'mon," she laughed. "I bet a hearty breakfast would do you good."

I stood there, staring.

"Clean yourself up and get dressed," she asserted, gently. "It's getting late. We'll miss the waffles."

I could not move.

"Brian. Let's go! Take a shower. We're going out."

I remained in shock, but I shuffled up to my bedroom and complied. Before heading back down, I hesitated and looked in the mirror at my thin face and tired eyes. The word *BIPOLAR* still appeared across my forehead, but in that moment it seemed faded, shallow.

I don't remember if I enjoyed my breakfast with Sarah, or what we talked about, or even if we talked. The significance of that excursion was that it was the first of several, and the start of my return to the land of the living, the world beyond the front door of my townhouse. Sarah's compassion, her willingness to brush aside how selfishly I had mistreated her and support me, brought forth the self-respect I desperately needed to see beyond my seclusion. In our discussions, she never spoke of our past relationship, my sudden termination of the life plans we had begun making together. That was behind us, and she had moved on. Instead, she reminded me that the future had not yet been decided, and if I could endure my present distress, happiness would one day resume.

Her empathy was as selfless as it was kind, and it cut through the depression that had buried me alive.

Steve and Sarah communicated often as they supported me in my recovery, and as they did, a tightly-bonded friendship formed between them. Steve kept my family apprised of my progress, and they were beyond grateful for the commitment to my health that both Steve and Sarah were making. Mom and Joy wished they could have visited more often than just an occasional weekend to support me in my recovery. But given their family and community responsibilities that just wasn't feasible, as much as that weighed heavily on their hearts and minds.

Other than my circle-of-trust friends, nobody else in my nearby social scene knew about my bipolar episode, and that was just the way I wanted it. While I was beginning to accept my illness, I was not remotely comfortable with exposing it publicly. At all. So much so that I kept dodging my local friends' invitations to meet up in fear that they might sense something was wrong with me. I continued working on that "very large software project," and though I can assume, now, that some friends knew something had happened given how much time had passed since they had seen me, I convinced myself that they hadn't.

I wasn't confident, and I wasn't fully reengaged in the life I once knew, but every day I was a little bit better. I took my meds, ate healthy meals, and attended regular therapy sessions with Marty. I started strumming my guitar and playing my piano again, conjuring a joyful ambiance inside my townhouse that had been absent for too long. With Steve's help, I also began running.

"You can do this, Talarczyk," he said. "And I'll run with you as often as you need me to."

On my first attempt, I could barely reach the half-mile mark without gasping for breath, but I wept with gratitude as the air filled my lungs and the desire to run further reconstituted itself.

It wasn't a smooth road by any means, but my improvement was palpable. I had regained enough self-assertiveness to push through my body's physical limitations, and the ubiquitous shame my mind continued to battle. When my illness tried to take my thoughts away from me, to convince me that my life would forever be constrained by its power over me, I was able to reason with it and subsequently with myself.

I'll be okay, I told myself. *I'll figure it out.*

When I was strong enough, I finally went home to face both Joy and Mom directly. They welcomed me with loving enthusiasm, offering emotional sustenance I had rejected for too long. While I was prepared for their reaction to me, I was entirely unprepared for my reaction to them. I readily indulged, even embraced, the support they offered. While the guilt I retained for disrupting their lives endured, I willingly shed my independence, willingly divested myself of all defenses and plunged myself into their care. We never talked about bipolar disorder directly; it was way too soon for that. But as I played scrabble with Mom, went shopping for baby clothes with Joy, and helped Greg assemble the crib in which Jason would soon be sleeping, I felt as if I were reclaiming my role in my family, reconnected to our traditions and values. I was "Beej" again, and that felt good.

Still, that first trip to North Haven after my episode was difficult for me. Marty and I had just started to unwind the psychological triggers of why my illness had chosen to surface for the first time, and it became clear that my father's death was indeed the root cause. Returning to our home on Ezra Street where his ghost was still hiding behind every coffee mug I used, every closet that I opened, brought back the anxiety that I had worked so hard to shed. But I pushed through the mental adversity and my fear of restimulating my depression.

I returned from that trip home with a different mindset about my illness than when I was last there, just out of the hospital. The promise I made to Mom that I would stay on my medication and continue to see my therapist would be kept. That felt good, and now that I had accepted my diagnosis, I wanted to learn more about it in any way that I could.

I started my research at the local Barnes & Noble bookstore and was shocked to see how much literature existed about bipolar disorder. There were histories of bipolar, scientific studies of bipolar, personal memoirs, self-help books, "survival kits," and stories of people who, sadly, did not survive. I purchased as many of them as I could fit in my backpack and threw myself into my research with academic zeal, highlighting passages and taking copious notes.

Without surprise, the clinical rhetoric depicted people just like me who lived normal lives which were suddenly obstructed by mania, depression, despair. Symptoms often surfaced in patients' mid to late twenties – exactly my age. Psychotic experiences were far less common but even more debilitating. On the other side of such episodes, people found themselves confused and terrified, losing their jobs, losing their friends, losing all confidence, and needing extensive therapy.

The further I read, the more I saw myself in their stories, which both enlightened and horrified me. On one hand, processing the social struggles people have while wearing their Scarlet B justified my own shameful feelings on the matter, as if I were a member of some special genetic fraternity. On the other, all of the misery and despair depicted sent my anxiety straight through the roof.

When I ran out of reading materials, the next phase of my bipolar research encompassed climbing up the Scecina family tree to see what I might find hidden among the thick Slovakian branches.

While it was agonizing to compare myself to Uncle Danny after first being diagnosed with bipolar, once I had a better grasp of what had transpired, and following Marty's guidance, I wanted to learn more about him. With casualties still mounting from my bipolar identity war, I wanted to arm myself with as much hereditary information as I could to defend myself against any further assaults. Since I didn't feel comfortable extracting that military intelligence from Mom in fear of opening up old family wounds, I turned to the Scecina whom I knew would be willing to provide it.

My Aunt Diane.

Diane, my mother's younger sister, lives in Bellingham, Washington, a quiet coastal outpost near the far western Canadian border. With my business savings still flush, I took a trip to visit Aunt Diane and my Cousin Jonathan in Bellingham. When I arrived, they greeted me with enthusiastic affection. We cooked Slovakian delicacies together – pierogies and halupka, kolachky cookies and cinnamon rolls. We visited several Native American arts and craft stores, ate strawberry pancakes at Aunt Diane's favorite breakfast diner, and danced about the living room to traditional Slovak music.

One morning, Aunt Diane suggested the two of us go for a hike, and she took me to a local mountain park, where, less than a half mile into our trek, she confronted me on my bipolar struggles.

"Your mom told me you've been through a lot lately," she said without pausing as she led me up a steep hill. "Want to tell me about it?"

At first, I was stunned by her directness and didn't know how to respond. But as we continued meandering through the serene woods, breathing in the crisp, Pacific Ocean sea breezes as they wafted by, I opened up to her. I shared it all – my mania, my psychosis, my hospitalization, my depression. I told her how difficult it was to reengage in all the things I used to love doing, and my fear that my local friends in Virginia might find out about my illness and negatively judge me.

"I don't have the confidence to interact with them the way I used to," I said. "And I don't know when I will."

Aunt Diane listened without interruption, and once that was all off my chest, I solicited information about her experiences with Uncle Danny. What were his manic episodes like? How often did he have them? Did he ever experience psychosis? I was hoping to learn how to cope with my illness, and I wanted reassurance and advice. Instead, I received something far less complex but no less palliative.

"Everyone has something they have to deal with, Bri," she said. "And some of it's really tough. The trick is knowing what you're up against. So now you know what your stuff is, figure out how to deal with it."

In Aunt Diane's mind, there was no antidote to hardship but to confront it. On the surface, her guidance was as clear as the gentle river flowing down the backside of the mountain where we stopped to snack on energy bars. But the actions required to follow it were not.

"How do I do that?" I asked.

"I can't answer that for you, Brian," she replied. "Nobody can. You've got to figure that out on your own. Just be patient with yourself as you do, and remember, time heals all wounds."

Time, Dad. That's what I need. Time.

When we finished our hike I felt refreshed yet still conflicted. Patience had never been my strong suit, and a lot of time had already passed. Nevertheless, I left Bellingham with a sense of purpose and a desire to keep pushing forward, to continue my pursuit of confidence and clarity.

On the flight back to Virginia, I jotted Aunt Diane's advice down on a scrap of paper, and beside it, a list of local friends with whom I should reconnect. I would not share my mental woes with them. I would continue to keep them on the outside of that. But I would proactively engage with them, I promised myself. I would stop dodging their invitations to meet up for dinner, to play soft-ball, to shoot pool at the pub down the street. I would seek connection and attempt to enjoy their company.

To do all that required something I did not want to do, but felt it was necessary to preserve myself: lying about my health.

The truth would not be revealed, at least by me, and as I reentered my social scene, I donned a double identity. Visible Brian was a thriving, happy, jovial guy – busy with his career and self-suffi-cient. Shrouded Brian was hesitant, languishing in his temporary retirement, terrified of going back to work. I was in a constant state of contradiction. I wanted to be with my friends, but I did not want to socialize. I wanted to be alone, but when I was, I was painfully lonely. Every emotion hit me with blunt force, yet I remained numb.

My double-identity played out in nearly every social encounter I found myself in. Halfway through sharing an entertaining meal with friends at a restaurant, I would escape to the bathroom and barricade myself in a stall to evade the foreboding that suddenly overcame me. On the golf course, I would enjoy the camaraderie of my friends on the tee-box at the beginning of every hole, but not as much as the subsequent walk alone to hit my ball up the fairway. Returning to a summer beach house we had rented in Dewey Beach, Delaware, I found pleasure in drinking beer and listening to live music and laughing late into the evenings, but it was the release through my long, isolated morning runs along the shoreline that brought me there.

Throughout the summer and fall, my social anxiety lessened, but the double-life I was living persisted. To mask the internal torment my web of lies incited, I modified my external appear-ance. I shaved my head.

It was far from a bold move. My hairline had been receding for years, and I had contemplated doing it many times before. Now, I needed a new physical identity to hide the one I was struggling with internally. I needed to look in the mirror and see something other than bipolar disorder. Going bald was a desperate attempt to establish that distinction, to give myself a new sense of self.

After I shaved for the first time, I took a picture of myself in the mirror and emailed it to Mom.

"I like it, Beej!" she responded. "You look sophisticated and strong."

I was far from either. I was scared and desolate. But I was at least moving forward.

While I could not bear to discuss the trials of my double-life with anyone, Marty was an invaluable help as I navigated its murky waters, and with each therapy session, I became more comfortable opening up and heeding his advice. Knowing that the mental illness research I conducted was pivotal to the acceptance of my illness, he encouraged me to continue reading and loaned me several books from his personal library, including clinical texts exploring the biology of bipolar disorder – the latest genetic composition theories and chemical makeup analysis. Much of the research was beyond my rudimentary understanding of the human body, but it was comforting to learn how much attention scientists were giving the illness. Perhaps one day there would be a cure, or so I erroneously thought at the time.

In addition, Marty recommended another tool to help me process the intense flashbacks from the psychotic phase of my episode which my post-traumatic stress often yielded. Although I didn't know it at the time, his suggestion would become one of the most critical elements of my long-term stability and management of bipolar disorder.

"Brian, do you like to write?" he inquired.

"I used to in high school and college," I said. "But I haven't written anything since. Why do you ask?"

Marty walked into an adjacent room and returned carrying a notebook. He sat in the chair beside me, opened it up to the first page, wrote my name, and handed it to me.

"Writing down any recollections you have of your episode can help you process it," he said. "For many people who have a mental illness, keeping a journal is a powerful coping mechanism."

I had heard this before. Back in the hospital at Yale, my psychiatrist had mentioned writing as one option in the development of my "wellness plan" – especially given the severity of my psychosis and the need to process any PTSD I might face. The desk drawer in my room had even been stocked with pads and pencils. But none of that registered with me at a time when I was in a state of pure denial.

"What should I write about?" I asked Marty.

"Why don't you start simple," he replied. "Just jot down some of the things you experienced between Thanksgiving and Christmas."

I was both skeptical and apprehensive, but later that evening I nestled into my favorite reading chair beside my fireplace and scribbled down thoughts into the notebook. My scattered entries were rather vague at first, although not because I couldn't remember anything. My "temporary insanity" was far from temporary – the psychotic movie was as accessible as the thousands of MP3 songs I had illegally downloaded from Napster when the internet first began showing promise. But it was difficult to externalize my experiences. In doing so, I felt as if I were formally proclaiming my mental abnormality – embracing the reality that parts of my brain functioned differently from others; further affirmation of an illness that I had finally accepted but fervently didn't want to be associated with.

I was excited to share what I had written with Marty. However, to my surprise, he was reluctant to read it.

"This is your journal, Brian," he decreed. "This is your opportunity to examine yourself. You don't need to share it with anyone, including me."

I was thoroughly disappointed. I thought he had given me a homework assignment, which I had diligently completed and wanted to turn in to be graded.

"But I want you to read it," I replied. "I want to talk to you about it."

"In that case, I will. But only because you're asking me to."

Marty sifted through my journal entries, petitioned a few basic questions, and listened intently to my responses. As I was leaving, he put his hand on my shoulder and congratulated me on my achievement.

"Brian, I know this wasn't easy for you," he said. "Be proud of what you've done, and if it helps you cope with your illness, keep writing."

I took his advice, and in the months that followed, I continued documenting my manic and psychotic escapades. I "stuck to the facts" as Marty had suggested, chronicling the What and the When and the Where but steering clear of the Why or the How whenever it made me feel uncomfortable. I also avoided the more difficult topics, especially the darkest days of my depression and anything whatsoever to do with my father. *I'm not ready for that*, I told myself. I would get to that in due time.

The process of documenting my journey through madness wasn't necessarily empowering as Marty noted it might one day become. But it was certainly liberating. I had developed a conduit through which my PTSD could be released; a channel for self-reflection; a place where I could tell the truth about myself since I was headstrong on lying to everyone else. Writing in my journal wasn't a magic bullet for mental wellness, and it still isn't today. But it is one of the tools that helps keep me focused and centered on what I need to do in my life to remain healthy.

Looking back at those early pages of my journal, I can see my soul resurfacing. While the real substance of my struggles, my father's death, is absent from the narrative, my sense of self, my aspiration to reclaim the life I once knew is prevalent. The main character is yearning to break out of the cage that his illness has locked him in, and to reclaim the self-confidence that has prevented him from doing so. As he re-engages with his local community of friends and a social scene that brings him much day-to-day pleasure, he envisions the time when his professional footing and the enjoyment derived from his career returns. He is keeping his mother and his sister on the outside of his bipolar identity battle, but he has recognized their concern and embraced their love.

For the time being, that was enough.

PART VI

Suppression

Wednesday, May 2nd, 2001

I sit at the dining room table and straighten out the off-white tablecloth. Mom enters carrying her old Scrabble box, a remnant of her youth and her prized possession. She takes a seat and places the box between us. I lift up the top and pull the board out very carefully, making sure I don't rip the masking tape that holds the center crease together. It would be sacrilege to do so. Mom has preserved her Scrabble game over the years as if it were an original copy of the United States Constitution.

I do not feel like playing Scrabble this morning, but Mom insists. Since she rarely insists on anything, I oblige her. She needs this diversion, I tell myself. Or perhaps she thinks I need this diversion. Either way, I agree to her request as it would be disrespectful to dampen her spirits any more than they already are.

We pick our letters and begin placing tiles. I struggle to concentrate and focus on shorter words so I don't hold the game up, regardless of how few points I receive. Halfway through the game, my brain stalls, and I decide I need a break, some time alone.

"Mom, can we finish this later?" I ask, politely. "I'd like to go for a run."

"Sure, Beej. Enjoy yourself."

I lace up my sneakers, grab my iPod, and head out. I do not have a route planned. I just know I need to run and for a while. Long enough to pretend that Dad hasn't died, to convince myself that this is just another trip home to visit Mom and him, to eat New Haven pizza and drink Foxon Park birch beer and watch the Yankees.

I run down Saint John Street – a good place to start, I think to myself. I climb the short hill and cross through our town green, past the old cemetery where my friends and me used to play hide-and-seek. I cut over to the cross-country trails in the woods behind North Haven Middle School, where my teammates and I used to compete. The pathways are wider now and further cleared, making it easier to see the jagged rocks and dangerous tree roots popping up from the ground where I had once tripped and sprained my ankle.

From there I head over to the recreation complex and meander in between the little league baseball and softball fields in Montowese Park where I spent much of my youth. Distant memories hurl at me like pitches in a batting cage: all the seasons that Dad coached me; the summers when I was home from college, coaching beside him; the tournament game when I struck out with the bases loaded, ending our quest for the division championship; the conversation Dad and me had in the car on the way home – his gentle reassurance able to contort the worst possible defeat into a victory of some kind. His coaching super-power.

The early morning sunshine and the pleasant harmonies streaming into my ears propel me onward through the streets of my hometown, through more flashbacks of my melodic childhood.

I run over to Cloudland Drive, where Marcia used to live, and climb the long, steep hill that leads up to her house. I reach the top and turn around to take in the magnificent view of North Haven off in the distance – the quaint community in which I grew up, where most of my family still resides. All my aunts and uncles and cousins who showered me with affection and nurtured my innocence for as long as they could before I moved away. My innocence that is now shattered.

My unplanned trek eventually leads me to the baseball field on Bailey Road just a few blocks from our house, where the North Haven Junior Varsity team is practicing. I take a break from my run and sit in the bleachers to watch the boys take infield and outfield practice, just like Dad used to do.

As the coach hits the ball to right field, each player shifts around the diamond with precision: the 1ˢᵗ baseman to the infield grass, holding his arms up for the cutoff throw; the 2ⁿᵈ baseman to first; the shortstop to 2ⁿᵈ; the outfielders to each of their respective backup positions, and the pitcher behind home plate in case there's an overthrow.

The catcher yells "Cut 2" and the 1ˢᵗ baseman rifles the ball to 2ⁿᵈ base. The shortstop catches the ball and slaps his glove on the ground to tag out the imaginary runner.

That is the beauty of the game, I think to myself. That's what makes it unique. It's a slow, deliberate dance. A classic waltz – three beats to a measure, three outs in an inning, nine stanzas from beginning to end. Everyone gets a turn to take the lead on the dance floor, and everyone shuffles around them gracefully as they do.

Now my dance partner is dead.

He's lying stiff somewhere in a cold, dark morgue, and he's not coming back.

Dear Kids,

The list of things I'm not proud of in my life before I met Mom is long and distinguished, and all the lying that I did following my bipolar diagnosis is near the top. But please know that at the time, I was ashamed and desperate, and the stigma of my illness made me even more so. I needed to break free from those constraints, to live my life on my own terms, and sadly, lying was the only recourse I believed I had to do so.

Love,

Dad

Throughout the fall and winter of 2002 - 2003, I continued to resist going back to work. I still wasn't ready, I told myself. I needed more time to heal. Luckily, I had the financial means to cover my monthly expenses as well as all the hobbies and leisurely activities I focused on instead of working. I went to the gym regularly, travelled around the country to visit friends, took piano lessons, and read. A lot.

Eventually, my business coffers were depleted, and I was forced to liquidate assets to buy myself more time. Trading in my sporty Mazda hurt, but it was a necessary sacrifice. I drew what I could from my 401k retirement savings, but I was too young to have much there. After that I turned to credit cards to pay my expenses, but I knew that could only last for so long.

My one remaining asset was my townhouse. Thanks to the housing boom that was sweeping the nation in the early 2000's, I knew I had equity in my property. I loved my house and wanted no part of selling it. However, without other alternatives, eventually there were only two options, and I hated both of them: I must overcome my anxiety and return to work, or I must sell my townhouse and move. Where I might go, I didn't know, which scared me as much as the idea of working. But after much deliberation, moving became the path of least resistance. Or rather, the easy way out.

I was reluctantly off to the next chapter, running away from nobody but myself.

My departure from Northern Virginia would do nothing to reduce the web of lies that I had been telling Mom and Joy and all of my friends about my business failures. In fact, it accentuated them. Liar, liar, pants on fire. Again. I needed to justify my sudden desire to relocate, but I also wanted to preserve my identity as a successful entrepreneur. I had no reasonable answer to offer anyone who might ask why I was suddenly uprooting my life. Selling my house because I was flat broke and lacking the fortitude to work didn't fit my carefully crafted professional persona.

While assessing the local real estate market, I found a perfect rationale. House prices had skyrocketed even higher than I assumed. 70% returns on short-term investments. Cashing out on the substantial equity in my property was a worthy justification, and I spread that false narrative with precision. No longer was I a failed business owner. I was a smart investor. A financial guru.

"I don't know why everyone isn't doing this," I told Joy on the phone after the first open house which drew over 30 people. "These market conditions won't last forever."

What an asshole I was.

I'm sorry, Dad. Please forgive me.

As I expected, the house went under contract right away. There were multiple bids, each higher than the next, and all were well over the asking price. After the closing, I would have enough cash to avoid working for quite some time. But what I wouldn't have was a place to live. For that, I had no plan. I just knew I needed to leave.

Even though I had been largely hesitant about being home, my first impulse was to move there. Mom was safety personified, and Joy and Greg could provide a welcome blanket of compassion. I could taste the security of being back in Connecticut, wrapped in familiarity – living among several of my circle-of-trust friends from UConn who had settled there, playing softball with my cousins and former high school teammates, maybe playing in Greg's blues band again if he let me. Perhaps, I thought, my dad's haunting absence might even provide a modicum of reassurance. I could help Mom around the house. Take care of the yard. Build her a new back patio. Become her regular Scrabble opponent again.

The idea of returning home was enticing. . . and simultaneously terrifying. Back in my family bosom, I would have to come clean about my inability to work and all the other lies I had been telling. Further, the thought of living in my father's long shadow re-invigorated my self-recrimination and shame, the perseverating need to punish myself for my insanity. My embarrassing illness.

I couldn't go home. There was no way I could live with me there.

Next, I was convinced I should move far away. As far as possible. To Colorado or California, to Hawaii or Europe. *How far do I need to go to get out of my bipolar fishbowl?* Moving somewhere distant would give me a clean slate, allow me to leave my disgraceful past behind me and start anew. But I knew I would have to take control of my phobias and go back to work at some point, and it would be easiest to do that within reach of the Washington D.C. area where I still had a few connections.

I began a thorough search, investigating towns within a comfortable radius of the Capitol. I was looking for somewhere quieter than the hustling and bustling of Northern Virginia, an escape from the stifling bumper-to-bumper D.C. Beltway traffic and fifteen-dollar mixed drinks. I desired an enclave similar to Bellingham, where Aunt Diane had settled down, with hiking trails to explore and running routes free of cars racing by. A place where life was not in any great hurry, where I could move more slowly and not stand out.

It only took a couple weeks of searching before I found exactly what I was looking for in the tranquil, Chesapeake Bay community of Annapolis, Maryland.

It was the perfect choice. Just a short drive east of D.C., Annapolis was – still is – quiet, almost sleepy – congenial and cozy in the way only a small town can be. Even though I knew few people who lived there, I felt safe living in the shadows of the U.S. Naval Academy where Steve went to school, and enamored by the town's rich history and military traditions. I was certain that Annapolis was the place my broken soul had been craving. I could break away from the D.C. white-collar rat-race for the time being, yet remain connected to it for work opportunities down the road.

Instead of purchasing another house right away which would cut into my savings, I rented an enchanting apartment in the historical district adjacent to City Dock, Annapolis's downtown area. City Dock is like a Disney version of a quaint, mid-Atlantic island town. Lined with boats tied up to piers, candy shoppes and Bloody Mary bars, artisanal coffee bistros and all-you-can-eat crab buffets, the area is as relaxing as the gentle waters that flow around it. I was mesmerized by its charm and serenity from the day I arrived.

City Dock became my personal sanctuary, my healing home, and I snuggled gratefully into the conviviality of the neighborhood. In the early morning, I would wander to my favorite cafe to buy a large cup of freshly brewed coffee, then settle onto a park bench beside the water to watch the sun rise over the Bay and read the newspaper. I kept busy during the day by writing in my journal, taking photographs of historic buildings and fancy sailboats, trying my hand at acrylic painting. In the evenings, I would stroll back through downtown and have a craft beer with some of the locals, sit for a while and listen to acoustic guitarists play Jimmy Buffet and Van Morrison covers.

Ensconced in my new life in Annapolis, I felt that I was, to all practical appearances, downright normal again. My peaceful surroundings had transformed me. My separation from my hectic life in Virginia had healed me. My escape plan was successful, and I felt free again. Optimistic. Healthy. My social life was back in full swing as well. I had formed abating relationships with City Dock musicians, with whom I jammed and occasionally played out at the bars. I made other new friends, engaging in easy, stress-free relationships, and I remained in contact with many of my old friends in Alexandria and Baltimore, whom I regularly invited to visit me.

Feeling secure and confident in my new surroundings, I finally went back to work, although only part-time, to help a friend who was struggling to meet his client's software development demands. The job was mundane and didn't pay well, but it felt good to participate in something beyond my hobbies each day. I was far from ready to work full-time. My anxiety over making such a permanent commitment persisted.

My relationship with bipolar disorder was following a similar, part-time path, although I didn't see it that way. I thought I had fully conquered the beast, or at least the most difficult challenges were now behind me. I had accepted my illness, had taken some strides in managing it effectively. But I remained by no means comfortable with it, and I kept it buried in the closet, out of reach from nearly everyone but Marty. Slowly but surely, I stopped writing in my journal as well. I had exercised everything out of my mind that I needed to, I decreed. No longer was there a need to scratch old bipolar battle scars. Yes, I had the same mental illness as Uncle Danny, but I wouldn't let it get the best of me. I wouldn't become a burden to my family repeatedly as he was. My episode was a one-time deal. I was healthy, and I would remain so.

Part of my belief that I had everything under control was my steadfast commitment to taking my medication. *All my health requires is to stay on lithium and I'll live well and prosper*, I told myself. Marty had reminded me, repeatedly, that drugs were just part of the equation to remaining balanced, and while I didn't completely dismiss his warning, I also didn't fully internalize it. Some time had now passed since my episode, and I hadn't experienced any of the bipolar highs and lows that the illness can produce. At the time, I saw drugs as the biggest contributing factor to that. Bad idea.

Such erroneous logic was, in part, learned from Mom, who routinely associated Uncle Danny's wild mood swings to whether or not he was taking his meds. Or, at least, that was how she explained Danny's erratic behavior and frequent hospitalizations to Joy and me as teenagers.

"Uncle Danny stopped taking the medication that keeps him out of trouble," she'd tell us. "He's back in the hospital again because of it."

Take the medication, and you'll stay out of trouble.

It was as easy as that, right?

Wrong. But I didn't know any better back then.

Nevertheless, I was proud of my vigor and wanted to share it with Mom, to assure her she needn't worry about me anymore. I invited her to Annapolis and we had a wonderful time together. We toured the Naval Academy, bought "Nap-Town" souvenirs for Josh and Jason on City Dock, and caught up on some long overdue Scrabble matches. Mom was as impressed as I with the beauty and calm of Annapolis. But my overall health and happiness is what seemed to impress her the most although her feelings on the matter were as elusive as all of the lies I had been telling.

"It's nice to see you so restful, Beej," she said as she took hold of my hand while we sat on a bench beside the water one afternoon.

Restful.

I wasn't exactly sure what she meant by that, but I knew by the seriousness in her expression and the tightness of her grip it was bipolar related. Was she congratulating me for pushing through my depression and becoming more stable? Was she probing me for more information about my current mental state? Was she wondering if I was taking proper precautions to prevent another manic / psychotic episode from recurring? I didn't know, but I didn't inquire any further.

Whether or not I was being "restful," that was as close to a discussion about my mental illness as Mom and me had since I was first diagnosed with bipolar disorder. For all intents and purposes, there was nothing that needed to be discussed, a sentiment we both shared at the time. My feelings on the matter were as pervasive as my hatred of the Red Sox. I had successfully escaped from my bipolar fishbowl, and there was no need to dive back into the murky water.

I don't blame my mother for not engaging me in discussions about my mental illness. One hard lesson I've learned from my bipolar experiences is that assigning blame to anyone, or anything, is a futile, and often selfish, endeavor. At the time, I was deliberately steering clear of talking about anything related to bipolar disorder, with anyone. My illness was a thing of the past, a relic residing in my previous life in Virginia. Other than with Marty, exploring how "restful" I was or wasn't being was off-limits. Besides, everything was normal again, what needed to be discussed?

The truth is, it's difficult for any of us to internally confront what we don't externally expose, and at the time, I was hyper-focused on not exposing anything that was emotionally destabilizing. That was especially true for my mental illness, as well as anything whatsoever to do with my father's death. I swept both subjects under the rug and moved on with my life.

Together, Mom and I buried the evidence, although in retrospect, it was me who had committed the crime. If I were to blame anyone, I would blame myself.

W hen my apartment lease came to an end, I made what I perceived as a giant step in my personal maturity: I left my City Dock sanctuary. I would remain close by, not move too far away from the safe haven where I had regained my strength and revived my spirit. But it was time to get a place of my own and settle more permanently into the serene town I had come to adore.

The housing market remained red hot, but I was lucky to find a property that was unexpectedly inexpensive, largely because it needed a tremendous amount of work. Built in the 1960s, the house had never been remodeled once since. The bathroom wallpaper sported sparkling silver butterflies arranged in seahorse shaped patterns. The pink kitchen tile was laden with mildew. It was clear the previous owners were life-long smokers; much like my childhood home which was cloaked in cigarette smoke from my father's nicotine addiction, the entire place smelled like burnt onion soup.

"It's a hidden gem," my realtor said.

There didn't seem to be anything hidden about it whatsoever, but I was excited to take on the large renovation project, having one more excuse to avoid going back to work full-time.

Despite having little income to show a bank, getting a loan to buy the house was surprisingly easy. A national lender offered mortgages through what they called a "No Doc Loan" program – one of the key contributors to the mounting economic crisis our financial markets were becoming exposed to in the early 2000's.

"With your high credit score, Brian, you don't have to provide any documentation to verify your income," my loan officer explained. "Just know that your interest rate may change slightly five years from now."

The arrangement was far from logical, but without a job, I couldn't have asked for a better deal. I signed the contract, packed all my stuff, and moved into my very own 3-bedroom colonial, albeit one that was barely inhabitable.

I would live in my new abode across town for three years, from 2004 to 2007. The house would become, on one hand, the place where I would reclaim the remainder of my self-confidence that my bipolar episode had eroded; on the other, the point in time when my bipolar self-awareness would become further suppressed. The house resided on Lury Lane, but it might as well have been called "Leery" Lane – a notion foretold by an unexpected announcement from Marty during my very first therapy session with him after I moved.

"Brian, I'll be retiring from my practice soon," he said. "It's time for me to move on to the next phase of my life."

I found his declaration both surprising and unsettling. While my rapport with Marty had started out rocky, over time he had become a trusted partner, the referee to an ongoing boxing match occurring in my mind – a heavyweight fight between my illness and my personal identity. Suddenly, I had to find a new doctor, a new confidant, and that was frustrating and terrifying. A new doctor meant that I'd be forced to relay my bipolar history, to answer questions about the pain and suffering I had thought I put well behind me.

All of my concerns would unfortunately prove true.

I did a web search for psychiatrists in the surrounding area and, for no other reason than his office was located in Annapolis, I chose a gentleman named Richard. I figured that if he were easy to reach, I would have no excuse to avoid therapy, and I would go regularly. It turned out that geographic proximity was the only thing easy about my new doctor.

Richard was Marty's antithesis. No laid-back acceptance, no gentle paternal prodding. He was an aggressive, arrogant know-it-all. His attitude was, "You're sick, and I'm going to tell you what you must do to make you better," and his practitioner style repelled me instantly. Even though I was feeling stable, Richard assumed I was fragile, and that stirred up all my old anger and bipolar self-doubt.

In the beginning, I had to meet with Richard once a week so he could "get to know me." It seemed like a fair request, given the newness of our relationship and the severity of the psychosis and depression I had experienced. But meeting him that often quickly became annoying.

"Listen, do you think we can dial these sessions down a bit?" I asked. "I haven't had any mental health issues in a long time, and I don't expect that to change."

"I can't do that, Brian," he replied. "I need to understand your bipolar history in more detail, and until I do, I don't feel comfortable just giving you drugs."

"But I've been taking lithium for a long time now, and my moods have fully stabilized."

"I understand that, but you need to let me do my job."

"Well, I think you're doing a poor job."

Jerk.

Unfortunately, it was Richard who wrote my prescriptions, and, having jumped over the first hurdles with him, there was no way I could face starting all over again with another doctor. So I swallowed my misgivings along with my lithium pills and stayed with him.

Losing my trust in my psychiatrist was a problem although I obviously didn't see it as one at the time. It was a problem because I would soon suppress the need to remain on a formal "wellness plan," and since I lived alone and remained emotionally isolated, there would be nobody around to point that out to me.

I was first introduced to this psychotherapy concept when I was hospitalized at Yale New Haven. Of course, back then, I thought anything with such a cheesy name like "wellness plan" was a crock of shit. Who needs a "plan" to be "well"? How about you just do the things that keep you healthy and make you happy and don't do the things that make you sick or sad? It's not that hard, people.

In short, a wellness plan is a contract with oneself to maintain one's mental health. Those who have a mental illness often have difficulty leading a balanced lifestyle. Bipolar disorder, in particular, lusts for emotional extremes – ultra happiness, and debilitating sadness – wherever and whenever it can. There are many things that can force someone with bipolar off a healthy track. Those are called "triggers." In its simplest form, a wellness plan is a list of those triggers, and beside each, the things one can do to prevent themselves from tripping over them.

My wellness plan triggers have evolved over time, but back then, Marty worked with me to identify three primary ones to watch out for:

1. Hyper-creativity
2. Loneliness
3. Overworking

Each of these could lead to an imbalanced biochemical and/or emotional state, which in turn could alter regular sleep patterns – the most critical element of my wellness plan, both then and now. Without sleep, my mind can't reset itself. Thoughts begin racing, and stress has no vehicle through which it can routinely release. Bipolar mania is never far behind.

Unfortunately, all three of these triggers would get pulled while I lived in my house on "Leery Lane," and given my assumption that my mental illness had essentially been cured, only divine intervention would prevent another manic/psychotic episode from recurring.

Thank you, Dad.

Trigger #1, hyper-creativity, was the first to get tripped.

To my delight, fixing up the house became my new excuse for not returning to work full-time. Armed with a sledgehammer and a Sawzall, I started knocking down walls that were blocking sunlight and building new walls to restore intimacy. Once the general layout was complete, I refinished the hardwood floors and painted each ceiling and wall which dissipated the horrid cigarette odor. Then, I renovated one room at a time, replacing worn base-boards, swapping out old light fixtures, installing new cabinets, building custom bookshelves – sparing no expense as I did.

It was a labor of love, and although I worked alone most of the time, I was never lonely or so I thought. The endorphin overload derived from my hyper-creativity masked my desire for connectivity and companionship. I thrived on the immersion, with classic rock as my soundtrack, caffeinated drinks as my sustenance, and creative energy as the driving source of my passion for turning old to new.

I was so engrossed in my renovation efforts that it never once occurred to me I was exhibiting hypomanic behaviors. During these activities, I'd lose track of time, finishing my electrical wiring or drywall sanding at 11:00 pm when I thought it was 8:00 pm. I'd skip meals without noticing until I was starving, forget to return Joy and Mom's phone calls until their messages showed concern and caught my attention, deprioritize my part-time work commitments until a co-worker pinned me down, pissed off.

Caught up in my artistic endeavors, I also never realized how sloppy my remodeling work had become. One afternoon I was playing guitar with a friend when we both heard a loud crash from upstairs. I ran up to see a 2-foot piece of crown molding on the ground which had fallen because I had forgotten to nail it to the studs. On another occasion, I was reading a book in a chair beside a cozy fire in my fireplace when the lacquer on the new mantle I had just installed started to smoke because I didn't give the top-coat enough time to dry. Thank goodness I was sitting right next to the fire at the time and extinguished it right away or the whole house could have gone up in flames.

Idiot!

Luckily, all the physical activities I was completing tired me out enough to maintain a steady sleep pattern, or there is no doubt my hypomania would have progressed to something much worse.

My romantic relationships during this time period were also going up in flames on a recurring basis – my wellness plan Trigger #2 – loneliness – wriggling into the limelight.

When I wasn't fixing up my house, I was going out with friends, drinking far too many gin and tonics than I should have for the lithium to properly function, and searching for a female companion whenever I felt alone, which was often. When I'd find her, I'd try to take things slow – convinced that I could date more maturely and shed my habit of serial monogamy. But soon enough, I'd grow tired or bored, abruptly break up with the latest woman of my dreams, and seek out the next.

I was sure my attempts at dating were, to some degree, in earnest, but in the aftermath of my bipolar episode, I was in no way capable of committing to any long-term relationship like the one I had previously cultivated with Sarah To do so, I knew I'd have to share the repercussions of my mental illness at some level – to be open and honest about the uglier parts of myself I kept hidden. But that wasn't going to happen. I had to hold back. After all, I didn't want to be judged, and I sure as hell didn't want to be pitied.

Back when I was still seeing Marty, he had attempted to show me the error of my ways.

"If you want to engage in a meaningful relationship, Brian, you must find a way to expose your past without feeling vulnerable about it."

Unfortunately, Marty was no longer around, and even if he were, I was so headstrong when it came to romantic affairs that I would not have taken his advice. Instead of revealing what was behind the mask, I closed down. What else could I do? I was inhibited by a false conviction: if anyone I dated knew the dirty details of my insanity, they would push me away. But by shutting down that part of me, I was actually doing the pushing.

My actions were egotistical and childish, but I could not stop to think what I might be doing to anyone else. Still, I was lonely. I lived alone in a large house, and I had way too much time and space to myself. I needed a consort, of any kind.

Enter Sammy.

On the heels of my latest short-term relationship fiasco, I visited a local animal shelter where a friend worked and huddled into the corner of one of the kennels was a cute Labrador/Beagle mutt. The instant that we looked at each other for the first time, I felt a strong, spiritual connection with the little guy, and I could tell he felt the same with me. The name tag on his crate said "Cinnamon," but I renamed him Sammy.

Unfortunately, Sammy came with some baggage. He had recently endured his own trauma, noticeable from multiple cuts and contusions across his body.

"What happened to him?" I asked my friend.

"Well, he escaped from his previous owner's house and was hit by a car," she said. "The driver hit and ran, and he nearly died."

The accident left Sammy with two cracked ribs. Making things worse, his owners, intimidated by the thought of caring for a damaged animal, surrendered Sammy back to the shelter without even paying the vet bill.

Because of his physical appearance and the potentially high cost of his long-term recovery, Sammy was virtually unadoptable and would soon be put down. The very thought of that made me ill. He was in every way damaged goods, just like I saw myself at the time, and I loved everything about him. He came home with me just a few days later.

To everyone's surprise, Sammy healed quickly, and after he regained his energy, we spent countless hours playing fetch in the backyard, and running through the nearby cross-country trails behind Annapolis High School. We visited the local dog park, where Sammy could socialize with other pups, and attended "Puppy Hour" at a bar on the City Dock, where he munched on free milk-bone appetizers while I drank beer and flirted with the bartender.

Everywhere we went, Sammy was friendly and easygoing, amusing every stranger with his carefree, whimsical temperament. He was easy to bond with, and I became obsessed with his slobbery kisses, his hyper excitement every time I left the house and returned. During the day, as I took business calls or worked on the house, it was reassuring to have him near me, curled up cozily on the sofa or his favorite living room chair. At night he slept at the foot of my bed and his presence calmed me, drove away any stress that work or dating or any facet of my life introduced.

Looking back, there is no doubt that being with Sammy helped off-set the hypomania that I exhibited from my exhaustive, hyper-creative home repairs and imbalanced dating routine. The responsibility of taking care of someone else beyond myself provided me with a daily structure that kept me balanced, precluding me from randomly leaving town for several days to visit friends I knew in

Cleveland or Miami or Houston just because I was bored, or lonely.

Of all the activities that prevented me from going completely off the mental illness rails, my continued dedication to long-distance running was perhaps the most pivotal. Rarely did a day go by when I wasn't running along the water, or running through the woods with Sammy, or running around the outer perimeter of the Naval Academy with fellow members of the Annapolis Striders Running Club I had joined. The miles upon miles of nothing but me and my music and the open road filtered out any mental disturbances. At night, my physically tired body had no issues falling asleep, regardless of what hypomanic strain I had unknowingly put on myself throughout the day, and I would wake up refreshed and centered.

Tire out the body, clear out the mind. Rinse, wash, repeat.

The same routine I remain on today.

Dear Kids,

It's not easy to confront your fears. And make no mistake, as confident and charismatic as some people might seem, everyone has them.

You can't wave a magic wand and overcome anxiety, but the first step in doing so is accepting it's okay to feel that way. I hope the sum of your experiences leads you to that conclusion much sooner in your life than mine did.

Love,

Dad

By the time I had regained enough confidence to take on a full-time consulting workload, over two years had passed since I had my bipolar episode. That's right, I hadn't worked a nine-to-five job in over two years. Making things worse, over that period I continued to lie to everyone about how great my career was going: Mom, Joy & Greg, my circle-of-trust friends – I had told them all two years of lies; my personal fake news blog for which I am still horrified and thoroughly ashamed.

Today, I do believe taking an extended sabbatical from anything can be beneficial if you're doing it for the right reasons. But I was not. I was on my professional hiatus for all the wrong reasons. I was steering clear of what I perceived as the root cause of my mental breakdown: Trigger #3 – overworking. *My professional life is the problem*, I told myself. *My career is to blame*. Back in Alexandria, I worked too much, then I couldn't sleep enough, then my genetic circuitry went haywire and I found myself in a loony bin. It was all work's fault, not mine.

Sure it was.

The proceeds from the sale of my townhouse in Virginia were significant, but after putting a ton of money into my house renovations, my savings were dwindling, and I had no other assets to liquidate as I did in Alexandria. Whether I liked it or not, it was time to confront my professional fears.

I had many struggles with this, but the most imminent was that I didn't know where to begin looking for work. My friend whom I was helping on the side didn't have any more work than what he was already giving me. I couldn't call up my old clients and beg for their forgiveness, nor would I ever tell them about my mental illness struggles that had caused my sudden departure. That was personal information, not professional. It would only tarnish my reputation further, I convinced myself, and I had already embarrassed myself enough.

With the help of a former colleague, one of the only professional relationships I hadn't burned to the ground during my episode, I obtained some Department of Defense consulting work.

"Brian, there's a position opening up on a Navy contract," he said. "It's a multi-year effort and they can use your skill set."

I was grateful for the offer. Even better, it allowed me to work remotely, something I strongly desired. Working from home was a good way to ease back into a routine, which was difficult at first. Concentrating on any single task for more than 5-10 minutes at a time was unexpectedly challenging. But once I got back into the swing of things, I came to enjoy the steady rhythm of my Monday-thru-Friday schedule and the software development challenges I was given.

As my full-time job stabilized and my social roots in Annapolis deepened, I felt officially anchored to a community that I treasured. For the most part, I was mentally stable, albeit luckily. My hypomanic periods were balanced out by music, social connectivity, and long morning runs attuned to the undulation of the gentle Chesapeake waters that surrounded me. I indeed felt *restful* as Mom had noted. Or rather, what I perceived restful to mean. More than anything, I was genuinely happy, and that's what mattered to me at the time. As long as I was happy, I assumed I was mentally healthy. Whether or not I was proactively managing my wellness plan didn't matter.

I'm back, Dad.

Throughout my time in Annapolis, I visited Connecticut regularly, never missing a Christmas or Thanksgiving or Easter meal back home. Mom and Joy's love and support were like a magnet, drawing me in and giving me strength whenever I felt I needed it. Although I didn't see it this way at the time, they, too, were a source of balance that offset the dangerous bipolar circus tightrope I was skipping across. On each visit home, time slowed down, and even though I was often only home for 2-3 days at a clip, that slowness allowed my batteries to recharge.

While Joy, Mom, and I were still avoiding discussions about bipolar disorder at the time, we were talking more openly about my father's passing, and for me, that was a step in the right mental health direction. Enough time had passed and I was more comfortable reminiscing about my dad. Whenever we gathered as a family, I was able to keep the emotional strain that had previously tainted our reunions at a safe distance. His sudden death still made me sad, however. I wished he were around to see the life I was leading, to visit Annapolis himself and play some golf, to come see my band play on City Dock. But I was no longer handcuffed to the pain that his passing caused me, and that felt good.

It was Marty who had first helped me understand how important it was to process the grief I endured from the absence of my father in order to successfully manage bipolar disorder for the long haul. While it took some time, I finally heeded his advice.

"Brian, you must tackle your bereavement," he had said. "Find a way to live with it, process it as your new reality, if you're ever going to feel whole."

Any event might have caused the breakdown I experienced, Marty elaborated, but because my dad's death was the initial trigger event of everything that had happened, I needed to find a place inside me where my grief and illness could co-exist without breaking me.

"How you accomplish that is up to you," he had said. "Only you can figure that out, but it's essential that you do."

I remember that discussion as clearly today as I did when Marty and I initially had it. We were eating hot fudge sundaes at an ice cream shop in Georgetown, taking a therapy session "road trip" as he called it. I also recall how conflicted I felt after returning home that day, the same sentiment that I had after leaving Aunt

Diane in Bellingham. Both of them had exclaimed it was me who held the keys to unchaining myself from the painful events which had unfolded. While I was busy searching for external signposts to guide me, they were both pointing me to my inner self.

I hadn't known where to begin dealing with my father's loss while I was living back in Virginia. His death was too fresh, and I was too entangled in my psychosis PTSD to act on Marty and Aunt Diane's mutual proclamation. But several years later in Annapolis, an opportunity for reconnecting with my dad presented itself, and I followed where I was being led.

Thank you, Dad. I needed this.

While chatting with a general contractor who was helping me with some electrical work, he pointed to a watercolor painting of Roger Maris I had recently purchased and hung on the wall in my family room.

"Do you like baseball?" he asked.

"I do. It's a passion of mine," I replied. "I played for a long time and also coached little league with my father for many years."

"Oh my God," he said, dropping his heavy tool bag which nearly landed on my foot. "I can't believe you just said that!"

I laughed.

"Why?"

"Well, I just became my son's little league coach."

"Oh, that's great. Congrats."

"No, it's not great. I only took the position because no other parent was willing to. I know absolutely nothing about the game."

He asked if I would be interested in helping him out, and I jumped at the chance.

Thus, I inherited a team of 11-14-year-old boys. They were a lively bunch, interested in everything except playing baseball. Since the truly talented players in town were on the travel team, our team was the Annapolis equivalent of the *Bad News Bears*. We consistently lost every game we played. Balls flew over the first baseman's head as often as they went past our catcher. But what struck me most was the great attitude all the boys had. They played their hearts out, and they lost with pride, always smiling, always enjoying running around and joking with each other. They knew they were terrible and didn't care. Neither did I.

We belonged to a league with only four teams, which meant that everyone made the playoffs. We went into the postseason expecting the same negative outcome every regular season game had produced, but somehow we won our first game. We got our boost when our star player, Gary, hit a towering grand slam down the left field line in the bottom of the last inning. The explosion of excitement – whistling, screaming, hooting, hollering – from the team and all the parents was deafening. I was in shock but happy for my deserving kids.

In the championship game, we faced the best team in the league, a group of private school kids from a nearby town who played together year-round. They had beaten us by double-digits in every previous game, and everyone expected the pattern to repeat. Before our kids took the field, I sensed some unusual nervousness among several of the players, so I pulled the boys into a huddle.

"Don't look at the scoreboard," I said. "Just be relaxed and enjoy yourselves as you've done all season. And I'm going to help you."

To ease the tension, I shook things up with a few youth sports coaching maneuvers I had learned from my father. I moved the infield to the outfield and reversed the batting order from last to first. I sent them all out to their positions with Twizzlers and Snickers bars. Then, I shocked everyone by making our youngest player, Teddy, the boy with the slowest fastball in the league, our starting pitcher. Teddy didn't have speed, but he had spunk. He knew he wasn't nearly as good as the other pitchers we faced, but he loved being on that mound.

What occurred next was nothing short of a Christmas miracle in the middle of June. The parents couldn't believe what was happening. Neither could I. The pitches Teddy threw over the plate were so slow – more like underhand bean bag tosses than little league fastballs – the other team could not manage to hit them. When they did make contact, they inevitably hit the ball right at our players, who inexplicably survived the first six innings without making a single error, or dropping their candy.

It was all unfolding too perfectly to be true, but then it wasn't.

Spunky Teddy lost his spunk, walking several batters in a row. Then, he gave up three runs, which forced me to bring in Gary, the only relief pitcher we had left. Clumsy and flat-footed, Gary had a good swing, but he was a wild pitching choice. He threw the ball really hard, but he had limited control of where it went. Predictably, he gave up two more runs, and suddenly our six-run lead was down to one, with two outs and the bases loaded.

With all eyes on Gary, the poor kid looked noticeably stressed and in desperate need of calming down. I called timeout and walked slowly to the mound, looking at the ground, keeping my head hung low. I had a trick up my sleeve, one more strategy right out of Big John's storied little league coaching playbook. I didn't know if it would work, but it was worth a try.

When I reached the mound, I squared my face into the most serious expression I could muster and looked Gary right in the eye.

"Why did the chicken cross the playground?" I asked him in earnest.

"What?" He was confused. "What are you talking about?"

"To get to the other slide," I said, retaining my stern look. "Get it?"

He was befuddled and stood silent.

I continued. "Why was 6 afraid of 7?"

No reply.

"Because 7 ate 9," I said. "Come on, Gary, that was an easy one."

This time, he cracked a half-smile. But it was obvious he was still tense.

"Why couldn't the bicycle stand up by itself?"

"Why?"

"It was two-tired. Get it? Two – Tired?"

Gary finally laughed, which was good, because I couldn't remember any more of my Dad's corny dad jokes. But I could tell Gary's mind was as far away from baseball as it could be, and that was the point.

"You look relaxed now. I'm glad to see it," I said, handing him the ball. "Now go throw three freakin' fastballs as fast as you can straight by this batter so we can all go out for ice cream and celebrate."

And that's exactly what he did.

Standing alone watching our players pile ecstatically on top of Gary, listening to the jubilation among parents and friends, I raised my arms, looked up at the sky, and wept.

I miss you, Dad.

Dear Kids,

Being with both of you out on the baseball and softball fields remains as important to my mental health as playing guitar and running and date-nights with Mom continue to be. Over the years, coaching has kept me connected to our local community as well, and has yielded many close friendships.

Getting to share my love of baseball with you and your friends is one of my favorite parts of being your Dad, just as it was for mine, and I'm grateful to both of you for granting me that privilege.

Love,

Dad

My bipolar meltdown and subsequent extended recovery put many things in my life on hold, for a long time. One of those was an excursion to Slovakia that I had planned for Mom and me as a present for her 60th birthday. Now that I had returned to feeling like myself again, I was excited to join her in visiting several relatives with whom she had corresponded throughout her life but had never met in person. It was there when Mom and I had our first conversation about bipolar disorder since the day I was diagnosed.

In the new old-world setting of Eastern Europe, Mom and I were able to step out of our practiced mother-and-son roles for a bit. Things we never talked about before were easy to discuss, and I took full advantage of the opportunity to be her adult peer rather than her mentally ill son. As we travelled from town to town in our rental car, Mom shared stories of her life that I had never heard before: spring break vacations to the Bahamas she took with friends in college; men she dated before meeting my dad. I clung to everything she offered as if I was climbing a steep rock cliff leading to the origins of her silent serenity I had forever admired but never fully understood.

In the shadows of her parent's Slovakian upbringing, I also learned a lot about Mom's own. To my surprise, and utter captivation, she even talked about Uncle Danny and how close they were as kids.

"Danny and me used to play hide-and-seek together in the woods behind our house," she shared one rainy afternoon as we sipped tea in a small café in Bratislava. "There was a huge oak tree he used to climb to the top of, and even though I knew he was up there, I could never find him."

Insulated by the innocence and delight of her childhood memories, there was neither mention of the mental illness struggles Uncle Danny experienced later in life nor the arduous times the family endured while supporting him through recovery. She spoke in playful glee with a smile as bright as the fields of purple and yellow tulips that blanketed the rolling fields between each town we visited. In that safe space, we both felt comfortable letting the elephant out of its cage, albeit briefly.

"How are things going with bipolar disorder, Beej?" she asked. "How is all that treating you?"

I was surprised to find how easy it was to talk with Mom openly about my episode, my illness, my progress. Moreover, it was quite comforting to hear her share some of her feelings about everything that had happened as well as the occasional concerns both she and Joy still had regarding my overall health and mental stability.

"You've overcome some terribly difficult things, Beej," she said. "We are happy for you, but everything that happened was so distressing, we worry sometimes."

Had it been several years earlier, Mom's apprehension would have summoned all the insecurities and shame that had plagued me. Now, however, I was proud of my recovery, confident and strong, and her empathy did not bother me. I didn't feel pitied. I appreciated her concern, and I understood where it was coming from.

I started to respond, but she cut me off and continued.

"You are very different from my brother Danny," she said. "You may share the same illness, but other than that, I don't see many similarities between you and him."

"What do you see?" I inquired.

"It's not about what I see," she said. "It's how I feel. Even when Danny seemed to be doing really well, I feared he would stop taking medication and fall apart again."

A tiny tear formed in the corner of her eye, a rare expression of emotion from the Zen matriarch, the rock of our family. I reached across the table and grabbed hold of her hand.

"I understand that," I said. "But I'm not going to let that happen."

In an effort to assure Mom that my life was, indeed, very different from Uncle Danny's, I described all of the activities that were presently bringing me joy and peace in Annapolis: the dining room table I was building in my workshop; the new, healthier diet I was trying out. And now, I wasn't alone. I had Sammy with me. She needn't worry. I was happy and healthy.

All of my projected stability aside, there was one thing I knew Mom needed to hear, and before we left the cafe, I delivered it.

"Mom, I promised you that I would never miss a dose of my medication," I said. "I haven't, and I never will."

We both cried. Then, we stood up and embraced.

It was only a brief conversation, but since the day I had walked out of the psych ward at Yale New Haven Hospital, I had never felt so free.

The time I spent with Mom in Slovakia was a world apart, a retreat into pure love and contentment. I was stress-free, and I remained so for quite a while upon my return. Then, I faced the inevitable reminder that no mental illness idyll lasts forever.

In a work meeting one morning, my client gave me some startling information.

"I'm very sorry, Brian, but we're facing big budget cuts and I have to let our consultants go, including you."

After working with the same team of engineers for several years, being pushed out was wrenching. My success was a large part of my self-esteem and coping with being suddenly unemployed yielded a spate of professional insecurity. It also brought on some extreme, unexpected anxiety.

Instead of confronting that and searching for new work, I once again ran away from it. Just as I had done in the aftermath of my bipolar episode, I shut down my laptop and filled my days with leisurely activities: playing golf, hiking with Sammy, fishing with friends out on the Bay. While doing so, I tried to convince myself that I wasn't avoiding going back to work – I was, once again, recuperating. I was taking it slow and ensuring my next professional move was well-conceived. With enough time, my confidence would return.

It didn't.

Instead, my plan backfired. My anxiety elevated and with it, came a new round of depression.

At first, I was hopeful it would be temporary – perhaps last a day or two. I had determined this wasn't a bipolar episode; no mania or psychosis had preceded it like before. *Nothing to worry about*, I told myself, *just a minor setback*. And this time I wasn't alone. I had Sammy. His fidelity and warm snuggles would help me through. If I just isolated myself from the outside world for a bit, I would bounce back.

Sammy and I spent a couple of days on the couch in my living room with a continual stream of old movies playing on the television in front of us. We ventured as far as the backyard to play fetch, and for the time being, Sammy's love and companionship kept my depression from taking full control. I felt like I was winning. Then, a couple of days turned into a couple of weeks, and my social life refused to let me have my way.

First, it was a fellow City Dock musician: "Brian, where have you been? We have a gig this weekend. Can you make it?"

Then, it was the little league coordinator: "Brian, can you help umpire tonight? One of the guys is sick."

Then, it was the head of a local environmental non-profit organization for which I was volunteering: "Brian, we need the website updated as soon as possible. Can you please call me back?"

Remaining isolated was, at the very least, socially awkward. I wanted no one to worry about me, and I most certainly did not want to talk with anyone about my emotional struggles. But after several weeks of avoiding everyone, I sensed their concern, which furthered my anxiety and deepened my depression.

I was also angry. My medication wasn't working. Why the heck wasn't lithium keeping me balanced? I did not expect my meds to instill a life of eternal happiness, but I did assume they would prevent any deeper level of sadness like the one I was experiencing. They weren't, and that pissed me off.

I needed to talk to someone, but I didn't know who that might be. I couldn't stomach discussing my despair with Richard. The same was true for Steve and my other closest circle-of-trust friends. And Joy and Mom were off limits. I had been stable for so long, and I needed to remain so in the eyes of everyone.

It did not take long for flashbacks of my bipolar episode to invade the cave I was hiding in. Images from my near suicidal nightmare preoccupied my mind, as if I had been transported back in time to my townhouse in Alexandria, curled up on the floor of my bedroom in filthy pajamas, using the sun's rays seeping through a window to thaw my frigid body. I fought the images off, telling myself that this time the demons were not going to get me. But they kept encroaching, and the closer they got, the more I shut down.

I was no longer winning. I was failing, at everything. I had failed at my job. Now, I was failing at my community obligations. I stopped vacuuming and doing laundry. I stopped reading, eating healthy, seeking connection. My life was all one big utter failure, and nobody but me was to blame.

Eventually, the ghosts consumed every aspect of my life, and in my mind, there was only one thing left to do.

Go. Run. Far away.

And this time, don't look back.

It was time to move. Again. I was terrified of leaving Annapolis, the town that I had fallen in love with – the City Dock community and the surrounding area that had breathed life into my drowning soul. But I just couldn't stay. The walls were closing in, and I needed to get out.

Deciding where to move was like a scene straight out of *Groundhog Day* as if I were Bill Murray going through the exact same decision process as I did when I left Alexandria. The truth was that once again, I instinctively wanted to move back home to be near Mom, to nestle into the safety of her vigilant care, and to be near Joy and Greg, to lean on them for emotional support and have a front row seat to watch Josh and Jason grow up. But I knew I would have to be financially independent, and the technology sector of the Connecticut job market was far too limited.

Remote jobs were also scarce back then, so I began to think about reasonable compromises. Somewhere closer to home but also close enough to a larger market for work.

One of my circle-of-trust friends lived in Boston, and I enjoyed visiting her there on multiple occasions to see Yankees / Red Sox games at Fenway Park, to attend New Year's Eve celebrations and Springsteen concerts. Although Dad would be appalled to think of me living in the epicenter of Red Sox Nation, the idea of moving there seemed comfortable. However, I had no interest in living in the city.

"There're many smaller, quieter towns in the suburbs," my friend told me. "If you look around, you'll certainly find the right one for you and Sammy."

Thus, my departure from Annapolis began with a road trip. I drummed up the physical and emotional strength to leave the confines of my house but only for the purpose of finding the place where Sammy and I might escape to next. With a bag of dog food and a suitcase full of clothes, we hit the road.

Over the course of two weeks, we visited several dozen towns. I was in search of perfection, somewhere like Annapolis — a community where I could sip pre-dawn coffee on a park bench and watch the sun creep up over the Atlantic Ocean. Finally, toward the end of our excursion, one North Shore location checked all the boxes: Salem, Massachusetts.

Only a short train ride from Boston, Salem had a vibe that was not dissimilar from Annapolis. A harbor community that boasted a young adult population in a refurbished, upscale downtown, Salem had a vibrant arts and music scene, plenty of running routes beside the water, low-key bars, and a large dog park. On top of all that, it came with the moniker "Witch City" – the Halloween capital of the world, where all wizards and warlocks were welcome, any time of the year. The mystique of that alone had me fervently intrigued.

Salem was the place, and now all I needed to do was find a house to move to.

Before returning to Annapolis, Sammy and I met with several realtors, visiting every property that was on the market. I was discouraged at first. The ones along the water were well above my price range. Others further inland were either too run-down to purchase, or not run-down enough, lacking any character whatsoever. However, one home in a historical neighborhood just a short walk from downtown Salem stood out. It was the home where the next chapter of my life with bipolar disorder would be written – the next beautiful, wretched, exhilarating, terrifyingly glorious chapter.

A cozy little clapboard house on a fateful street in Witch City. Walter Street.

W hen I was first diagnosed with bipolar, and for quite some time after, correlating spirituality with bipolar disorder in any fashion was like eating one of my mother's beloved cucumber, raw onion, and mayonnaise sandwiches – it just wasn't going to happen. But as my relationship with my illness expanded, so did my perception of spirituality and in a healthy fashion.

When I think about the psychotic phase of my bipolar episode, I try to think of it in two ways. They are the polar opposite of one another, but they both have equal merit.

The first is the obvious, physical one: my psychosis was horrifyingly dangerous. My psychotic exploits nearly killed me. The second is spiritual and deeply personal. While the things I was doing were treacherous, the reason I was doing them was not. The impetus of my psychotic adventure was to spiritually reconnect with my father – to speak to him, to be with him once again – and my psychosis was the conduit through which I was able to make that otherworldly connection.

I wish there was a way for someone who isn't genetically predisposed to psychosis to experience the depths of its natural power – in a safe and secure environment, of course, and without LSD or another hallucinogen as the catalyst. Natural psychosis is difficult to describe in a tangible cause and effect manner, but a conversation I once had with my friend Orus helped put the phenomena into more practical context. Actually, just about everything I discussed with Orus helped frame things more practically, and poignantly. First, let me tell you why.

Orus and I met at an open house held by the nursery school which both of our young children attended and we quickly became close friends. The impetus of that was our joint love of music and specifically playing the guitar. A few weeks later, we formed a "Dad Band" with several other musicians – a stoic acoustic ensemble comprising limited musical talent, but a wealth of dad joke humor and the mutual enjoyment of sitting around a campfire drinking cheap wine, talking about our inadequacies as fathers and husbands, and occasionally jamming a few Tom Petty and Led Zeppelin songs.

Sadly, shortly after we met, Orus was diagnosed with myxoid liposarcoma – a rare, aggressive cancer leading his doctors to predict that he might only have a few months left to live. While the biological evidence appeared conclusive, Orus refused to believe it, or rather, he chose to live his life to the fullest during whatever time he had left if his terminal diagnosis proved true. Because of that mindset, Orus transformed his three month death sentence into six heartwarming, memorable years for himself, his wife and four children, his parents and other family members, his co-workers, his fellow Dad Band members, and all of his friends. In that time, he "teased out every possible moment of meaning and fulfilling experiences as [he] sought to enjoy the life [he] had, instead of fearing the death that some day comes for us all. . ." – the last words he left us in the obituary he penned for himself just before he died.

In those difficult, yet inspiring six years, Orus and I had many intimate conversations. Alongside talking about his cancer treatments and the occasional moments of hope, we also talked about my bipolar experiences. During one of our discussions he asked me what it felt like to be psychotic. Other than Marty, and then eventually my wife, nobody else had ever asked me that before. It was a difficult question to answer, so I did what I often do when I don't have a good response to an inquiry: I answered his question with one of my own.

"Well, when do you feel the most spiritual?" I asked him.

He sipped on his glass of cabernet and thought for a minute.

"Music," he said. "Sometimes when I'm listening or playing, the right lyrics at the right time speak to me, spiritually."

I know that feeling as well. There have been many moments in my life, and not just when I was psychotic, when a certain song has come on the radio at just the right time with just the right lyrics, and I believe I'm receiving some clandestine message being delivered just to me. My skin tingles, and I feel enlightened as my mind processes the substance of the message, why it is being sent, and who might be sending it. Sometimes I feel the message so strongly that I become obsessed with it, and I lose track of what I'm doing in the moment.

I would describe the outset of psychosis similarly. Now, just imagine that feeling not going away. Imagine staying in that spiritual moment for several minutes. . . then perhaps hours. . . then perhaps days – your heart receiving handfuls of cosmic messages through song lyrics and tv shows and social interactions and other mediums all at once, making you feel like the world is evolving around you and you alone. In that abstract headspace, reality simply fades away, and in its void, you begin to define your own reality – your own song, with your own lyrics. Then, you distribute your message to the physical world around you from the psychotic place to which you have transcended.

I hit the pause button on my spiritual soundtrack for a long time after my father died and I was subsequently diagnosed with bipolar disorder. I did the opposite of what Orus chose to do after his doctors told him myxoid liposarcoma would soon end his life. I let my fear and shame dictate the road I travelled instead of listening for the spiritual music and following where it directed me. I wish I hadn't because I'm sure I missed many messages that my father, and others, sent to me along the way; messages of beauty, and also warning.

PART VII

Resurgence
(OR AS I LIKE TO CALL IT, "STRIKE 2")

Thursday, May 3rd, 2001

I t's the middle of the afternoon, and Mom and I are watching *The Price is Right* on the game show network. Bob Barker is soliciting bids from each of the two contestants during the show-case showdown. Mom plays along.

"I say $8,500," she says. "How about you, Beej?"

I'm barely paying attention but pretend that I am to appease her.

"That sounds about right. I'll say $8,900."

The retail value is revealed. It's well over $12,000. Not even close.

Outside, I hear Joy's car door shut, and she steps into the house. She gives me a hug then hands me two trays of leftover lasagna and birthday cake.

"I brought you this because Greg will eat the whole thing if it's in our refrigerator," she says. "That's the last thing he needs."

I chuckle and thank her.

Mom retrieves her pocketbook from the kitchen counter and puts on her sneakers. She and Joy are going to the Milford Mall to purchase new outfits for the wake and funeral. They both don't have anything appropriate to wear, they say. They want to be comfortable during the events, they say.

"Are you sure you don't want to come with us, Beej?" Joy asks. "We can stop at Men's Warehouse for you if you want to buy a new suit."

"Yes, I'm sure," I reply. "Sarah will bring up some clothes for me from Virginia."

Mom doubles down on Joy's empathy and not-so-subtle concern.

"Are you sure, Beej? We'd love to have you join us."

"No, that's alright. I might go hit some golf balls at the driving range."

After they walk outside, I follow shortly behind them. I do not want to be alone in this house. I can't be alone here. The silence makes my skin crawl, and I have no appetite for birthday cake.

I shuttle across town to Sleeping Giant Golf Course, to Dad's weekend retreat. His holy temple, where he sought absolution after a week of working hard at a mundane job that he abhorred. I grab a beat-up driver from the rack, fill a bucket with balls, and walk to the furthest tee box to separate myself from the other golfers. I place a ball on the tee and drive it far and straight. A good start. I hit another one with the same result. I hit a dozen more, just as composed, until Larry, the part-time groundskeeper, gets into his caged cart and begins driving around to pick up golf balls.

I pause and remember a fun game Dad used to play with me.

"Beej, if you hit the cart before I do, we'll stop for root beer floats on the ride home," he'd say.

I aim my stance at Larry and strike my first ball well, but it hooks sharply to the left. My second slices to the right. My third dribbles on the ground just a few feet in front of me. My fourth launches over the mesh screen protecting golfers playing on the ninth hole, nearly hitting an older couple walking up the fairway.

I stop the game.

I walk up to the tiny clubhouse to buy myself a soda. I stroll around, sipping on my Dr. Pepper and examining the course memorabilia. The main room is like a Hall of Fame for the Sleeping Giant Men's Club, which Dad helped found. He was voted in years ago, and a picture of him hangs on the wall from the year he won the club championship. He is holding his small trophy and smiling ear-to-ear as if he had just won The Master's and he's about to receive a green jacket from the previous year's winner.

Before I leave, I stand on the empty first tee. I'm reminded of the day I first played with the new metal driver Dad gave me for my birthday when I was thirteen. I remember it was a Sunday because I rarely played with Dad on Sundays. Each Sunday I was in church with Mom and Joy, squirming in my seat, ignoring the words from our appointed elders which I didn't understand, thinking about the juice and cookies I'd have at the break.

But that Sunday was different.

On that Sunday I was with Dad, worshiping in his temple. Playing alongside his weekly foursome, his own congregation. Listening to their witty conversations, their joyful hymns. Watching their putts trickle into the hole like grateful amens.

That Sunday I held my new birthday driver in the air as if it were a sword, and I, an onward Christian soldier, following Dad around the course like a loyal disciple, comforted that there, in his presence, God was all around me.

I wasn't thinking about Walter — my father's absent father — on the day I moved to Walter Street in Salem, MA in the spring of 2007. I wasn't thinking about anything other than running away from the stultifying depression I experienced in Annapolis. *Escape to somewhere new and everything will be normal again*, I told myself. The excitement of the adventure will revitalize you, Brian – keep your haunting past from haunting you. Just push forward, and all your troubles will go away.

Sure they will.

Regardless, I was happily surprised by how much my excitement for beginning the next chapter of my life back in New England had alleviated my depression. Virtually overnight, my confidence returned and I felt back in control - ready to confront any obstacles that stood in my way. Even when the softened real estate market prevented me from selling my house, I didn't let it bother me. I just found renters and moved onward. But there was still one emotional barrier to cross before leaving town: saying goodbye to friends and co-workers.

Over the course of a decade, I had become very close to many people in the Washington D.C. – Baltimore – Annapolis triangle, and as much as I needed a fresh start, I had mixed emotions about leaving them. Without any relatives in the Mid-Atlantic, I had made them my representative family, and I couldn't simply watch them fade away in the rear-view mirror.

I struggled with how to approach each of my friends, how to explain my sudden desire to remove myself from a community which everyone knew I adored without sharing my struggles with depression. But that wasn't going to happen. That secret remained tucked away. I needed an explanation, but I didn't have one. What I did have, however, was my old playbook of deceit, the same one I had used when I left Alexandria. The same one I had been using since the day I was first handed my Scarlet B. This time around, the web of lies I spun was even more intricate.

I'm sorry, again, Dad.

At a farewell lunch with some work colleagues, I told them I was offered a new job in Boston that I just couldn't pass up. . . "I'm getting out of government contracting business and moving to the private sector. It's far more exciting and pays much better."

During a send-off gathering at a City Dock restaurant, I told a separate group of friends that I was quitting technology and going into the real-estate business. . . "My Annapolis property is the first in my residential portfolio, and I've already got my eyes on a few more in Massachusetts."

For my fellow musicians, I was joining an old college buddy's band that had regular gigs in downtown Boston. . .

For my baseball parents, I was returning to New England for the changing of the seasons I had missed for far too long. . .

By the time I had finished my disgraceful bon voyage tour, my plan had worked, at least in my eyes. Each of my friends received a song I assumed they wanted to hear, and I had an album of greatest fiction hits to propel me forward. But it didn't matter. All of that would soon be a distant memory.

There were two people that I couldn't lie to, at least not completely: Mom and Joy. They knew me too well, and I felt they would both see right through my duplicity. That being said, nothing prevented me from avoiding some of the truth, and in particular, the depression I had experienced. Mom and Joy didn't need to know about that. It would only make them worry, and I had already made them worry enough. What I did share with them was genuine, and during a brief stop home on my drive up to Salem, I ensured they knew how I felt.

"I'm ready for a change," I said. "And I miss you both. I want to be closer to you."

Both Mom and Joy were just as confused by my sudden relocation as my friends were, but they didn't challenge me on it. In hindsight, once again, they both wished they had. I do, too. But such open communication about my illness still wasn't happening, and it wouldn't happen for some time.

I should have known that my life on Walter Street was going to be some combination of spiritually illuminating and grimly painful but not because of the name of the street to which my exhaustive house search had led me. When I drove to the house with the keys for the first time, there was a black cat with beady yellow eyes sitting on the front stoop, staring at me, and purring so loudly I could hear him from the driveway.

A black cat, in the Halloween capital of the world, awaiting at my doorstep to welcome me to Walter Street.

Dad, really?

Sammy nearly jumped out of the car to chase the scrappy little feline. Looking back at everything that happened in that house now, perhaps I should have let him.

As it turned out, the black cat was owned by my kind, delightful neighbors who lived across the street. His name was Herb, and he was quite popular in the neighborhood as he roamed the streets for scraps of food anywhere he could find them. There's a chance, I guess, that Herb was, indeed, sitting on the porch to cast a "Witch City" spell onto Sammy and me. But his primary intention was to get an afternoon treat from the previous owner of the house who fed him each day when she returned from work – a ritual I learned about from my neighbor later on.

Even though I was, once again, unemployed, it wasn't difficult to secure financing for the house thanks to a second "No Doc Loan" my bank had graciously offered me – another line of credit extended from my already overleveraged property in Annapolis. I had become the poster child for the "No Job? No Income? No

Problem!" mortgage debacle that would soon bring our entire financial system to its knees. But I didn't care. Like all the lies I had been telling, my latest loan, even if semi-fraudulent, got me where I needed to go.

Built in 1849, my new abode was a sweet little Greek revival in a cozy neighborhood just a short walk from downtown Salem. The property had been well-maintained over the years but still required several renovations. Tearing down old kitchen cabinets and installing new appliances kept me occupied during the day while I searched for a new job. As much as I didn't want to start working right away, I needed the income. Without the proceeds from the sale of my house in Annapolis that I was counting on to keep me afloat after the move, my credit balance was once again approaching rock bottom.

Without any work contacts in Boston, I called a headhunter.

"Hi, I just moved to the area and I'm looking for some temporary consulting work."

"I'm happy to help," she said. "Why don't you tell me a little bit about yourself and your career first before walking me through your resume?"

Tell you a little bit about myself and my career.

Hmm, where do I even begin?

It took a while, but the headhunter found me a job in Medford on the North Shore, just a short distance from Salem. It wasn't the remote position I had hoped for, but it was only twenty minutes from my house, and my new client gave me a generous allotment of autonomy. Better still, I found the technology work interesting. The job entailed building software for the automotive industry, something I knew little about, but with the help of several gracious co-workers, I quickly understood and enjoyed.

In short order, Salem felt like the perfect place for Sammy and me to settle down. We had new friends, generous neighbors, and a whole new world to explore. My drive home whenever I wanted to see Mom, Joy, and the rest of my family was just a couple of hours, and I visited often. I wasn't as close to them as I would have been if I had moved back home, but as I sat beside them watching Josh's school plays and Jacob's little league games, our relationship was becoming closer to what it had been when I was growing up.

Always faithful to my promise to Mom, and still believing that so long as I stayed on my meds I would circumvent any deeper depression, when I ran out, I found a new therapist, Cindy, and continued taking my daily dosage. I would have preferred to stop seeing a psychiatrist altogether. In my mind, I would never meet another Marty, never develop the trust I had placed in him with any other doctor. But once again, I was held hostage by the prescription pad.

Cindy's therapy practice was located in the basement of what used to be an old church before it was converted into a small business office building. It was cold and dusty down there, but thankfully she was neither. She was kind and approachable, always wearing a t-shirt and jeans to our sessions that complemented her spiked purple hair and laid-back personality. She was also knowledgeable, particularly with medications to treat mental illness.

"Brian, studies now show there can be negative side-effects of taking lithium for an extended period," she said during one of our first sessions. "Though it is uncommon, the drug has been known to cause kidney damage."

I was appreciative of her medical insights, but I'll be honest, I felt like an idiot. In all the years I had been taking lithium, I had never thought to question its biological implications. Nowhere in my initial research were such cautions ever mentioned, or at least none that I had stumbled upon. In addition, given that the drug is comprised of salt, and one of the most common medications used to treat bipolar disorder, I just assumed there was nothing I needed to worry about. Apparently, I was wrong.

"We're going to slowly switch you over to lamotrigine," she said. "It's a second-generation drug that has no side-effects, and it will also be better for your overall metabolism."

I was nervous about changing medication at first – fearful it wouldn't be as effective and cause my depression to resurface, but Cindy thoughtfully walked me through it, and her relaxed, trust-worthy rapport put my mind at ease. However, when she suggested we explore the more complicated facets of my wellness plan, my bipolar history, my family or personal relationships, I immediately shut down.

"I'm fine," I would tell her. "Just fine."

And I was fine. For a while. Until fate intervened once again.

One day I noticed that Sammy had developed a bump on his nose. I made an appointment at the vet. By the time we got in to see her, the bump had grown substantially.

"Brian, I'm very sorry to tell you this, but Sammy has cancer. A voraciously aggressive cancer which is inoperable."

I had no choice but to put Sammy down.

My little buddy, my floppy-eared cuddle bug, was suddenly gone. My healing companion, who had nursed me as I nursed him back from near death, who had filled my days with the most sincere, unconditional love I could have ever imagined, had left me. No more long runs through the woods. No more dog park playdates and nighttime snuggles. My heart splintered into myriad, lacer-ating shards. It was like losing my father all over again and just as unexpectedly.

Mom came to Salem and stayed with me shortly after. She understood my attachment to Sammy and wanted to support me as I processed my loss.

"I'm so sorry, Beej," she said when I met her at the train station. "What can we do to honor Sammy?"

We picked up Sammy's ashes and brought them to Furlong Park, a quiet enclave beside the Danvers River just a few blocks from my house, which Sammy and I frequently visited to play fetch and skim rocks. There, I took off my sneakers and socks, waded into the water, and scattered the dust from the urn all around me. Back on the beach, Mom and I sat on a blanket, and she held me as I cried in her arms, watching the remnants of my beloved furry friend dissolve into the receding ripples of the water.

———

In the months that followed Sammy's death, I leaned on my area friends for support as I worked through my sadness, and I let Mom talk me into acceptance. Despite my fear that the shock would trigger another battle with depression, I got past the immediate emotional strain, renewed my commitment to work, and got steady on my feet. I let Joy in to help as well when I needed her, and I felt like I had successfully weathered a major crisis. However, when I wasn't with them, I was suddenly aware that once again I was alone.

For the first time in several years, the only pulse beating under my roof was my own. Without the sound of chew-toys being mangled and water being slurped, the quietude in my house was deafening. Motivated by the silence of my loneliness, I began dating again. Soon after, I met Pam.

Pam meandered into my life just as I was beginning to trust myself to care for someone beyond a dog and myself. A neighbor recognized a synchronicity in our personalities – our affectionate sarcasm and crafty wit – and brought us together at a Halloween party.

"Nice to meet you, Brian. I'm digging the muscles," Pam said, chuckling at my Hanz and Franz costume – an oversized gray sweat suit stuffed with crumpled newspaper.

"It's nice to meet you too. Can I buy you a drink?"

Pam's short brown hair, cute, tiger-striped glasses, and sassy smile immediately caught my attention, and she was instantly a comfortable, reassuring presence. We had much in common. We shared an appetite for travel and adventure, a disdain of the political sphere, and a mutual appreciation for stand-up comedy. I was captivated by her *laissez-faire* attitude towards circumstances beyond her control, something I struggled with in all facets of my life at that time.

It didn't take long for Pam and me to be a committed couple. Part of the charm of our relationship, at least for me, was that we saw one another only on weekends. A new job took Pam to Portland, Maine, about a 90-minute drive north of Salem. One of us would visit the other every weekend, arriving with a backpack of clothes and a bottle of wine. The relatively short, long-distance relationship suited both of our independent natures. We were a devoted couple living generally separate lives. The arrangement was safe, giving both of us space to explore our own interests with the approving backing of a steadfast partner.

Over time, I trusted Pam more and more, and as our relationship evolved, I even opened up to her about my mental illness, albeit on a superficial level. I never provided her with any of the dirty details of my episode, never shared how extensive my psychosis was nor how deep my depression ran. I was afraid that would scare her off, so I downplayed the severity of my experiences and all of their psychologically damaging repercussions including the trail of lies I had told. I was managing my illness on my own, and I was good at it.

Stupid decision #1.

The bipolar tight-rope I was walking across alone had been wobbling for years, and allowing someone to assist me in the management of my illness is exactly what I needed. But I couldn't recognize that at the time. It was easier to diffuse the power of bipolar disorder by dismissing its relevance.

"It was a difficult thing to deal with back then," I explained to Pam matter-of-factly. "But other than taking my pills, I don't really think about it that much anymore."

The news did not seem to deter Pam at all. She seemed to pass no judgment, and I found her genuine empathy comforting. Of course, she only had half the story, which was fine by me. What good would it do to tell her any more? How could that possibly better our relationship? And why open a wound that was healed? There was no need to dive any further into something that happened over seven years prior to our meeting.

Stupid decisions #2, #3, and #4.

The geographic distance between Pam and me gave me the freedom to explore my own opportunities, and around the same time, my professional life took an upward leap.

Pleased by my performance with some project management responsibilities I was given, a senior executive at my client's company extended my contract and asked me to join a newly formed research and development division – a group of industry experts creating a state-of-the-art automotive technology platform.

"Brian, we need a strong leader to help us build this thing," he said. "It's the number one priority for the company, and I can't think of a better person for the job."

The technology was similar to the Blue Force Tracker telecommunications work I had done for the U.S. Army earlier in my career, only better. It was cutting-edge and complex – an early version of what Uber and Lyft would use a decade later to track vehicles across their rideshare services. I was ecstatic and did not hesitate to accept the offer.

The technical challenges we faced, exacerbated by the tight deadlines our executives dictated, often kept us in the office well-past normal business hours. We'd order pizza and drink beer in our secluded "war room" as we worked through each phase of development. As the pressure from management to improve the design increased, I saw Pam less. But Pam knew how exciting my job was to me and fully supported my efforts. She, too, was very busy with work that often required extensive travel to Europe and Asia.

One afternoon, our boss came barging into the conference room, overtly excited.

"Guys, I've got some unbelievable news," he exclaimed with his arms flapping. "We have our first big auto manufacturer opportunity. . . It's go time!"

He led us all to the boardroom where the CEO of the company had brought in a delicious spread of food and several bottles of champagne. After shutting the door, they told us that our firm had been selected to bid on a multi-year contract with a major Japanese conglomerate.

"If we win, our software will be installed in hundreds of thousands of vehicles!" he exclaimed. "After the deal goes through, there'll be big financial incentives for all of you."

Some extra money was enticing. By this time, the mortgage crisis had severely diluted my net worth which was now mostly tied up in real estate. My bank even cut off my credit line using a corporate solvency clause buried somewhere in the fine-print of my lending contract. My "free money" days were over.

As the company executives shuttled between Boston and Tokyo, my team shifted into overdrive to support the effort. Relentlessly focused, intensively dedicated, we put in a couple weeks of nonstop work. No days off, no weekend breaks, no family fun nights were allowed. I was exhausted, but I pressed on, unaware that I was increasingly hypomanic. No one there knew my history and had no reason to be on the alert. Pam was 90 minutes away and in the dark. Mom and Joy were even further, and my monthly therapy session with Cindy had just lapsed.

My hypomania simply grew stronger with every passing sleepless night. Tired as I was at the end of the day, I could not slow down the wheels turning inside my brain. I was in overdrive, obsessively focused on my responsibilities to the company and the tiniest details of our software: vehicles scrambling through busy cities;

transponder data failing to reach our servers; break the code, fix the code. . . break the code, fix the code. Nothing tired my body or relaxed my mind, and I found myself giving in to the sleeplessness. I'd stop tossing and turning in the middle of the night, get out of bed, turn on my laptop, and get back to work.

Oblivious to any impending doom, my work got sloppy, just as it did during my first bipolar episode. I began writing rambling, incoherent emails. I strutted about the office like a mini-monarch, congratulating colleagues on jobs well done, offering high-fives to superiors, presumptuously engaging strangers I met in the kitchen or while waiting for the elevator. Though I noticed winces from a few people, I did not recognize how bizarre my behavior was. Wrapped up in my overstimulated, bipolar narcissism – my propulsion to becoming king of the kingdom – I was in no way cognizant of anything beyond my hyper-creativity and the work objectives given to me. As far as I knew, I was successfully executing my tasks, meeting deadlines, achieving milestones, solving problems. What could be wrong?

One morning, I arrived at work flushed and out of breath as though I had run multiple heats of the hundred-yard dash. Without inhibition or fear, I strode into a senior executive's office like a colossus, a Caesar among the plebians.

"Hello, Alex," I chortled. "I just want you to know that I am ready to take on any new challenge you might suggest. I can deliver whatever you and the company could possibly need. If you want me on your full-time staff, I'm ready to sign on anytime you say. I'll leave you with a copy of my resume, and you will see that I am the best candidate you are likely to meet in this lifetime."

An hour later, one of my team members found me sleeping under a conference room table. I sat up and laughed. "Yeah. I just thought I should take a short cat nap before our status meeting."

That afternoon, my manager called me in to talk about the incident with the senior executive and sent me home to get some rest. Instead, I went home and doubled down on my work activities, which by now were completely incoherent.

Pam had left several voicemail messages that I had not returned, and by this time, she was calling me incessantly. She could tell something was off, kept asking me if I was okay. Finally, we connected.

"Of course, I'm okay," I laughed. "My client is just counting on me to help shepherd this big deal through, and I can't let them down!"

"You're sure? I don't know. . ."

"Ha-ha. Trust me. I'm fine," I said. "But if I don't finish my work, I'll never get up to Portland to see you this weekend! I'll call you again tomorrow. . ."

I did not call her.

I like to think of myself as someone who learns from his mistakes. And that's important, because I make a lot of them. As my second bipolar disorder episode began ramping up, obviously I hadn't learned from my past mistakes. In fact, I had charged directly into repeating the same one I had made at the outset of my first episode: overworking – the importance of avoiding wellness plan Trigger #3 now a distant memory. All wrapped up in the excitement of professional challenges and financial incentives being dangled in front of me and my co-workers like a hypnotist's medallion, I was simply unaware of my imbalanced, abnormal behavior, which was escalating at an unprecedented pace.

Shortly after talking with Pam, I began drawing my first psychotic inferences and zealously responding to them. The first involved an old companion – the reincarnation of a soulmate, whose loss had never been far from my consciousness.

Sammy.

Trotting through my backyard one morning, I saw Herb, my friendly neighborhood feline. I scurried out to pick Herb up, brought him inside, and after he settled, I gave him a tour of my house. In my bedroom, he leapt up on to my bed and sat upright, just as Sammy used to do in the mornings as I changed out of my pajamas before our walks. I took that mental cue to heart, climbed up into the attic, and opened several storage boxes in search of Sammy's old collar. When I couldn't find it, I constructed one out of my belt and secured it around Herb's neck. Surprisingly, he didn't resist, which made me feel like I was on the right track. Next, I raced down to the basement and cut a short length of rope to use as a leash. It was all coming together quite nicely.

"Ok Sammy, let's go!"

Sammy, I mean Herb, and I trotted over to Furlong Park. The tide was out so I brought him down to the rock-lined beach, then skimmed a tennis ball across the shoreline, expecting him to fetch it once I let him off my makeshift leash. Instead, he bolted up the rocks, across the park, and back to his familiar territory.

As I stood there looking out at the same river inlet where I had released Sammy's ashes, flashbacks of the two of us rushed through my mind and brought me to my knees. I sobbed and prayed.

Sammy, give me a sign, give me anything...

Nothing came, so I left the park and began jogging back to my house looking for Herb. Along the way, I saw my neighbors walking their dog. I sprinted over to them, squatted down, and pleaded for direction.

"Sammy, tell me what to do," I said, nearly out of breath. "Tell me where to go."

This time the instructions were clear.

Go to the graveyard, he said.

The graveyard. My first clue.

The game was on.

I avoided the questions my neighbors began to ask and sprinted up Walter Street and into Greenlawn Cemetery – a large grave-yard adjacent to our neighborhood with smooth, shaded path-ways that I ran through frequently. I weaved in and out of the tombstones, meticulously reading the inscriptions, looking for patterns of words or letters or punctuation to guide me.

The initials of the name on the first headstone were "L" and "P." I don't recall all the details of what happened next, but by the time I completed my intense clue-searching among other head-stones, burial tombs, and a family of ducks gliding across a small pond, I had the message I was brought to the cemetery to receive.

L. A. P. T. O. P.

I dashed home and grabbed my work computer. At the top of my email inbox was a message from someone in my client's HR Department. Perfect. I read it several times.

"Hi Brian, we've been trying to reach you, but you haven't returned our messages. Can you please call me?"

In all my time working for the company, I had never received an email from this man. This must be the next message. But what is he really asking me? Or rather, what is he trying to tell me?

Wait. . .

Our software. . . our telecom platform. . . has it been tracking my every move? Did they secretly place a transponder somewhere while I was in the office? Are they all watching my location shift on the big-screen television in the conference room?

Hold on. . . how can that be? Where could they have hidden it?

I cycled through every possibility. The device couldn't be in my laptop bag, or if it were, I hadn't been carrying it around with me. Perhaps it was in the jeans I was wearing? No, that didn't make sense. . . I always wore khakis to the office. Where could they hide it?

Wait a minute. . . my sneakers! I had kicked them off late one night. . . could someone have cut a tiny hole in the tongue and slipped in a microchip?

Fuck.

Fuck! Fuck! Fuck!

I threw my sneakers in the trash, put on an older pair, and dashed down the street, back to Furlong Park. I hid behind the rocks along the beach, hoping nobody had seen me. There, I received another voice command, resonating from my chest cavity and bursting into the forefront of my improperly functioning brain at the speed of light.

Go downtown.

I made my way to downtown Salem where I searched for one clue at a time near each of the tourist attractions: the Witch Museum, the *Clue* mansion, the House of the Seven Gables. I rummaged through the trash barrels scattered around the main shopping strip, engaged in a lengthy conversation with the bronzed *Bewitched* statue. I ran into the Hawthorne Hotel, sat on one of the plush couches in the lobby, and collected as many tourist flyers as I could hold.

More clues appeared in various forms scattered around the downtown area – plastic straws, small pebbles, a lost key ring, words and images on takeout menus. I shoved them all into the pockets of my jeans until there wasn't any more room then darted back to my house and arranged the puzzle pieces on my bed. As I placed the last clue, the message could not have been any more succinct.

PORTLAND!

Right. Pam. She had asked me to come visit. Was there something there I needed to find? Was she part of this? Had she been part of this all along?

I grabbed my keys, hopped in my car, and sped to the northbound interstate. The hum of the tires on the highway and the music on the car radio hypnotized me. Soon, I no longer heard any of them. All sounds were contravened by a familiar voice.

It's time, Beej. You are ready now, and I, too, am ready . . . to anoint you. . .

Yes, it was time for my father to return once again.

I'm coming, Dad. I'll be there soon!

The speedometer of my car teetered at 90 miles per hour all the way to Portland. With each passing exit, the alternate reality I had previously contrived – Sammy's rebirth, my client stalking me, Pam's potential involvement – had fully dissolved. There was only looking forward into a new, singular psychotic portal, a delusion that my father was coming back for me as he had once before. Although this time there would be no mortal conquests involved. No government agents to impress nor terrorists to defeat. Those were earthly presuppositions. This was my spiritual destiny.

My Father, who art in Heaven, hallowed be thy name...

Thy kingdom come, thy will be done, on earth as it is in Heaven...

The third day was finally upon us. The stone in front of the tomb had been pushed aside.

I was crucified on the day Dad died, but three days later, on my birthday, I was reborn... and now the time has finally come to revel in his mercy and grace, deliver the world from evil, join my father on his throne.

I heard the same scripture repeat itself in my mind, the one from the book of Saint John: *For God so loved the world, he gave his only begotten Son... Whosoever believeth in him shall not perish, but have everlasting life...*

I am the only begotten.

I am the chosen one.

It was a bright, sunlit spring afternoon, and by the time I arrived in Portland, it was the middle of the day. When I got out of the car, I took off my sneakers, rolled up my pant legs, opened my shirt, and walked through downtown Portland, smiling at everyone I met. I held up my hand to stop traffic when I crossed each street, engaging drivers who were honking their horns and screaming at me.

"Hey asshole – get out of the road!"

"Why do you use such profanity, sir? I am the Son of Christ. Come follow me."

No one followed.

I ambled through the waterfront area, moving deliberately, tranquilly, touching the hands of all I met in restaurants and bars, small stores and merchant clusters. At the Harbor Hotel, I entered through the lobby and went directly to the first-floor where I knocked on doors, calling to Peter, Mark, Matthew, and Luke to join me.

After a security guard escorted me out, I strolled to a neighborhood park beside the ocean, where tourists strolled and fishermen cast lures into the surf. I squeezed in between a loving couple on the beach and put my arms around their waists then stepped out in front of them to pronounce them man and wife.

Next, I waded into the water and performed a baptism on a small log I found washed up on the shore. Then, I raised my hands to the sky, closed my eyes, and walked slowly into the water until it was up to my chin.

Dad, should I go further? Are you out there?

From behind me, I heard a woman screaming. "What the hell are you doing? Get back here, you're going to fucking drown!"

Her tone startled me. *Maybe she needs my help.*

I swam back to shore, but by the time I got there, she was gone.

Now soaking wet, I stripped down to my boxer shorts and took off for a several-mile, barefoot run on a path that eventually led to Pam's apartment. Pam was not home yet, so I let myself in and ran a warm bath. Blood from my scorned feet mingled with the water. I cleaned them with a washcloth and soap, just as I would my disciple's feet. I laid back in the tub, closed my eyes, and temporarily fell asleep.

I was awakened by a lovely woman, who kneeled down next to my reclining, cleansed body. I reached out and touched the light on the top of her glowing head.

"Oh my God Brian, are you okay?"

My relationship with my illness is littered with regrets. I've been told by therapists, friends, girlfriends, Greg, Joy, Mom, and my wife repeatedly that I shouldn't regret my self-preserving behaviors as I fought my bipolar identity war. But I do, deeply. Time is a precious commodity, and I wasted so much of it hiding from the people I love instead of embracing the love they offered. I don't regret having a mental illness. I can't. The presence of bipolar disorder in my genetic makeup is outside my control. But I have deep remorse for all the selfish acts I committed while failing to manage it properly – acts that hurt all those who gave me the support I needed to do so.

I am not the only one who has regrets pertaining to my bipolar episodes. Joy, Greg, and Mom have several regrets, too. The most prominent occurred right here in the middle of my second episode when Pam came home to her apartment to find me sitting in a bloody bathtub. She immediately called Joy to tell her I was in trouble, and she wasn't exactly sure what to do.

If you ask Joy and Greg and Mom what they *should have* done but *didn't* do at that moment, they'll tell you they should have taken me to the nearest hospital as quickly as they could. They should have placed me in the hands of medical professionals to evaluate the severity of my imbalance and treat me appropriately. But they didn't, and in hindsight, they wished that they had.

So why not?

The short answer is they knew how much I had despised being in the hospital during my first episode, and they didn't want to subject me to that again if they didn't have to. Joy in particular was afraid I would become belligerent if I was forced into a psych ward again – adamantly opposed to receiving the professional treatment I desperately needed. Her fears would unfortunately come to fruition a few days later.

Instead of taking me to the hospital, Mom came up to Salem to help Pam get me stabilized while Joy and Greg attended to Josh and Jason and put a plan together for how to handle the sudden disruption. It was a futile endeavor to keep me calm, but I give Pam and Mom credit for trying. As psychotic as I was, stabilizing me wasn't going to happen with a couple extra doses of lamotrigine which they gave me after correctly assuming I had missed taking my meds over the previous few days. Trying to relax me with their collective maternal gentleness also had little effect. Those were band-aids for a bipolar papercut. I was mentally hemorrhaging, and there was no end in sight.

I'll be there soon, Dad. Please wait for me.

Over the next 24 hours, things got worse. Much worse. As incoherent as I was, I didn't like being told I couldn't roam freely as I normally would – as my unfettered, psychotic mind defiantly wanted to. When I couldn't stand it anymore, I screamed at them, repeatedly. . . so much so that both Mom and Pam feared I would become physically violent and barricaded themselves in the guest bedroom.

That was the last straw for everyone. It was time to get me to a hospital and pronto. They all agreed I had become a danger to myself and others, and no matter how angry I might feel about being hospitalized, it was essential to force me towards professional help.

Given the indignant state I was in, Pam and Mom didn't feel comfortable transporting me to the hospital on their own, so Greg was put in charge. He, too, was nervous about how I might respond to being wrestled into the hospital and solicited some assistance from the ringleader of my circle-of-trust friends.

Enter Steve again, stage left.

Steve heard the concern in Greg's voice and immediately stepped away from his work and social responsibilities in New York to drive to Salem. Together, Greg and Steve persuaded me to take a ride with them to Salem Hospital, but it wasn't easy.

"I don't think this is necessary," I told Greg. "There's nothing wrong with me. Why don't you see that?"

"Let's just get you checked out at the hospital, Beej," he replied. "If there's nothing wrong with you, we'll bring you back."

The chairs in the waiting area outside the emergency room at Salem Hospital were hard and cold, and the bright, fluorescent lights were dizzying. I shifted around in my seat, trying to get comfortable, but my soaring adrenalin made sitting still impossible. Eventually, I gave up and paced around the lobby.

My mind remained psychotically entangled, bouncing between the reality of my pending hospital containment while still playing the role of the almighty Savior preparing to die on the cross. In that bewildered state, I did not understand why Steve and Greg, my beloved Apostles, had brought me to a hospital.

Is there someone dying who needs to be saved? Are there followers to assemble among the doctors and nurses and patients?

"We just have to wait to be admitted, Beej," Greg said. "Hopefully it won't be much longer."

Admitted? Admitted to what? The Holy Temple? The Kingdom of Heaven? That made no sense. I would lead Greg there when the time came not the other way around.

I walked over to a vending machine near the side-entrance and studied its contents, hoping to find answers to my questions among the rows of candy bars and gum packs. None surfaced immediately, but something reminded me of the clues I collected as I ran around downtown Salem. Before leaving for Portland, I had hidden them in various places around my house. Now, I was compelled to retrieve them.

Greg and Steve had not taken their eyes off me for a second, and I felt like I was melting. Finally, someone called them over to a reception desk, and I grabbed the opportunity to bolt out the door.

The details of what transpired next are fuzzy at best, but I do recall dodging several cars as I sprinted across the hospital parking lot and through several busy intersections in downtown Salem. Eventually, I ended up at my house and collected all the rocks and takeout menus and other clues then charged up the stairs to my bedroom and rearranged them across my comforter. It did not take long for Steve and Greg to find me. As livid as they were, they approached me calmly.

"Brian, let's get in the car and go back to the hospital," Greg said. "That's where you need to be right now, okay?"

Next thing I knew I was weightless; bright colors swirled about me as my trusty disciples walked me down a long corridor bathed in soft celestial light. Beyond two large steel doors, my Lord's assistants greeted me. I answered their many questions, certain that soon they would reveal my father waiting for me on a silver throne.

A tall, brawny man and a female nurse led me to a private room. Greg trailed behind us carrying a small duffel bag. The nurse handed me a couple of pills and a glass of water. I swallowed them and, shortly after, collapsed onto a soft, down featherbed.

My head was spinning, and for a moment I thought I was going to throw up. Then total darkness. Silence.

The following morning when I awoke, the line between delusion and reality became even blurrier in my drug-induced haze. On one hand, I was angered for being forced into the hospital against my will, and I wanted to leave, badly. On the other, despite the nay-sayers dressed in white coats telling me otherwise, I was still certain that all was unfolding exactly as had been biblically ordained.

Not too much longer, Dad. I just need to break free from these shackles. . .

Without the freedom I desperately desired, it didn't take long for me to express my disgust for the environmental constraints imposed on me by hospital protocols.

"I'd like to get some fresh air," I said to my doctor. "Can I do that for a few minutes? I won't run away or anything."

"But you already ran away once," he replied.

Crap. He had me there. But I couldn't let him know that.

"I'm not sure what you're talking about. Can you please just let me leave?"

He was not moved.

That afternoon, I tried being on my best behavior, hoping that would change my doctor's mind and get me released. I took the handful of pills they gave me without questioning what they were. I responded to every suggestion or demand by a hospital worker with a "Yes, sir" or "Thank you, Ma'am." I even participated in "puzzle time," where we split up into small groups to assemble various sections of a 5,000-piece puzzle. Though in the back corners of my psychotic mind, we were searching for clues to how the world would end as prophetically described in the book of Revelations.

During the next session with my doctor, I repeated my request to leave the ward, but my furlough was once again denied.

"I'm sorry, Brian. You need to understand that you're going to be here for a while until we can get you stabilized."

"Get me 'STABILIZED'? What the hell does that mean?"

"It means that. . ."

"Fuck you. I know what 'stabilized' means," I screamed.

That put an end to my days as the second coming of the Lord.

From that point forward, I adopted a persona that refused to mollify anyone. If they would not let me out of there, I would not take my medications. I would not change out of my pajamas or take a shower. I would neither be quiet at night nor meet with my doctor in the morning. I did everything I could think of to show them just how "UNSTABLE" I could be if they were unwilling to grant me liberation.

"I'm a United States citizen, goddamnit! Freedom is my fucking birthright!!!"

During the next few days, a whole new side of me erupted. I became aggressive, petulant, verbally abusive. I reverted to a preadolescent self that had never before manifested. In the cafeteria, I flung food and giggled as it splatted across the table. In group therapy sessions, I stuck my tongue out at the coordinator whenever she asked me a question then looked around the room waiting for my fellow patients to giggle. I climbed on furniture and had to be coaxed down, called people names like "Psycho" and "Retard," and told the head nurse to "talk to the hand" whenever she reprimanded my behavior.

At the height of my uncivil disobedience, I exhibited intense rage and banged on the locked metal doors leading out of the ward until my fists were bruised.

"GET ME THE FUCK OUT OF HERE!!!"

Two orderlies pinned me against the wall, dragged me into a private room, and strapped me down to a padded gurney. I continued screaming at them as they tightened the leather straps over my legs, arms, and chest. Then a doctor came in with a large needle, held my leg steady, and injected it into my thigh. My pierced skin stung like hell.

"FUUUUCCCCKKKKK!!!"

Several hours later, I awoke from my tranquilized sleep, nauseous and disoriented but at least more relaxed. I wasn't in my bed where I expected to be, but no longer was I bound to the gurney. I stood up, walked to the entry door, and pulled on the handle but it was locked. My rage instantly returned. I felt like an animal trapped in a cage. I certainly was acting like one.

"You cocksuckers! You can't do this to me. This is fucking America! I have Constitutional rights!!!"

After getting no response from the staff and exhausting myself, eventually I had an epiphany. Divested of all choice, they had me. I was a prisoner.

***

After I calmed down enough to be released from my temporary solitary confinement, the orderlies brought me back to my room. Given my abhorrent, aggressive behavior, I lost my privilege of roaming the halls. But I had my voice, and I used it to appeal to my fellow incarcerated patients.

"They can't keep us here forever! We must stand united against these despicable oppressors!!!"

When I wasn't screaming, I was crying – burying my face in my pillow so nobody else could hear, asking myself questions that my forced isolation prevented me from asking Mom and Joy and Pam. Why are they doing this to me? What can I do to prove to them that they have dropped me off at the gates of hell?

From underneath the covers of my small, rickety bed, I yelled and cried and yelled and cried until there was no breath available in my lungs, no tears left to fall. They, indeed, had me, and there was nothing I could do about it.

Alone in my room, the sirens of ambulances pulling into the hospital brought forth horrid memories of being locked up in Yale New Haven Hospital during my first episode. Although the rules of the ward were the same – no belts, no shoelaces, no computer, no phone, no time outside – my situational awareness was drastically different. This time I knew what was happening. I knew the daily, mind-numbing routine. I knew the roles everyone in the hospital played, including my own: the mentally sick slave. But having that context didn't make anything easier. Just like the first time, I felt helpless yet simultaneously enraged and still occasionally psychotic – the extensive drugs unable to bring me fully down from my immaculate ascent up the rocky face of Golgotha.

Joy arrived one morning and sat beside me in the visitor's lounge. She gave me some unsettling news.

"Beej, the State of Massachusetts is going to lock you up in a facility probably worse than this one if you don't start cooperating," she said. "You have got to focus. Whether or not they do that hinges on your behavior in here, and I'm telling you, nobody else can help you with that. YOU have to save yourself."

My blood pressure blew up. I leapt from my seat and stormed the room.

"What the fuck are you talking about, Joy? They can't do that."

"Yes, they can, and they will if you don't change your attitude."

I was livid and punched one of the lamps.

"I don't believe you, and I don't believe them. They're bluffing. . . screw all of them!"

"Beej, you need to calm down and listen to me," she said, now standing up herself. "This is not an idle threat. They're ready to commit you involuntarily to a mental institution for a minimum of three months, and they have the full authority to do it."

"That's bullshit, Joy. Total bullshit."

"It's not, Brian. You need to get that through your thick head. You're not in control here, and the worse your behavior gets, the sooner they're going to send you away."

I wanted to scream. I wanted to jump through the window and run like hell.

Fuck them.

Eventually my rage settled and I sat back down, contemplating my predicament. Joy sat beside me, and slowly, her voice began to break through. The same parental voice that could talk me down from the occasional hissy-fits I threw as a kid, the gentle pleading that convinced me to eat the food I resisted or to let go of a bad idea I had latched onto for no apparent reason. I could hear my older sister speaking, and I wanted to listen.

"They can do it, Beej. I'll fight it with every ounce of breath I have, but I can't fight them without you."

Now she had my attention.

"Your behavior sucks. You have got to stop screaming and acting like a lunatic. That's not you. I know that, and to be honest, I think even they know that, but you're not giving them a choice. I am begging you. . ."

Looking into her sorrowful eyes, I imploded with tears. She wrapped her arms around me.

"Listen, Beej. You got this. You can make yourself well."

"I dunno. . ."

"Well I do. You're smart. You're strong. And you're not alone."

"Yes, I am. I drive everyone away."

"That's not true, Beej. I'm here. Mom's here. Greg and Pam and Steve are here. You have an army of friends who are here for you. You can be well. You just have to want to. And you gotta stop acting like an asshole."

Joy pulled me even closer, refusing to let go, even when our visiting time was up. Her supplication had swallowed me whole, and in the warmth of her embrace, I felt safe.

After she left, I spent the rest of the day alone in my room, processing the ultimatum that the hospital administrators had spelled out, and Joy's plea for my cooperation.

Can they actually do this?

Can they keep me locked up in a cage against my will for as long as they're threatening?

Extending my hospital nightmare any further was petrifying. I could not bear to think of being restrained any longer than I already had been, let alone for several more months. The sheer thought of being forced to endure isolation and disgusting food and no sunlight for that length of time amplified my fears. I needed to comply. Just like my first time in a psych ward, I had only one ticket out of there, back to my independence, back to the life I once knew.

I had to let them win.

Dear Kids,

Now that I've shared the details of my psychotic belligerence with you – my pounding fists and kicking and screaming and hospital staff restraining me – I sincerely hope that neither of you have a different opinion of me. This is something that has immensely worried me, but it's imperative that I don't hide anything from you about my bipolar experiences. You need to know the truth, the whole truth, and nothing but the truth about them, as apprehensive as that makes me feel.

Love,

Dad

Outside of my second psychotic episode, I can count the number of times I have been physically violent on one hand. Actually, I can count them on one finger. When I was in sixth grade, one of my good friends, Robby, tackled me on the playground while we were playing two-hand-touch football during recess. I stood up and shoved Robby. Then, he shoved me back. Then, I tackled him to the ground. Then, Robby put me in a headlock, punched me in the stomach, and walked to the other side of the school grounds before the on-duty teacher noticed anything had happened.

That's the extent of my violent behavior. An adolescent squabble with a childhood friend, which I, of course, lost.

When I was growing up, violence wasn't tolerated in our peaceful compound on Ezra Street. The "spare the rod, spoil the child" paradigm has shifted over generations, but even when it was more acceptable back then, my mom and dad forbade the mere thought of ever hitting us to get their point across. My dad was appalled by violence, avoiding conflict of any kind, at all cost. Mom had similar opinions, and between them, our family aggression boundaries were firmly established early on – boundaries that Joy and I never once attempted to cross, except for the time Robby pissed me off on the playground.

I, myself, struggle to reconcile my uncharacteristically violent behavior during my stay in Salem Hospital. Was that me acting in a fit of madness and rage? Was that me who nearly became a ward of the state because he was considered a material threat to himself and society? Well, it wasn't anyone else. It wasn't some actor portraying me. Those were my malevolent words and my audacious, forceful actions – nobody else's. Then, of course, it wasn't me, per se, or at least any version of me that I've ever manifested outside of that experience in the psych ward.

Bipolar imbalance can be caused by many things, but it is often driven by external stressors and the lack of internal control to handle them appropriately. My external stressors have changed over time, but more recently the most prominent ones threatening my emotional balance have been derived from parenting. As loving and honest and respectful and well-mannered as both of my children have been since the day they were born, being a parent has introduced many challenges to managing bipolar disorder. While I've never exhibited physical acts of violence towards my children, maintaining my resolve as I've learned how to maneuver through their own young, irregular emotions has been difficult. It's obvious to me, and probably to my children, that my wife is much better at that than I am. Well, she's much better at a lot of parental responsibilities, but especially that one.

I will say, adhering to the parental statutes I've established in my wellness plan over the years has become easier with time. Parenting itself hasn't become easier, not by a long shot. I often feel as clueless today as I did the first time I changed my son's diaper and managed to smear foul-smelling diarrhea all over our living room couch and rug. As my children have grown up, the problems they've faced have grown bigger, and I haven't always known how best to support them. But my ability to recognize my mental imbalance stressors and control my emotions before they get the best of me has certainly improved.

I'll be honest. It desperately needed to.

I have a section of my personal journal devoted to parental imbalance. It's entitled "PARENTAL IMBALANCE." A catchy rubric, eh? Within this section is a list of all the times I've lost my temper, or was otherwise materially off-kilter, since my children were born. The entries serve as a reminder to me of how important it is to maintain equilibrium as a father and subsequently how important it is to learn from the times I flirted with bipolar danger. This self-reflection isn't as squeaky-clean as I'm making it sound, of course. I often repeat my bipolar mistakes. And sometimes, the things I write down disgust me. But the process of documenting these behaviors forces me to continuously ask the question "is that me?" – or better stated "do I want that to be me?" – and that's a good thing.

Most of my emotionally imbalanced parental ugliness occurred when my children were much younger, and I was much younger. Back then, I tended to yell at them more frequently when I couldn't get them to follow my instructions to get in the car, or brush their teeth, or refrain from squirting ketchup all over the counter and floor. On a number of occasions, five in all to be more specific, I yelled at them so loudly that they leapt back, startled and afraid of my sudden, explosive verbal aggression.

When I look back on these journal entries, I feel terrible. Neither of my children deserved that. They were just doing what they should have naturally been doing as kids: being imbalanced. I was not doing what I should have been doing as an adult with bipolar disorder, as any adult should: maintaining my balance and patience.

The most aggressive of these instances occurred when my son was three years old. My wife was away for the weekend, visiting her girlfriends in Boston. I had just put my daughter down in her crib for the night, which was a struggle in and of itself as she screamed in my ear while I rocked her back and forth. Then it was time for my son and me to read *Curious George Rides a Bike* together, his favorite book at the time, and for him to go to bed following. He had a lot of energy that evening, more so than usual, and he refused to come to his room. He ran up and down the upstairs hallway, screaming and shouting, and I was afraid he'd wake up his sister. When I ran out of patience, I yelled "STOP IT!" at the top of my lungs. He was so scared that he froze dead in his tracks, after which I scooped him up, carried him back to his room, and forced him to sit beside me in his toddler bed.

We both calmed down soon after and enjoyed reading all about

Curious George's bike riding adventures, but I was remorseful for my aggressive, imbalanced behavior.

Part of my bipolar struggle today, especially when it comes to parenting, is trying to understand which imbalanced behaviors are induced by my illness and which are just normal emotions that the stress of parenting generally introduces to all parents. That ambiguity is difficult for my black-and-white brain to discern – the part of me that tries to put everything in its own separate container. But after some extensive reflection, I've come to believe it's a little of both. Having bipolar disorder, I am predisposed to disorderly moods and emotional imbalance. It's hard to refute that losing my temper as harshly as I did when my children were younger isn't, at least partially, responsible for that. But to be honest, I just don't know.

What I do know for certain is that the strong, trusting partnership my wife and I have formed over the years is the key ingredient in my ability to control my bipolar mind's lust for rapidly fluctuating moods, and in turn, keep my temper in check when it comes to parenting our children; when it comes to just about everything, actually. Patience is indeed a virtue, and one she exemplifies more than any person I've ever met. I'm lucky to have her in my life, and she could not have entered into it at a better time.

PART VIII

Solitude

Friday, May 4th, 2001

The wake is over, and I am so glad. I couldn't look at Dad lying there in the casket any longer – his chubby face covered in makeup hiding his deathly blue skin-tone; his tight white dress-shirt and necktie choking him. I couldn't shake anymore strangers' hands or give any more hugs to family and friends who came to pay their last respects – all three hundred of them according to the sign-in book.

The after-party at Uncle Joe's house continues late into the evening – all of my aunts and uncles and cousins and Dad's closest friends are gathered, eating and drinking and helping each other process our collective sadness. Nobody wants to go home. Doing so would be too final. Nobody wants to surrender to life without Dad.

I lean back on the plush couch in the living room beside Sarah, who drove up from Virginia early this morning and will stay through the funeral tomorrow. I am thankful she returned in time to help me mentally prepare for the wake. I am thankful she is in my life and will be there for me when I return to my townhouse. I cannot move forward alone.

Uncle Joe enters and pulls me up from the couch. He hands me a glass of scotch and guides me to the kitchen, where a small group of Dad's friends are gathered. This is Dad's posse, his brothers from The Village, who do not see each other as often as they used to but remain as close as they were when they first met in Saint Michael's Elementary School. As though I were the newly crowned king, they stand in unison and raise their glasses as I enter the room.

From the hearty laughter I've walked into and the near-empty bottles of liquor on the table beside them, I know they've been telling old stories of their childhood escapades – the same stories I

235

have heard hundreds of times before, every time the posse has gathered. But I don't mind hearing them again.

Lenny, Dad's closest friend, goes first. "Bri, did ya know your father almost didn't graduate from high school?" *he asks as he laughs and lifts his drink in homage.* "It's true! Me an' him were pool sharks. We cut math class and our other afternoon classes to hustle all the guys at the pool hall."

I am incredulous, despite the fact that I already know how this story concludes. But I play along as if I don't.

"Didn't he get in trouble with Grandma?" *I ask.*

"Nope," *Lenny cackles.* "Well, not at first. He was a hell of a typist, snuck into the school office every semester and changed his report card Ds and Fs into Bs and As. It took a while, but when your grandmother found out, she went to the school and persuaded the principal to pass him. Then, she chased his ass home and beat him bloody with a soup ladle."

We all laugh. That was Dad. Big John – the child who never grew up.

Not to be out-storied, Uncle Joe chimes in. "Didja ever hear the one about 'Spindletop's Best'?"

Of course, I have. But Uncle Joe needs the microphone right now, and I am happy to give it to him. I shake my head. "No, I haven't. Who the hell is that?"

He stands up and tells the story. "Spindletop's Best was a race-horse, a 40-1 longshot, who, according to the neighborhood's most popular bookie, was about to run his best race ever. The bookie convinced your dad to go door-to-door and persuade everyone to contribute to a money pool he called 'the bet of a lifetime.' Your dad was a master salesman even then, and everyone bought in."

Uncle Joe pauses to take a sip of his seven-and-seven. As he does, I prod him on further. "So what happened?" I ask, already knowing the answer.

"Well. . . Spindletop's Best came in dead last – nearly 20 lengths behind the winner. Brian, I bet that horse is still running!!!" Uncle Joe declares, and laughter explodes once again.

Drinking and storytelling take us well past midnight, and as tired as I am, I wrap myself in the solace of everyone's company. Giddy memories temporarily stave off the emptiness and abandonment I feel as well as my anxiety that continues to loom about delivering the eulogy in the morning. A speech which I still haven't prepared. A tribute to the father that I loved and am not ready to lose.

Dear Kids,

I don't want to frighten you, again. But I don't want to sugar coat the effects of acute bipolar depression, either. Just remember, like the many stories I've told you about my father over the years, this one has a happy ending.

Love,

Dad

J oy left Salem Hospital that day fearing I would ignore her stern warning and deeply saddened by what the State of Massachusetts administrators might do if I did. She also felt as if I might never speak to her again, which saddened her even further. Her assumption of how defiant I might become if I was hospitalized had proven true, and since she was the person on the receiving end of my explosive reaction to the hospital's not-so-idle threats, she felt as if I blamed her for everything. That couldn't have been further from the truth. I blamed the hospital for their erroneous protocols, not her. But given my rage, she had no way of knowing that.

Our intense fight divided Joy and me in a way that had never happened before. Never. In our entire lives, we had barely ever argued, let alone screamed at one another as we did in the visiting area that day. Given the parental role she played in my life, I had always done what Joy asked of me without questioning her edict. Now, not only was I questioning it, I was infuriated by it, and as she returned home to Greg, Josh, and Jason – to making school lunches and watching little league games and teaching Sunday School – a dark cloud followed her. Would our relationship ever be the same again?

Mom was certainly sad and had some remorse as well, but much less than Joy. She was on the periphery of hospital legalities which Joy took point on due to her seasoned experience as a lawyer. Mom also had her "Beej Blinders" on, as Joy once referred to them – her belief that I, her Prodigal Son, could do no wrong. But Joy knew better. She understood the depths of my stubbornness and never once had she worn blinders, of any kind, especially when it came to co-parenting me.

What neither Joy nor Mom understood at the time – what I myself didn't understand – is that my outward rage had less to do with being contained against my will than it did with the inward shame I carried for being a burden to both of them, for displacing their lives. . . again. Yes, I resented every aspect of my hospital constraints, but that wasn't the root cause of my angst. After many years of repairing my identity as an independent, mentally healthy, professionally successful adult, I felt as if I was back to square one – back to being trapped in my bipolar fishbowl – back to being a baby bird with two broken wings. Even worse, now I was being labeled a danger to society; a leper to be locked away; a caged animal. What repercussions would that have? Would Joy and Greg and Mom ever be able to look at me any differently?

How about you, Dad?

When the stronger medication I was given finally had an effect, my rage depleted. But that did not occur overnight. It took nearly a week, and during that period, I remained defiant and abusive – each incident bringing me one step closer to becoming a ward of the state. My psychosis eventually diminished as well, and with the help of my doctor, I garnered additional context surrounding my insanity and the abstract play into which I had cast myself and others. But the effort required that I disentangle from the truth, and that exhausted me. Then, my guilt and shame fully consumed me.

Emerging from playing the role of Jesus only added to my distress. Where was my father when I needed him the most? Oh right, he was dead. My spiritual connection to him was just a temporary illusion, conjured from a mental illness I had long forgotten about. And where did my honorable disciples, Greg and Steve, go? Ahh. . . back to Connecticut and New York. . . back to their respective lives that my insanity abruptly tore them away from. And last but certainly not least there was Mother Mary – sweet, innocent Pam, now dating a fucking lunatic.

Once firmly grounded in reality, I found myself drowning in contrition for my tirades. I had disrespected the hospital staff, and by doing so, I had dishonored my family, my girlfriend, my closest friends – everyone. How could I be such a fuck-up? And how would I ever get past that? There were no acceptable answers to those questions, but I knew the first step towards self-preservation was getting out of the hospital. Once there, the blinding spotlight on me would at least be dimmed, I told myself. Free from all these barriers, I could hide again.

The key to being released from the psych ward in Salem Hospital was the same as Yale New Haven Psychiatric Facility: good behavior.

"Brian, if you follow all the rules, it will greatly help your situation," my doctor said. "It also wouldn't hurt to make amends with our staff."

I followed his advice, and as I engaged with puzzle time and light exercise and other social activities, I apologized to the on-duty nurses, psychiatrists, and security personnel for the way I had treated them. Each accepted without judgment, downplaying how much of a self-entitled, uncontrollable train-wreck I had been.

During my second week in the hospital, I continued my compliance – willingly participating in every group therapy session that they offered, even if I didn't want to, and I swallowed every pill I was administered, even if I didn't know what it was for. I would do anything to be released from my imprisonment, to exit center stage and hide behind the closed curtain separating me from the audience; retreat to my dressing room where I could be alone.

There was one stark difference between my second hospitalization and my first: I had a stronger support network outside my immediate family and Steve to aid me in my recovery, and I am so glad I did.

Pam stayed at my house and came to the hospital daily, encouraging me to listen to my doctors and trying to keep my spirits up as best she could. Steve filled my circle-of-trust friends in on everything that transpired, and each of them took turns providing me solace in their own way. Those who lived locally visited me, bringing me books to read and new music to listen to. Another friend came up from Connecticut with a pizza from Pepe's. Others, who resided far away, called me on the pay phone to let me know they were thinking about me and asked how they might be able to help.

Each of their visits and phone calls ended with the same sentiment, and each time they conveyed it, I cried.

"We're here for you, Brian. We'll always be here for you."

I welcomed my friends' comfort but even that did little to curtail my perception of myself as a social outcast and a bipolar burden. I would forever be that friend, that son, that brother who couldn't take care of himself and needed their help. I would forever be Uncle Danny.

As for reconciling my relationship with Pam, I didn't know where to begin. I was completely humiliated. Ever since I had shared my mental illness with her, I had prided myself on ensuring I had it all under control. Now, here I was, locked up in an insane asylum, not in control of anything.

"I'm sorry Pam," I conveyed, repeatedly. "I don't know what else to say. Thank you for everything you're doing for me."

Pam showed only genuine empathy for what I was going through, but I had difficulty getting past that. Each time she sat with me in the visiting area, I only saw a woman who wanted to run from the hell I was putting her through, and even though she told me that was the furthest thought from her mind, I didn't believe her. If I was her, I wouldn't want to date a mental maniac, let alone a dangerous one – someone that might physically harm her if my illness ever resurfaced in the way it just had. I would have run away and never looked back.

At the end of my third week on the ward, I had improved enough to earn my release, which both delighted and terrified me. I would be free, sure. But free for what? Free to deal with the aftermath of the tornado that had, for a second time, ripped through every facet of my life and my family's lives? Free to dodge emails and phone calls from co-workers with whom I had made a total fool of myself? Free to be engulfed in the next phase of the episode. . . the dark side of my illness. . . the inevitable abyss?

Knowing what I was in for did not make it any less unnerving. After my first episode, there was a several-week period before my depression took over. During that time, I felt – dare I say? – fine. Drained by everything that had happened, but stable. Now, out of the hospital and resubmerged into my life, the same pattern was repeating. Each morning, I awoke expecting to feel the dagger of misery plunged into my belly, but it didn't happen. I went for long walks around the neighborhood with Pam. I went grocery shopping and cooked meals. I played my guitar. Things seemed normal. So normal, even Cindy was surprised.

"You look great, Brian," she said. "I wasn't expecting this, given the severity of what you've just gone through."

Since I was now a repeat offender of psychiatric incarceration as well as a patient who exhibited intense fury, my hospital release stipulations were much stricter than they were after my first bout of madness. I was required to meet with Cindy every day at first, then at least 3 times a week for another month. She, in turn, submitted weekly summary reports of our therapy sessions to Salem Hospital and other State of Massachusetts' administrators. If, at any time, anyone questioned my mental stability, I could be hauled into court and involuntarily taken back to the hospital.

I was in no position to challenge the arrangements, but I despised every aspect of them. Driving to Cindy's office every day and answering the same set of questions over and over was dreadful.

"How are you feeling today, Brian?"

"Fine."

"How would you describe your mood?"

"Good."

"Are you having any suicidal thoughts?"

"No. Can you please stop asking me that?"

"I'm sorry. I'm required to."

Re-entering my Salem social scene was just as discomfiting. While I was in the hospital for an extended period, Pam made every attempt to save face and keep my meltdown a secret from my local friends by spreading a good cover story, but I was certain people saw right through that.

"Brian's dealing with some family issues right now," she had said. "He'll get back to you as soon as he can."

In my mind, there was no doubt people knew something significant had happened to me. Like my first episode, I looked like crap. My skin was pale, my eyes sagged, and I had lost nearly 15 pounds. I had also disappeared for several weeks, even abandoned a good buddy on a trip to the Delaware Shore over Memorial Day weekend at the last minute. I avoided seeing everyone as long as I could, but doing so only made me more culpable.

I had one significant obligation which heightened my anxiety the most. Before my episode, I had planned a surprise birthday party for Pam, inviting many of her friends and several of mine to my house to celebrate. Now, I was nervous about being surrounded by so many people but even more so about what anyone might think if I suddenly cancelled the event. I couldn't cancel. I had to assure everyone that nothing was wrong with me. Nothing at all.

The night of the party, while I was out to dinner with Pam, everyone gathered at my house. When we walked in the front door, the lights came on and all of cur friends emerged.

"SURPRISE!!!"

Pam leapt back, but I leapt furtier, instantly realizing that I wasn't prepared for so much social stimulation, and my anxiety immediately went through the roof.

I wanted to leave my own house right then and there, but I knew that wasn't an option, so I mingled around the crowd for a while, avoiding speaking to anyone as best I could. I sipped on a glass of wine, hoping that would contain my nerves. It didn't. The party chatter elevated. The music got louder, and all conversations blended together. I felt dizzy and began to sweat. Eventually, I could no longer constrain my anxiety. I absconded upstairs, shut my bedroom door, sat on the floor, and cried uncontrollably.

Shortly after the party, Pam returned to Portland, and in my seclusion, it did not take long for the vampires to return and begin sucking the guilt-laden blood from my veins. The mental paralysis came quickly, and there was no question as to what was happening. Within a short period of time, a deep depression engulfed me.

I could never have fully comprehended the expression "down the rabbit hole" had I not descended into that awful darkness. I was aware this time, saw myself falling, like Alice, into a cavernous pit, unable to catch myself on any protrusion along the way. At the bottom, all the doors were locked, barring my escape. I had to feel my way around, endure the pain from the sword plunged into my soul, succumb to the hopelessness overcoming me, and hope that one day the dark abyss would tire of me and spit me back into the light.

Just as they had before, vivid flashbacks of my psychotic adventures haunted me as I lay crippled in my bed: walking through the streets of downtown Portland as the chosen one; presiding over a fictitious wedding and baptism; standing in the cold ocean water up to my neck. I hid under the covers to evade the vibrant images of letters inscribed in gravestones, tourist attraction pamphlets, blood trickling out of the cuts on my feet into the clear bathtub water. I put my hands over my ears to silence the voices of insanity replaying inside my head, the audio cues that directed my theater of the absurd.

Once totally immersed in the gloom, my ambition turned to overwhelming guilt and self-loathing. Oh my god, what have I done? I have humiliated myself and every person who ever loved me. I am a complete, fucking failure. There is no resolution, no way out of this macabre bipolar sentence my gene pool has pronounced on me. My future will be nothing but one continuous cycle of mania and depression – bouts of madness for me, torture for Mom and Joy and anyone else within reach of the nuclear meltdown. There is only one thing that will release me from this godforsaken nightmare.

This time around, I had accepted the fact that death would be the more probable outcome, and I planned it all out in my mind. Once I set it in motion, I would not retreat from the act of propelling myself into eternal damnation. I was adamant that neither Mom, Joy, nor Pam should find my lifeless body. I had to simply fade out, remove myself from their lives, allow them to carry on without the burden of me. I needed to allow Joy to focus on raising and loving Josh and Jason, let Mom enjoy watching her grandchildren grow without disruption, and give Pam the freedom to get on with her life, date other men, be happy.

Just a mile up the road, there was a tall bridge which connected Salem to the neighboring town of Beverly. It spanned the Danvers River – a wide body of water with heavy currents that flowed out into the Atlantic. I ran over the bridge regularly on my longer North Shore morning routes. In my despair, it became clear that jumping off the Salem-Beverly bridge fit all my suicidal prerequisites. I could dive off at its peak in the middle of the night when nobody would see me, submerge myself into the depths of the river, let the water enter my mouth and nose. At that point, even if I wanted to save myself, I wouldn't be able to. The shore would not be within reach, and even if it were, I would not have the energy to swim there. I would simply dissolve into the strong river tide that would carry me out to the ocean.

I knew that my sudden, elusive disappearance would tear Joy and Mom and Pam apart. In the long run, though, they would be better for it. I believed that if I left them with an explanation, I could soften the blow, so I wrote a lengthy suicide note, spelling out all the reasons why I needed to end my life. There were plenty – me being such a burden to them at the very top. I would never let my mental demons cause them agony ever again, and there was only one way to ensure that. At the end of my note, I summarized my feelings in a single sentence: "I'm sorry, and I love you all."

When there was nothing left for the vampires to feast upon, my father returned to visit me in my dreams. I could not see exactly where we were, but he was standing in the water with his arms extended, the moonlight glaring down on both of us. He stood still, watching me. He didn't beckon me forward, but neither did he suggest I go back. He just stood there.

What should I do?

He didn't answer.

It's been fifteen years since I nearly fell victim to my suicidal despair in Salem, curled up in my bed, envisioning myself diving off that bridge. Looking back, it makes me sad to think of all the people my selfish decision would have hurt, and all the things I would have never experienced if I let my bipolar demons win. I grieve at the thought of never having met my wife and never having my children, never seeing them become the loving, thoughtful, capable human beings that they are. But as my suicidal ideations swirled around me, there was something inside my heart that kept me from ending it all – a tiny flame that remained lit, telling me that the joyful life which my family now shares together was somewhere in my future; that my story wasn't ready to conclude, and that my children's had yet to be written.

Amidst my hopelessness, at some point I recognized a double-layered truth within my depressed self-delusion: if I killed myself the way that I had planned, the women in my life would not find my body, but they had already found my inner self. Though it was my body that Mom and Joy and Pam served when they discovered me in my near-lifeless state and ushered me through my suffering, it was my soul they were protecting, my psyche they sought daily to massage back to health. Permanently removing that from their lives would bring pain far worse than what I had already put them through, and no elaborate explanation I left behind, no apology from the grave, would ever change that.

With the help of their unyielding empathy, I eventually crawled back into the light though that was something I had to do on my own. When depression runs that deep, one cannot be pulled out of the chasmic rabbit hole by others. Just as substance abusers are the only ones who can truly keep themselves from drinking alcohol or pumping heroin into their veins, I was the only person who could resuscitate myself from my all-encompassing depression. But had the people surrounding me not held my hand as I did, at some point, I am certain I would have leapt off that bridge.

I was alive, and that was good. But the dreaded Scarlet B I saw stamped across my forward was once again debilitating. After my first episode, I had made a promise to remain healthy, to not let a second one occur, to never put Mom or Joy or anyone else in my life through that horror again. I had broken that promise and lost their trust. Luckily, the steadfast women in my life never looked at it that way. They simply saw a beloved son, brother, boyfriend in need of help, and they did not hesitate to provide it.

Eventually I got back on my feet. The clouds of death parted, and sunlight returned. Superficially at least.

There were two core differences between my recovery from my second bipolar implosion and my first. The most prominent one was that I knew when I was fooling myself. I recognized that although I was beginning to act normally, to engage with the world, to be interested again, I was, in large part, faking it. That recognition was further debilitating. How could I possibly fool others if I couldn't even fool myself?

The second was that I didn't have the financial means to avoid going back to work. Unbeknownst to me, my basic self-employment health insurance policy didn't cover extended mental health-related hospital stays, leaving me with towering bills and only a short grace period to repay them. Between that and the housing market crash which diluted nearly all of my real estate equity, I was in severe debt. I drained the remainder of my retirement savings to support myself for as long as I could, but soon that money ran out and I had to find work.

Procuring a new job proved nearly impossible once again, on many levels. The small network of professional contacts I had established from my consulting work on Boston's North Shore had been destroyed. And since I had burned the headhunter who got me my previous job, I had to find another one, which wasn't easy given the tight network in that professional community.

With the help of a small staffing agency, I was lucky to find consulting work for a mid-market bank headquartered in downtown Portland, just a short walk from Pam's apartment. I could stay with her during the week and return to Salem on the weekends to get my mail, cut the grass, and continue to assure my neighbors and local friends that nothing was wrong.

"Congrats, Brian!" Pam said when I shared the news. "I'll start clearing out some closet space."

Although I was nervous about the two of us living together, it was comforting to no longer be isolated in my house and be with Pam on a semi-permanent basis, and we quickly settled into a congenial routine. Once physically strong enough, I also started running again, finding tranquility in my early morning jaunts beside the ocean, watching fishing boats drift into the Atlantic towards the rising sun. I avoided running through the downtown area and the adjacent park where my Son of God escapades had peaked, but otherwise the routine activity helped rebuild my shattered confidence one mile at a time, just as it had done in the aftermath of my first episode in Virginia.

I thought at first that the job I took, a systems analyst position with the bank, seemed beneath me. However, the work proved to be both challenging and rewarding. Ironically, I was part of a team charged with collecting lending data for Federal regulators that might shed light on whom to blame for the disastrous financial collapse the country was reeling from in the wake of the 2008 housing crisis. From our research, it didn't take long to figure out that the "No Doc Loan" was a terrible idea for our economy and a key contributor to the global financial crisis which elected officials in Congress were still sorting through.

Over the course of several months, my professional self-assurance grew stronger as I was put in charge of a small team. In the office, I achieved the social stability I craved and a place to be myself without disclosing the self I preferred to conceal. I was proud of my collaborative contributions and genuinely happy. At least in my work life.

In my personal life, however, not so much.

While living in the same apartment with Pam was easy and enjoyable at first, over time the closer proximity began to suffocate me. There were too many opportunities for intimate discussions between us at a time when I was hyper-focused on battening down the emotional hatches. Our previous long-distance relationship had provided a perfect structure for that. Eating breakfast together each morning and sharing the same tube of toothpaste did not. Above all, my second episode had ruptured my spirit, and I had lost my ability to care for someone else.

I had to release Pam. Push her away. Dismiss her from my life. I erroneously believed that sequestering myself from the woman who had become close enough to infer what it was like to live inside my head would rejuvenate me.

Pam had to go.

As I was contemplating how and when to enact our breakup, I caught a lucky break at work. Well, lucky for me.

"Brian, our bank has been acquired by a larger financial institution," my boss told me. "Our division is being relocated to Newark, New Jersey."

"So what does that mean?" I replied, nervous I might lose my job.

"Well, the good news is you can work remotely as long as you're able to travel to our new office occasionally."

The timing could not have been better. No longer being required to work in Portland was the catalyst I needed to sever my relationship with Pam.

I no longer kept in touch with Sarah, my old girlfriend from D.C., who had helped save me from myself in the wake of my first episode. She was one of the many relics I left behind when I moved back to New England to start anew – my futile attempt to forget the awful, selfish way I had treated many people in my life, including Sarah. But I wish she were still around to remind me to approach my breakup with Pam with more gentleness and care for someone who also helped rescue me from my bipolar demise. Sadly, I did not. In fact, after all Pam had done to shepherd me through my recovery, I was even more insensitive and selfish.

On the heels of an argument over something petty that happened in the apartment, I simply packed my suitcase, told her it was time we went our separate ways, and headed for the door. Before I reached it, she grabbed my arm and begged me not to leave so abruptly. Her touch set me off, and I screamed at her.

"Just let me fucking go, Pam! LET. ME. FUCK-ING GO!" I shouted at the top of my lungs. "Just let me be alone."

That's all I wanted. To be alone.

I wasn't seeking freedom to date other women. It had nothing to do with anything Pam had done or hadn't done. I just wanted to separate myself from anything and anyone that required emotional connection. I needed to preserve myself in my own undisturbed space and time, sheltered from all reminders of my stained past. Sadly, Pam's feelings were not a factor in my decision. The valve of my empathy was permanently turned off. I could not have been more of a selfish prick if I had tried. I slammed the door behind me and never looked back.

Returning to Salem, the memory of Pam's eyes as she found me in the bathtub, spouting scripture, and rambling other illogical pronouncements haunted me relentlessly. No way would I allow myself to be in an intimate relationship ever again. I was not worthy of the love any woman might be willing to give, and as far as I was concerned, my effort to forge a lasting, satisfying partnership ended at Pam. I was destined to live a solitary life absent of loving anyone, including myself.

I was done.

In one of my therapy sessions, I mentioned to Cindy that Pam and I had broken up. She kept her questions to a minimum at first, but as time passed, she inquired if I had started dating again. Month after month after month, the answer remained no. Defiantly no. My mental illness had defeated me. No woman deserved me, and nothing I could do would ever change that.

Beyond dating, my breakup with Pam facilitated physical and emotional seclusion in nearly every aspect of my existence, including, unfortunately, my relationship with Mom, Joy, and Greg. My regular visits home dwindled quickly to occasional again, then only to holiday gatherings, where my absence might have led them to believe something was wrong. They each made every effort to maintain their presence, to keep all the windows of their unconditional love wide open, just as they had always done. I locked them tightly shut. I refused to be that son, that brother, that usurper who would forever drain his family's hearts.

As I had done in Annapolis, when I wasn't working, I was renovating my old house, replacing human connection with the use of my eagerly responsive table saw. I kept everyone but a trusted neighbor, a seasoned carpenter, out of sight and out of mind. Whenever I hit a part of any project that was beyond my remodeling skills, I turned to him, but otherwise I did the work alone with serious commitment to isolation and chastity. I confined my feminine companionship to the 70-year-old cashier at the local hardware store that I frequented for supplies. There was no room in my heart for anyone else.

When I got lonely, I turned to the virtual world for connection. Facebook had been around for several years, but by 2009, it was really starting to expand its gravity in our culture. People began taking advantage of the media aspects of the platform instead of just using it as a vehicle to keep in touch with distant friends or tell everyone they were in a "new relationship." Up until that point, I had accepted a few friend requests and shared some occasional sarcastic posts but didn't pay much attention to social media otherwise. Now, however, Facebook became my primary means of remaining connected to, well, just about everything and everyone.

Why socialize outside my house if I didn't need to?

Why talk to someone if I could just send them a message?

Social media allowed me to remain connected to humanity on my own terms yet retain my staunch independence. Further, I could present a fabricated version of myself and be seen in the image I created; project confidence and strength rather than anxiety and self-loathing; photoshop any bipolar blemishes out of every picture I posted of myself.

Facebook was self-preservation personified, and I was all-in.

Alongside hiding from any real, physical connection with humanity, I also got back into long-distance running, and, for the first time since high school, I began to approach it competitively. For years, I had run against nobody but myself, adhering to Steve's humble, tortoise-inspired advice "slow and steady wins the race." I had always approached "PBs" – Personal Bests – as exactly that. Personal. Now, I saw the sport as a way to strengthen the confidence I needed within my detached livelihood. Suddenly, finishing ahead of 200. . . 500. . . 1,000 other people became my primary objective during races. Running was no longer about the journey, the harmony of my controlled inhales and exhales in tune with the early morning calls of playful seagulls and crashing ocean waves. It was the destination I sought, the medals I hung around my neck, the assurance I was better at something than all the other runners. . . who didn't have bipolar disorder. Then, I felt better about myself.

The local community from which I disassociated myself included my musical collaborators as well. By then, I had met several musicians on the North Shore, had joined them on stage at various venues for open mic nights, and attended concerts with them regularly. But now I had no desire to share the pleasure of music with anyone but myself. I rearranged the songs that bands and I had jammed over the years to be played solo. I went to open mic gigs alone and left early if anyone I had previously played with showed up. I sold the majority of my stage equipment – my PA and speakers and microphone stands. I no longer needed any of it. I no longer needed anyone.

I had become a one-man-band, in every way I could cleverly fashion.

Surprisingly, or perhaps sadly, over time, my new normal became comfortable. If you had asked me then, I'd have told you I was happy. As the one year anniversary of my second bipolar episode approached, I found myself curled up in the safety of a comfortable peace of mind. I was confident again, mentally stable, and entirely alone. I thought I was exactly where I wanted to be.

And then I met Kim.

———

W hen I first tell people about my bipolar experiences, they typically ask two very specific questions regarding how I manage my mental health:

1. Do you take medication?
2. Do you see a therapist?

It makes sense that people want to know these two things as that is how mental health is generally positioned in our society: doctors and drugs. Talk things over with a doctor. . . get some drugs. . . get past whatever is ailing you. Damn, I wish it were that simple! But the truth is that it's not. For those who have a mental illness there are a plethora of factors involved in maintaining equilibrium.

Both of these questions I get asked are straightforward, but their answers are complex, at least to me. Let's talk about Question #1 first – "Do you take medication?" The answer is yes although not for the reasons that you might think.

There's a common perception that drugs play a significant role in one's ability to manage a mental illness, or at least that's what we're asked to believe from all the pharmaceutical advertisements portraying physically fit men and women whose lives are ever-so-happy because of their medication as they jog slowly along a sandy beach or push their kids on bicycles down a sidewalk. While we watch them do these things, we disregard the five-hundred sixty-two potential side effects being rattled off because a) the smiles on their faces betray no anguish whatsoever, and b) how can there legitimately be five-hundred sixty-two side-effects of anything? The drug manufacturers are probably just being overly cautious, right? There's regulatory legalities; they're just protecting themselves; no need for concern.

From my experience, psychiatrists support this notion as well. All of the medical and psychiatric professionals I have encountered over the years have ensured me, in one fashion or another, that my meds are an important element of stabilizing my moods. Some, like Marty, have placed less emphasis on medication than others, but none of them have ever said, "ya know, we're not exactly sure if drugs will help you at all, but why don't you take them anyway?"

For over two decades now, I haven't missed my daily dosage of bipolar medication for several reasons. First, following my own research on the matter, I now trust medical professionals when they tell me there are no negative biological side effects to lamotrigine, the drug I remain on today. If there were, or if future research proves otherwise, I would feel differently. Second, who am I to question a psychiatrist's therapeutic directive? I'm an IT professional and a management consultant, not a doctor. And lastly, from a bipolar perspective, my moods are generally stable and have been for a long time now. It would be irrational to believe that drugs haven't played a role in that, at least to some degree.

Still, I do question *how* effective my medication is, particularly in preventing the more severe aspects of my mental illness, including psychosis. When I had my second bout of madness in Salem, I had been taking my medication every day for a long time. Obviously that didn't prevent me from flying high as a kite when the psychological opportunity presented itself. Was that because drugs aren't what prevents psychosis? Or perhaps I was taking the wrong drug to prevent psychosis? Or. . . did my psychosis have nothing to do with drugs at all? Maybe I was just asleep at the bipolar wellness plan wheel, suppressing the power of my illness, and there was nobody around me to recognize my dysfunctional behaviors and step in before they got out of hand.

For how my illness has manifested itself in me, I would say it's the latter. Drugs aren't the main driver of my mental stability, by far. In my humble opinion, the balanced lifestyle I strive to maintain

far outweighs any medication I put into my body. When I tell people this, I've found my disclosure often makes them uncomfortable to a degree. What do you mean drugs aren't the cause of the effect? What about the people jogging ever-so-happily on the beach and the bicycle pushing parents? Look how happy they are.
..

Now let's talk about Question #2 – "Do you see a therapist?"

The answer to that is no, and when I tell people that, they often feel as uncomfortable as they do when I share my beliefs on the effects of medication. Maybe you feel that way too, so let me explain.

I would never deny the efficacy of clinical therapy for anyone who has bipolar disorder, or any other mental illness, or for anything, really. Marty was critical to my recovery from my first bipolar episode, guiding me through my bone-chilling suicidal ideations and the long road to stability which followed. But after Marty retired, my experiences with Richard, and then Cindy, were very different. I drew no relief or promise from seeing either of them, I only did so out of necessity for getting my drug prescriptions. In 2015, when my primary care physician told me that he'd be willing to prescribe me lamotrigine since I hadn't experienced a bipolar episode of any kind in quite some time, I jumped at the opportunity to free myself from therapy sessions I despised, and I haven't looked back since.

So why don't I see a therapist anymore?

Well, in a way I still do. Sort of. I do open up to other people about my bipolar challenges – my successes and failures as I work to stay on my wellness plan. These days, the people I open up to just aren't licensed professionals. They are my family and my closest friends. And as my children grow older, I hope to discuss this with them, too.

I recognize not everyone who has a mental illness is as close to their family members and friends as I am today. I certainly wasn't for a very long time. I also recognize that my perspective is derived from many years of sitting in a therapist's office, talking to Marty about my bipolar challenges and my wellness plan, which I initially developed. . . with him. But today, that's how I feel, and that's who I talk to whenever I need to.

With the exception of Marty, the first person that I ever felt comfortable opening up to about the dirty details of my bipolar experiences was my wife, although my ability to do so would not come easily. Skeletons hiding in the attic of one's mind for as long as mine had been don't just walk out on their own.

PART IX

Submission

Saturday, May 5th, 2001

I sit on the stone front stoop, listening to the squalls of early morning birds calling to each other as they start their day. Mine began with a cup of black coffee and some ibuprofen to shake the cobwebs off my slight hangover. I can still smell subtle hints of whiskey seeping out of my pores, the residual effect of Uncle Joe's post-wake gathering.

Mom and Sarah remain asleep upstairs, tired from getting home as late as we did last night. I awoke early to write down the words I will say in the church later this morning. I want my remarks to be meaningful. I want everyone to know how much I love Dad and how much he loved all of them. But I don't know where I should even begin.

How do you summarize a lifetime of memories into a few paragraphs?

What do you say if you're angry?

Why did Joy and Mom ask me to do this?

Why did I agree to it?

I scribble down the first thoughts that come to mind on an 8.5 x 11 inch sheet of paper. They are vague, but they are something. I fold the paper into quarters and tuck it into the pocket of my hoodie. I sip on my coffee and return to listening to the sounds of spring, hoping nature will perhaps offer words that are more eloquent.

Mom opens the screen door, steps outside, and sits beside me.

"Good morning, Beej," she says. "How did you sleep last night?"

"Good," I say, lying.

I put my elbows on my knees and lean forward. Mom rubs her gentle hand up and down my back. I want to cry. I want to let out all of the sadness and frustration and anxiety that has built up all week – the emotions I've refused to release. But I can't. I need to remain strong. I need to be the 'man of the family' now that Dad is gone, even though I'm not sure what that means.

We get dressed in our black attire then drive to the funeral home. When we arrive, Joy and Greg are standing on the sidewalk beside the long row of pink tulips that Mom admired. The limousine awaits us with its lights on, and Joy and I climb into the back. Mom follows and sits between us.

"Okay, here we go," she says as if we're young kids about to fly on an airplane for the first time.

As we pull out of the parking lot, Mom reaches down and takes hold of Joy's hand then mine. She tilts her head back, closes her eyes, and takes a long, deep breath through her nose. She holds the air in her lungs for several seconds then exhales through her mouth, slowly. She does this several times, and with each gentle release, my anxiety lessens.

We park in front of the church, and as we step out of the limousine, a sudden, strong wind chills me. I fold Mom's arm into mine to keep us both warm. I walk her inside to the front pew, kiss her on the cheek, then return to help carry Dad's coffin. They told me I didn't have to do this. They told me there were plenty of pallbearers willing to assist. But I would not let them do this without me.

The church fills quickly, all the way to the back on both sides of the aisle. When everyone is settled, the priest opens with a few kind words about Dad, and his voice echoes throughout the large chamber. I pay attention initially, but my mind drifts away when the Catholic ritual calls and responses commence: the our-fathers-who-art-in-Heavens; the peace-be-with-yous and also-with-yous. I take out my eulogy notes and go over them. Joy notices and puts her hand on my shoulder. Her touch energizes me, makes me feel like I'll get through this.

When the priest calls my name, I climb the steps to the top of the altar and stand behind the pulpit. I adjust the microphone to a proper height. The church is silent, and a light sweat forms on my brow as I feel everyone's eyes on me. I tune them all out and stay focused on Joy as I clear my throat to speak.

"On behalf of my mother and sister, we appreciate everyone coming today. My dad would be humbled and grateful, even if you're a Red Sox fan."

Some light laughter fills the church which pleases me, although it's not as much as I had hoped and I quickly carry on.

"I've struggled with what to say here this morning. There's so many things I'd like to tell you about my father, but I'm not sure where to begin."

Tears threaten to fall, and I pause to recompose myself.

"But after spending this past week at home thinking about him, there are two words that come to mind: 'Thank You.' I have a lot to be thankful for when it comes to my dad."

I look down at my notes, averting my eyes from everyone. I stay focused there, take a deep breath, and continue:

"Thank you, Dad, for believing in me, for standing behind me, no matter what."

"Thank you for providing for me and making me provide for myself."

"Thank you for letting me grow the way I chose to grow."

I raise my head and focus my attention back on Joy, attempting to channel some much-needed strength as more sweat forms on my forehead.

"Thank you, Dad, for yelling at me when I needed someone to rein me in."

"Thank you for never pushing me to win and showing me how to lose."

"Thank you for being proud of me, even when I wasn't proud of myself."

I turn and face Dad's coffin at the bottom of the altar. I wipe the tears that have formed in my eyes and stand up straight. I unclench my throat and speak from deepest part of who I am:

"And thank you, Dad, most of all, for teaching me how to be a father."

Dear Kids,

Over the years, Mom and I have both told you a few things about how we first met. But now it's time to tell you how we fell in love, because I'm not sure where my illness might have taken me if we hadn't. I certainly wouldn't be here sharing my bipolar experiences with both of you.

Love,

Dad

I t was a humid morning in late spring, 2009, when I awoke at
5:30 a.m. for a long run before work, stepped out the front
door, and began stretching. Across the street, I noticed this cute,
lean woman in running attire pressing her hands against a tree,
doing the same.

"Hi," she said softly.

"Hi," I replied. "I'm Brian."

She let go of the ankle she was pulling on to stretch and pointed
to herself.

"Kim."

That was the extent of our first conversation. After we both
finished our warmups, Kim tightened the pony tail of her mid-
cut, light brown hair and ran up Walter Street toward Greenlawn
Cemetery. I went the opposite way down to Furlong Park.

I had seen a moving van deposit new neighbors at the duplex
apartment across the street a while back, but I had not noticed this
woman before. Barricaded behind my house renovations, I hadn't
noticed much of anything beyond paint fumes and drywall dust.
But now, for reasons I didn't understand, I was fervently intrigued.

The next morning, my alarm again woke me at 5:30 a.m., and I
went outside for another run. As I was stretching, Kim came out
of her apartment. I was excited to see her and this time I didn't
hesitate to engage.

"Out for another run?" I asked.

She nodded. "Yup. Training."

"For what?"

"First marathon."

"Oh, cool."

Then, silence. I studied her, coyly, as I continued stretching – mesmerized by her lengthy tan legs and muscle-toned arms.

"How many miles today?" I asked.

"Just a few."

"Same here," I replied.

I was lying. With a big race coming up in New Hampshire in a couple of weeks, I had planned to do at least double my usual pre-work run. I didn't intend to lie, but the words flowed out of my mouth without forethought, as did my next inquiry.

"Want some company?" I asked.

"Sure, why not," she said. "But I'll warn you, I'm not a fast runner."

"Don't worry, neither am I."

Another lie. With all the competitive racing I had been doing, I was now running sub-seven-minute miles. But I didn't want to be a show-off. Even though we had just met and only a few words had been spoken between us, somehow I knew that wouldn't have gone over well with Kim – an intuition that would certainly prove to be true.

Other than some casual small talk, neither of us said much along the route she had planned, a short jaunt up to Bishop Fenwick High School and back. We just matched strides, got into a rhythm that felt good, and kept an eye out for cars passing by. When we finished, we both smiled, said goodbye, and then retreated into our respective houses.

That night I set my alarm for 5:30 a.m. again and leapt out of bed when it went off the following morning. Kim had done the same, and shortly after, we met outside. This time, she was the first to speak.

"Interested in another one?" she asked.

"Sure, why not," I replied, attempting to be casual.

Along our second run, we talked a lot, each embracing a mutual desire to learn more about the other. Where did you grow up? What college did you attend? What do you do for work? To our mutual surprise and pleasure, we had more in common than we would have guessed. We were both raised in Connecticut, not that far away from each other. We shared a passion for sports beyond running – from soccer to baseball to tennis and golf. We had both earned our undergraduate degrees in communications, had enjoyed our classes in marketing, advertising, and public speaking, yet neither of us had pursued careers in the field.

In the weeks that followed, Kim and I continued our morning runs together, and as the miles in her marathon training regimen increased so did our knowledge of one another's lives. I learned all about her mom's tennis skillfulness, her dad's "Daddio" carpentry work, and their support of her love for soccer which she played from the age of 5 all the way through college. She shared her obsession with beating her brother Chris at basketball when they were kids, and how her sister Amy and she were born smack dab in the middle of Hurricane Gloria – fraternal twins eager to embrace life from the very beginning, regardless of the torrential weather. Every run afforded each of us a level of intimacy that we weren't prepared for yet didn't shy away from.

In addition to Kim's kind, reserved demeanor, and the single, mesmerizing dimple flanking her hallmark smile, what I remember the most about my initial encounters with her is that I didn't question them. At the time, there were a lot of reasons why I should have – all stemming from my devitalizing bipolar episodes and the life of eternal solitude to which I had formally committed myself. But everything about this naturally beautiful woman who had moved into the apartment across the street and just happened to be training for a marathon, already had me smitten, and never once did I allow my vulnerabilities or self-doubt to interfere.

Thank you, Dad.

Thank you, thank you, thank you.

Our morning runs together became routine for several more weeks, but I still refrained from asking Kim out on a formal date, as did she. Then, one Saturday afternoon I ran into her at Trader Joe's while grocery shopping – her cutoff-jean shorts and retro Rolling Stones t-shirt stopping me in my tracks.

"Hey there, what ya making?" she asked, perusing the ground beef and raw onions in my basket. "It looks yummy."

"Homemade pasta sauce," I replied.

I saw my opportunity at last. As nervous as I was, I swallowed hard and dived into an invitation I had been trying to extend to Kim for weeks.

"Why don't you come over for dinner tonight? I mean, you and your roommates. All of you. Pasta at my place."

Kim came for dinner. Without her roommates. We ate spaghetti and meatballs in my newly renovated sunroom and chatted for some time afterwards. It was a lovely, relaxing evening. As she would later disclose, she went home sated and at least slightly more interested in me. I went to bed glowing with anticipation.

In one way or another, everything about Kim was different than any other woman I had dated previously. Beyond her glowing beauty, I was captivated by her warmth, her propensity to always listen before speaking, her maturity and simplicity. I had never met someone so humble and reserved yet simultaneously as fiercely driven as her. Above all, I was enchanted by her practicality and overt directness. She was the opposite of me in that regard, or at least the person I was at that time. Beyond just my illness, I was masking anything that interfered with the confident, successful persona I wanted to project to the world. She, on the other hand, was self-assured in whichever shoes she wore, and repulsed by dishonesty, which she made readily apparent when we finally went out on our first official "date."

By the time Kim and I sat across from each other at Leslie's Retreat, a hidden burgers and fries joint on the edge of our neighborhood, we knew so much about each other from our runs together that it felt like we'd been in a relationship for years. The conversation was enriching and comfortable, until Kim made it very uncomfortable, at least for me.

"So why have you been lying to me?" she asked, abruptly.

I sat back in my chair, stunned.

"What do you mean?" I replied, anxious. "Lying to you about what?"

"About being a slow runner."

I remained quiet, unsure how she might have known.

"There's this thing called the internet, ya know, and it told me you placed 16th in a field of 2,000 runners a few months ago."

I turned bright red, embarrassed, and squirmed in my seat.

"I'm sorry," I said. "I didn't mean to lie, I just wanted to continue our runs together, and I was worried if I told you the truth they might end."

"That's cute," she said, nodding her head and flashing a half-crooked smile. "But don't ever lie to me again."

"I won't. I promise, Kim."

I promise, Dad. And this time I mean it.

After our first date, she and I fell into a delightful routine. Each evening, one of us would venture across the street after work to invite the other out for a walk along the Danvers river, or over for a barbecue, or down to the local pub for a beer. We spent the summer easing into a relationship that neither of us could remember beginning. It never seemed like we were dating. We just gently burrowed into one another's lives and nestled there.

I fell hard and I fell fast, but I didn't think of it that way. I was just following my soul to where it was leading me and successfully preventing my mind's obsession over my selfish, shameful, crooked past from getting in the way. Kim, on the other hand, by nature a cautious, pragmatic person, understood exactly what was happening. While she was only 24 years old at the time and wasn't looking for a committed relationship, she was convinced that I was the one even before she understood why.

As summer waned, Kim's training led to the inevitable taper for her marathon. I was excited to be there for her, to support her. As I had anticipated, she was confident in her ability to run 26.2 miles after completing every precise step in her four month training program. After running with her for several months, I would have loved to participate in the race myself, but I didn't want to overstep. This was Kim's race, her moment to shine, and I wanted her to enjoy it alone. Looking back, I recognize even that was a step towards becoming the more humble man she was subtly asking me to be, the man I certainly was not at the time. Far from it.

The marathon was the Adirondack Distance Festival, an annual run held each Fall at Schroon Lake in upstate New York along a course that encircles the eponymous lake. Kim's parents and I dropped her off at the starting line; then we shifted around the lake together to cheer her on from various viewing points, handing her cups of Gatorade and Gu-packets and orange slices. As we waited for her, the three of us laughed and bonded. My obvious enthusiasm for my new girlfriend and their undeniable pride in their daughter conjoined and made us feel comfortable with one another.

We learned a lot about each other that day – family histories, family traditions, family expectations – but the most important thing we learned was that we belonged to a mutual admiration society with Kim at the center. By the time she crossed the finish line, I already felt accepted into her family and fully at ease.

Following the marathon, I could not wait for Kim to meet Mom, Joy, and Greg, and predictably, each of them instantly accepted her.

"I love her, Brian," Mom said. "And I see a glow of youth in your eyes that I haven't seen in a long time."

"Looks like Kim cracked the Beej code," Joy told me. "I'm really happy for you. Don't mess this one up!"

I will do everything in my power not to, I told myself. *Don't be a moron, Brian. Listen to your sister. Follow her example. Focus on someone else's needs instead of your own.*

Be present. Be real. Step up.

As superstitious as it might sound, I got confirmation for my optimism and faith in my relationship with Kim during the 2009 World Series, confirmation that I was back on a healthy track, that I might not actually be a fuck-up, that I could let go of my past mistakes and a write a new chapter of my life with Kim. Maybe a whole new book.

The last time the Yankees had won the World Series was in 2000, which had turned out to be the last postseason MLB games my father and I ever watched together. They had made it to the Fall Classic twice since my dad had died – the first time in 2001, when they were defeated in Game 7 by the Diamondbacks, and again in 2003, falling short to the Marlins. But in the same season during which I had met Kim, something told me the outcome would be different.

I see you again, Dad. I can feel you in my heart.

Kim and I traveled back home to watch Game 6 in Joy and Greg's living room, where Mom, Josh, Jason, and me were all proudly sporting our #2 Derek Jeter t-shirts. Pandemonium broke out in the house the minute the Phillies suffered their final out, and we danced around the room until we collapsed in a jubilant heap.

After we settled back down into our seats, Joy handed out beverages, and Greg raised his glass. "This one's for Big John," he said, choking as the words came out.

With my arm around Kim, I repeated, "For Big John."

By the time the first snowflakes began to fall that winter, Kim and I were inseparable. Rarely did a day pass when we weren't running together, eating a meal, or falling asleep in each other's arms. We shared everything that was happening in each other's lives. She listened while I reflected on my work experiences, the challenges I faced while now managing some larger technology projects for my banking client. I enjoyed learning about her post-graduate studies at the University of Southern New Hampshire, where she was working towards her MBA. We grew closer and closer, and even though we had only been dating for a short while, it seemed like there was nothing we couldn't talk about.

Except bipolar disorder.

I could not make myself bring it up.

From the very beginning of our relationship, I had made a promise to Kim that I would never lie to her, a promise I still keep. So why didn't I tell her about my mental illness sooner? The simple answer is that I was afraid of losing her. I could not bear to lose this beautiful woman, this angel cast into my life, who had captured my heart and revived my spirit. She had enraptured me, and I trusted her, perhaps more than I trusted myself. But what if she couldn't deal with the ominous possibilities of what my mental illness might conjure? It was a long leap from sharing a bed to "We're sleeping on a powder keg, and who knows when it might explode. . ."

I had opened all the avenues to myself except that one, which I kept firmly closed. I did feel guilty about that. I was ashamed of hiding my meds in the back of the bathroom closet; never sharing where I was going when I saw my psychiatrist; leaving out the entire swath of my psychotic episodes and extreme depression from every intimate conversation. But my fear of losing Kim overshadowed my guilt. It was easier to just keep my albatross hidden.

Eventually, I succumbed to the internal burden I was carrying. As vulnerable as I felt about opening that door, I owed her that respect.

During a blizzard that held us captive inside my house, we stayed up late drinking wine and talking. Towards the end of the conversation, I fumbled with my glass then put it down and took her hand.

"There is something I need to tell you. Something I probably should have told you already. Something you need to know."

She smiled. "Go for it."

Was she indulging me? Was she encouraging me? I couldn't tell, but I pushed forward or at least tried to.

"Um, well, see. . ." I stuttered.

"Brian, just say it."

So I did.

For the next hour, I blurted out the whole, convoluted, demoralizing history of my mental illness – from my father's death and my first episode all the way through my second. My psychotic adventures. My hospital stays. The severity of my depression and near suicides. My guilt for all the lies I had told including keeping my illness a secret from her. My regrets about having hurt Mom and Joy and so many others in my life, repeatedly. I held nothing back, even the embarrassing admission that I had fancied myself Jesus Christ.

Through it all, I was afraid to look at Kim, but that didn't stop me. I just kept talking. As I did, she said nothing, never once interrupted me. She just sipped her wine, sat stock still, and listened until it was clear that I was done. Then, she sidled closer to me and took my hand.

"Hey, sounds like you've got a lot of stuff to deal with," she said. "You know what? I've got some stuff too. How about we help each other figure it all out. . ."

I took a deep breath and looked at the genuine commitment in her eyes. At that moment I felt more alive than I had in over a decade.

"I love you," I said for the first time.

"I love you too, Brian."

S everal years after Kim came into my life, I was in New York City for a financial services conference, and in a restaurant late one evening, I had a long conversation about alcoholism with my friend Gerry – a work colleague who is a recovering alcoholic. At the time, Gerry was in his early 40's and had been sober for about three years. Prior to that, he had been drinking heavily on and off his entire adult life, never able to stop himself from reaching for a bottle of gin or vodka, his two personal demons.

Before Gerry became sober, his alcohol addiction had full control over him, and as often as he attempted to reverse that control, he couldn't. He went in and out of rehab more times than he could count, forced to pick up the scattered pieces of his personal life and professional endeavors every time he did. But Gerry was finally on a healthy track, proud of his sobriety, and willing to openly talk about his addiction with his family and close friends like me. I was proud of him as well and humbled that he felt comfortable opening up to me.

Like my struggles with bipolar disorder, alcoholism had caused immense pain and suffering to Gerry and many people close to him, including his previous fiancée, an attorney from a rival financial institution. During our conversation, he poured his heart out to me about their unfortunate separation – a byproduct of Gerry's last alcoholic episode which landed him in an overnight jail cell one drunken evening. The two of them had been dating for several years and were madly in love, but their love could not repress the instability Gerry's addiction caused their relationship. Alcoholism had won, and both Gerry and his fiancée had lost. He moved out, and she moved on.

I learned a lot about alcoholism that night and even more in the following years when Gerry and I continued to talk about his addiction. I learned how difficult it was for Gerry to attend work events at restaurants, ever aware of the bottles upon bottles of beer and wine and liquor that surrounded him as he ordered a glass of club soda and tried to block the ignoble elixirs from his line of sight. He had gotten better at that over time, he said, but the desire to belly up to a bar and drink himself into oblivion as he did for so many years never went away.

I can relate to my friend Gerry's story, although perhaps not in a way you might think. After many years of reconciling my illness, I now consider bipolar disorder an addiction. The "high" that bipolar mania produces is as addictive to me as alcohol is to Gerry. My mind is hard-wired to crave the super-human sensations I will surely feel, the immortal power I will obtain as mania sets every neuron in my body on fire. That imbalance is as intoxicating to me as a shot of vodka is to Gerry, and its triggers are everywhere. Some days, I feel like Gerry sitting in a restaurant, surrounded by a thousand vampires threatening my mental sobriety. It would be easy to veer from my wellness plan, to go back to my old ways of running around trying to do everything all at once, and as quickly and creatively as my illness allows me to. But I know that if I do, I will lose control over my illness that I've had for a long time now, and myself and everyone around me would suffer from it.

Like Gerry's capacity to refrain from drinking, over time, my ability to recognize my bipolar triggers and prevent mania before it happens has gotten easier. Also like Gerry, my support network is my primary defense mechanism for controlling my addiction. At the time I knew him, Gerry attended Alcoholics Anonymous (AA) meetings weekly and attributed much of his sobriety to his friendships with fellow addicts that he met through his group. Whenever Gerry's desire to reach for a bottle got too intense for him to handle, he'd call his AA sponsor, and they'd meet up for coffee or a stroll through Boston Common. He lived alone, but he never felt alone, he said. There was always someone a phone call away to help him keep his addiction at bay and he made that call as often as he needed to.

One day, Gerry invited me to one of his AA meetings, and I gladly accepted. It was held in the lower auditorium of a Protestant church, and we were among fifteen or so people who attended. As I sipped on weak coffee and listened to Gerry and his fellow AA members discuss the successes and failures that they had maintaining their sobriety, I was comforted by their empathy, their practicality, their willingness to expose the harsh realities of their addictions, and their collective ambition to remain on a healthy track. Seeing up close just how proud they each were to have earned their one year, their five year, their ten and twenty years of sobriety tokens, was genuinely inspiring.

Towards the end of the evening, one gentleman stood up and described his sobriety in a way I've never forgotten. He said to successfully manage his alcohol addiction, he had to learn how to ride a see-saw. On one side of the see-saw was himself, and on the other were all the people in his support network – his wife, his family, his AA friends – all helping him keep his life balanced, helping him ensure the see-saw never rose too high, or dropped too low. His first challenge, he said, was climbing onto the see-saw. That is, he had to stop thinking he could manage alcoholism alone and allow others to help him. Then, he had to accept the fact that his sobriety would forever be a moving target, the see-saw would be in perpetual motion – ascending and descending at various intervals.

For him, not falling off the see-saw required working together with the people sitting across from him, talking to them, and letting them help him in his sobriety objective. Only he could prevent himself from jumping off the see-saw, he said, but the more he stopped trying to manage his addiction alone, the less he thought about doing so.

I can't think of a better analogy for how I manage my mental illness today. For years, I thought I could handle bipolar disorder on my own. There were plenty of see-saws to ride in the park, but

I chose to sit on the swings all alone. It wasn't until I met Kim that I realized just how alone I actually was and how afraid I had been to let somebody help me deal with my illness. My head was buried underneath so many layers of bipolar shame and guilt that I could barely see the horizon, let alone my inability to engage in a meaningful and fulfilling relationship – one in which someone else could help me manage my mental illness.

Of all the mistakes I have made in my life, that is arguably the one I regret the most.

Following my bipolar disorder disclosure to Kim, she made it clear she would be inserting herself directly into my wellness plan – supporting me in a way my singular lifestyle had never afforded. She started with a simple question: "How did you sleep last night?"

While the question itself seems straightforward, it was layered in complexities. Kim wasn't simply asking me if I had gotten a good night's rest; she wanted to know if my brain's reset button had been pressed – if my mind had turned itself off long enough to ensure my next day would be balanced, my thoughts clear and focused. She had researched bipolar disorder, extensively, and she understood that regular, undisturbed sleep was pivotal for me to remain healthy. What she was really asking me was whether or not I had my mental illness under control, and she expected me to answer with 100% honesty.

Of course, I didn't get that at first. Given the casual manner in which she posed the question, I just assumed she was being affectionate.

"I slept well," I replied. "How about you?"

But soon after, as she asked the question on subsequent mornings, I came to understand the deeper meaning behind Kim's repeated inquiry, one which she continues to ask me today and I am thankful that she does.

While it took some time to feel comfortable letting Kim so entirely in, her support soon became my main source of security and strength, particularly when it came to mending the close relationship I'd once had with Joy. On the surface, it seemed like Joy and me were reconciling that as we began helping Mom make plans for her retirement and older age – updating her will, aligning her investments, discussing options on where she might live when she was too old to maintain the house. But below that, our relationship remained fractured from the repercussions of my second bipolar episode and hospitalization.

Kim challenged me to confront my feelings on the matter, and while I remained uncomfortable talking to Joy directly about the events which unfolded, I made several attempts at bringing us closer. After every visit home to see Mom's lawyer and financial advisor, I requested the three of us have dinner together, or get ice cream, or even take Mom grocery shopping – anything that afforded us the chance to reunite our friendship and remind us of the deep love and respect we had for one another. Dinners and groceries and ice cream were superficial gestures without talking about the underlying causes of our disconnect, but it was a start, and without Kim's support, I wouldn't have had the strength I needed to persevere.

Kim's non-judgmental acceptance of my illness also provided me with the courage I needed to come to terms with my past mental illness trauma and envision a future for her and me. Whatever that future held, I knew that it meant together. Each of us had weathered failed relationships, and we knew what we wanted from this one: a partnership built on mutual trust, grounded by a healthy routine of exercise, recreation, work, and financial stability. She and I were in agreement about everything that mattered – we shared political views, social consciousness, spiritual beliefs, and a commitment to life-long learning. But there was still one very important topic we had never discussed.

Children.

Before my illness took over every aspect of my being, I had envisioned myself living the life that my family does today. I wanted to be a father like my own father – the "cool dad" who told fantastic dad jokes. I wanted to take my children to concerts and go for long walks on the beach, skip out of work early and throw the ball around with them and their friends as often as I could. Sadly, bipolar disorder and the severity of my episodes altered my faith in my ability to parent. What if I had relapses that injured my children physically or psychically? Even worse, what if my genes found their way into their DNA and the illness manifested in a similar manner as it did in me? How would I forgive myself for having inflicted that kind of pain and suffering on my children?

I was humbled by Kim's choice to weather any storms with me even though she might get hurt. She was an intelligent adult, one who could perform a risk analysis for herself. But a son or a daughter who had not chosen life, much less my kind of life?

Up until this point in our relationship, I had not shared my parental misgivings with Kim because the topic had never come up in conversation. Since we were singing our life together in perfect harmony, each of us assumed the verse about children was written in the same key. But we were wrong. So wrong that it nearly ended our relationship.

On the weekend before our second Thanksgiving together, Kim and I went on a romantic getaway in Kennebunkport, Maine. One evening we had a candlelit dinner in a cozy Italian restaurant. I was mellowed by the fire blazing in an old stone fireplace and the hints of cherry emanating from my red wine as Kim sat across from me, softening in the half-lit room. I was certainly not prepared for what she was about to say.

"Brian, I'm ready to get married and have a baby."

I had no words.

A marriage I was preparing for, a child I was not.

So much ran through my mind: the long, painful road to rectifying my relationship with my mental illness; my new lease on life; my love for Kim and my overall acceptance of myself. How would a child fit into any of what we had constructed, what I had overcome?

I took a deep breath and squeezed her hand. "I can't, Kim. I just can't."

Kim sighed. "You're afraid?"

"Petrified. I just can't do it. There's too much danger, too many risks."

"What do you mean?"

I pulled my hand back and leaned away from the table.

"What if my genes are passed along? What if. . ."

I broke down. She gave me a moment but then pressed on.

"There's nothing you could say to alter my notion of our future. You are the man I want to be with for the rest of my life. But I want children. Your children. I want us to be parents. Together."

"I don't see how I could –"

"It's not a topic for debate, Brian. If you won't be the father of my children, I won't marry you, and I will no longer be with you. I can't."

"You're giving me an ultimatum?"

"I am."

The discussion ended there. We finished our meal, skipped dessert, and returned to the hotel. To avoid talking about it any further, we went straight to bed and turned our attention to something mindless playing on the television. The silence between us was deafening, and when I could no longer contain my anxiety, I turned off the TV and spoke.

"Kim, I can't fathom losing you, but it's impractical for us to have a family," I said, hoping to appeal to her pragmatism.

"You're wrong, Brian, and this is not your decision to make alone," she said. "I understand your concerns, but I don't agree with them. I know we will be great parents. Whatever life dishes out, we will handle it together."

I had no response and remained quiet as she continued.

"Don't be afraid, Brian. Don't use your illness as a crutch preventing you from being the wonderful father that I know you will be."

My silence turned to tears then to a full-blown meltdown, and I retreated to a chair on the other side of the room to regain my composure. I put my hands over my face and took several deep breaths attempting to calm my nerves. It didn't work. The intensity of the argument was overwhelming, and I needed an exit.

"Kim, I don't know if I'll ever feel differently, but I need some time to come to a decision."

"That's fair," she said. "But don't take too long."

We returned to Salem the following morning and remained separated over the next few days, only talking to discuss our plans for celebrating Thanksgiving at her parents' house. We were taking separate cars as I needed to return from the long weekend early to complete some construction. The following Monday, a contractor would be installing a new wood stove, and I hadn't even begun building the stone hearth for it.

Sitting beside Kim during the holiday feast in Connecticut was unexpectedly difficult – something neither of us had experienced since we had first met – and it frightened me. Although we were surrounded by her charming, socially-engaging family, the mood between us was dark, and we both talked little. Fearing someone might notice, I returned to Salem right after dinner, even further apprehensive.

The wood stove project was more complicated than I had initially thought it would be. In addition to building the stone platform, my contractor asked me to cut several inches out of the interior of the old, wooden mantel to be in compliance with fire codes. Since the mantel was the original from the mid-nineteenth century, I cut slowly through the wood with my fine-saw, but the vibration caused some debris to fall from the inside of the fragile brick chimney. I reached my hand up behind the mantel to clear it out. Some brick fragments fell, and so did a small, flat, rectangular piece of metal.

I picked it up carefully and examined it. To my surprise, it was an antique photograph. Its outer edges were worn and rusted, but the image in the middle was crystal clear: two young children dressed in formal attire posing for the camera. A boy, probably nine or ten years old, standing upright beside his younger sister.

Their bright faces lit up the faded white background. Their eyes radiated warmth and looked through me, almost blinking as they discovered the light of day for the first time in over a century. Their stares seared my heart.

Thank you, Dad.

Dear Kids,

I have always refrained from giving you spiritual advice. That is your path to explore and your decision to make. But I will tell you this: when the universe sends you a sign, don't readily dismiss it. Open up the door and let the light shine in.

Love,

Dad

As I knelt there in front of my fireplace, I had no doubt that a spiritual portal had opened up and dropped that antique photo down the chimney of my old house in Witch City to deliver me a message. I also had no doubt the sender of that message was my father. But even that couldn't alter my convictions about never having children. I simply could not get past my fear of passing down my illness, of being responsible for inflicting the physical and mental anguish I had endured on to someone else. I needed that curse to end with me.

Kim wasn't going to let me off that easily, and she returned from Connecticut on Sunday afternoon armed with a litany of discussion points on the topic of having children. She did not want my hesitation to linger any further than it already had. She could feel me pushing her away, escaping to my previous life of solitude, and she would do everything in her power to prevent that. She recognized that deep down I wanted to have kids – a surmise based on the many childhood stories of my father that I had shared with her, the omnipresent role he played in my upbringing. She saw me as a man ready and eager to follow in his footsteps. But she felt that I would only be able to do so if I unchained myself from my shackled bipolar past.

That night, she came over with the intention of forcing me to take a good, hard, honest look at myself.

"Brian, I believe your fear of passing down your illness to a child has little to do with future anxieties," she said. "It seems to me that you still haven't come to full terms with your complicated history."

I was angered by her aggressive insinuation, but I also didn't know how to respond. I folded my arms in frustration and kept my mouth shut. She continued.

"Yes, you've survived two horrific bipolar episodes and pulled your life back together. But if you've done so in such a way that prevents you from living your life fully, how successful have you been?"

Now, I was both angry and emotional. I left the room to calm down only to return with aggression, prepared to convince her that she was wrong.

Before I could say anything, she cut me off.

"If your father were alive, what do you think he'd tell you?" she asked. "He's watching over us, ya know. He's here with us right now, Brian. He's listening to you and me decide our future together."

Her words penetrated my heart, and tears threatened to fall.

"You know what I think? I think he'd give you the same advice as he did on the day you left for college: Don't be fucking stupid."

Now, there was nowhere for my emotions to run, no hiding place. I collapsed on the couch and cried profusely, a broken man surrendering to the woman he loved and did not want to lose.

Kim sat by my side, put her arms around me, and held me until my last tear fell. Then, she told me what she knew I needed to hear.

"Remember, you're not going to do this alone, Brian," she said, softly. "Those days are long past. We're in this together, and together, we'll figure it all out as we go along."

She turned my head toward her and stared into my desperate eyes.

"We will raise strong children and arm them with the courage to face whatever life dishes out. If by chance that's bipolar disorder, we will support them just as your mother and sister have supported you."

I believed her. I believed in her. I just didn't believe in myself.

Luckily, Kim did. She had no doubt.

Throughout that winter, Kim and I continued talking about children, and she helped me push through my anxiety – one discussion at a time beside a blazing fire in my new wood stove. As smoke went up the chimney in the very room where a young boy and girl once huddled together when there was no other source of heat, so did my fear of what the future might hold for Kim and me as parents.

The revelation gave me a whole new belief in what I could achieve, a notion which transcended into my professional life as well. Since I could be more truthful with myself, I began to see that I had been hiding from advancement, from pursuing professional goals. My illness had been an excuse to shy away from looking for challenging work that would engage my talents and enhance my real potential.

I had long been afraid to seek work in Boston, though I knew that the career opportunities I sought were in the city. I was afraid of the commute, afraid I'd fall back into work obsession, afraid the stress induced by the speed at which the city moved might trigger another episode. Most of all, I was afraid I'd lose my closeness to Kim. She set me straight.

"Listen," she said in her take-charge tone. "You know how I feel about work. Too much is stupid. But if there're opportunities in the city that satisfy you, you should embrace them, not run away from them."

I took her advice. Armed with new resolve, I transferred my responsibilities at the bank to a colleague, accepted a new contracting job with a cloud technology company in Boston, and bought a commuter rail pass. When I stepped off the train at North Station for the first time, I was nearly paralyzed with fear. Crowds of people, hustling and bustling through tight, claustrophobic spaces, balancing coffee cups as they ran up escalators, angry with anyone standing in their way.

The persistent noise was perhaps the most difficult element to get used to. Blaring car horns and drivers yelling at slow-walking pedestrians made me uneasy. The piercing sirens of ambulances and police cars and fire trucks racing past me were the most difficult to deal with, conjuring occasional flashbacks to my hospital incarcerations, waking up in the middle of the night whenever emergency vehicles pulled into the ER.

It was an onerous transition, but settling into my job became less difficult than I expected thanks to my new, laid-back boss who protected his team from impossible deadlines and eminently valued work/life balance – prioritizing watching his teenage son's basketball games in the suburbs high above his work responsibilities in Boston. Still, the company I worked for moved as quickly as the customer data that transferred between its systems and I was perpetually on high-alert for stress.

To counter the intrusions, I joined a gym next to my office and began running on my lunch breaks – a temporary retreat in the middle of the day to calm my nerves and clear my head. I'd put on my headphones and run down to the harbor adjacent to South Boston. There, the calm waters surrounding Castle Island and Pleasure Bay silenced the nonstop clamor of the city, and after a relaxing shower at the gym, I'd return to the office refreshed, focused, ready to get back to my work and support my team.

It took some time to find a steady rhythm and balance my work life in Boston with my personal endeavors in Salem, but after I did, I achieved much success at my job. As that success continued, my boss added new management responsibilities.

"Brian, you've done great work for us," he said. "I've got a large project kicking off in Europe that I'd like you to spearhead. It will require some travel to the UK but I'll try to minimize that as much as I can."

I was nervous about being away from Kim and the tension that international work travel might invoke, but I found solace in an old, successful coping mechanism.

My journal.

At the time, I had not written in my journal since I was living on City Dock in Annapolis. After reading through the internal monologue of my first bipolar episode, I began describing the details of my second. On my flights between Boston and London and Amsterdam, I jotted down every minute detail of my hyper-stimulated escapades. While the horrid depictions of my depression and near suicide were difficult to put down on paper, I refused to back down from the beast, forcing myself to confront my inner-most PTSD disturbances.

With Kim now in my corner, writing in my journal wasn't just liberating as it had been before; it was empowering, just as Marty had said it might one day become. As the psychological intrusions flowed from the deep crevices of my cerebrum through my shaky hands and onto the blank paper, I became desensitized to my trauma – the process systematically exorcising my deepest mental illness demons in a way no conversations with therapists or family members or friends or even Kim ever had. As I did, I was also providing myself with a daily reminder of the importance of respecting my illness, never letting the ghosts creep up on me while I wasn't looking.

As the 10-year anniversary of my father's death and my subsequent bipolar diagnosis approached in April, 2011, I was in every way I could think of a new man. Or rather, a newly minted, better version of myself. After living with my illness for a decade, I was no longer inhibited by it. Kim's acceptance and counsel had finally freed me. Marty had once told me that I should stop blaming myself. With Kim's unwavering support, I finally began to believe him, at least to a degree that allowed me to reconnect with the self-love the vampires had stolen from me. I had also found a way to coexist with the stigma of bipolar disorder rather than being repressed by it. How others might perceive me became less important than how I perceived myself.

"You caught the gene, Brian," Kim said to me during a sunset picnic at Furlong Park one evening. "Tough break. But certainly nothing we can't manage going forward."

Accepting that truth was long overdue, yet had Kim not come into my life, I probably never would have. I had told too many lies to too many people. I had hidden behind the stigma of my illness for so long that any reconciliation was simply not within reach, no matter who tried to lead me to it. I had lost sight of who I was, adopted an identity that was not me, labeled myself "bipolar" – whole-heartedly ashamed of my Scarlet B.

I am not bipolar, I told myself.

I am Brian.

I have a mental illness. It's called bipolar disorder.

Although it is a component of my existence, it does not define who I am.

I am a son, a brother, an uncle, a boyfriend. I am a co-worker, a carpenter, a long-distance runner, and a musician.

Above all, I am human.

I am not bipolar.

As Kim and I began discussing marriage, there was something she insisted that we do before we embarked on the next phase of our relationship.

"Brian, I'd like us to talk to your family about your illness."

Her reasoning was multi-faceted. She knew I needed to continue making amends with Joy, the divide between us still looming from my second hospitalization. She also knew that I needed to talk with Mom on a more truthful, realistic level – one absent of my mother's "Beej Blinders" that were counter-productive to the collaborative management of my illness. But what motivated Kim the most was her pragmatic desire to see my mental illness through someone else's eyes other than mine. Up until that point, she only had a singular perspective, and to her, that wasn't enough.

"Brian, if I'm going to help you steer clear of danger, I need to learn more about what it feels like to be on the outside looking in."

Kim's request was difficult to get past, and at first, I was fervently against it – a knee-jerk reaction derived from a decade of avoiding the agony of pouring salt into old bipolar wounds. While I had grown comfortable in my own bipolar skin, at the time, I had no plans to discuss that with anyone but Kim, especially my family.

"I don't see the need for that, Kim," I said. "I don't want to hurt my family any more than I already have."

"You're wrong, Brian," she forcefully replied. "This isn't going to hurt them, and it will help both of us."

In Kim's mind, talking with Mom, Joy, and Greg about our collective bipolar experiences had little to do with dredging up past hardships. She was pushing me over the most critical hurdle to managing my illness in the future – talking about it with the people that I love, and as uncomfortable as that would soon become, I will forever be grateful that she did.

It took some time for me to overcome my apprehensions, but Kim persisted, and eventually I complied. For Christmas that year, Kim and I drove home for the holiday to have dinner at Joy's like we always have. As we ate beef tenderloin and sipped on Cabernet, the mood was light and the conversation entertaining. After the meal, Josh and Jason went off to play video games, and we adults gathered in the living room to continue our casual chit-chatting. When a break came in the discussion, I raised my hand shyly as if I were in elementary school requesting to go to the lavatory.

Greg laughed. "Yes, Brian? You'd like to say something?"

I closed my eyes and stammered, "Anyone want to talk about bipolar disorder?"

My unexpected request stunned the group into silence. Then, Joy stood up and came over to give me a hug.

"I'd like that," she enthused.

Mom smiled. "Sounds good to me, Beej."

"Me too," chortled Greg. "So where should we start?"

Where we started was from the very beginning, and the very beginning was my father.

Long before my first bout with mania and psychosis, my time in the hospital recovering, my deep depression and post-traumatic scorn, there was the sudden, heartbreaking death of a man we all loved. A husband with whom Mom had built a family, who knew exactly how to make her laugh. A father who treated Greg like his own son, whom Joy and I adored, and I refused to lose.

"I didn't want to let Dad go," I said. "I didn't know how to, and my mind couldn't stop thinking about it."

"We know, Beej," Joy said. "Looking back, it all makes sense. But in the moment, it was very confusing and it scared the heck out of us."

For the first time since I was diagnosed, we all openly shared our feelings about a hereditary illness that had imprisoned our family for generations. I started by apologizing with the fervor of an alcoholic at Number 8 of the 12-Step Program. I was remorseful for the pain I had caused, for the hiding, for my duplicity. I wanted their forgiveness.

"I'm so sorry for the struggles I have caused each of you. . ."

Joy stopped me. "There's nothing you should apologize for," she said. "Remember, you didn't choose your illness. It chose you."

Joy continued, clearly grateful for the opportunity to release feelings she had kept bottled up. Some of her admissions surprised me.

"You have no idea how guilty I felt," she said. "I wanted to support you, but I constantly thought I wasn't doing enough. When you remained distant, I thought it was because I failed you."

"No, Joy, I was running away. I thought I could –"

"I know, Beej. I do. I'm just telling you what I thought at the time. You were in so much pain, and I felt helpless."

When a break finally came, Kim smiled and raised her hand as if she were another kid in the classroom. Everyone laughed, and the intensity of the emotional conversation settled.

"Yes, Kim?" Greg responded.

"Prior to either of Brian's episodes, were there any warning signs?"

Joy and Greg looked at each other, attempting to recollect anything that might have indicated something was awry.

"There really weren't," Greg recalled as he looked over at me. "Beej, before the first one, when we saw you on Thanksgiving, we didn't notice anything out of the ordinary."

Kim listened intently, taking detailed mental notes.

"We talked to you a couple of weeks later," Greg continued. "You were excited about a business thing you were getting into."

"That's right," Joy added. "You were asking all kinds of legal questions, really excited. Maybe overly excited. But we didn't think there was anything to be concerned about."

Greg and Joy shared some of the regrets that they had about the way they handled my second episode in Salem. There were many lessons learned, and they wanted to ensure Kim heard all of them.

"We shouldn't have waited to take you to the hospital in Salem, Beej," Greg said. "We should have brought you there immediately and let the doctors give you proper treatment, regardless of our concerns on how hostile you might become. Thinking you would stabilize on your own was a mistake."

The conversation lasted well into the evening. We cried a little, laughed a lot. I poked fun at myself for some of the more amusing antics my psychosis had brought forth – self-deprecating humor intended to lessen my humiliation.

"I must have been a sight to see walking down the street with a cat on a leash. . ."

"I'm still paying off my credit card from my Christmas shopping spree. . ."

As we talked further, we looked for the positives in our collective experiences – what we had learned, and in retrospect, what we had, perhaps, gained. Joy and Greg commented that the stress my episodes incited had tightened the bond between them. They found a new strength in their relationship, and the challenges I faced expanded their obligations to Josh and Jason, whose hereditary line includes a mental illness.

"When Josh and Jason are old enough, we'll be talking to them about bipolar disorder," Greg said. "They need to know, and if you're okay with it Beej, we need to tell them what happened to you."

"Of course," I said. "You should tell them everything."

By the time we finished, it felt as though we had engaged in the most productive group therapy session possible. At the end, I made sure to share how much Joy and Greg and Mom's selfless support had meant to me, how it got me through my despair.

"Each of you played a part in saving my life. . . not once, but twice," I said. "Joy, when you eventually talk to Josh and Jason, make sure you tell them that."

Throughout the evening, as Joy and Greg and Kim and I talked, Mom sat silently listening. We were all aware of her watching us with her soft, wide-open eyes that whispered, "I hear you, and I feel you, and I love you all," but no words were uttered. After everyone had said everything that needed to be said, asked every question that needed to be asked, wiped away every tear that needed to be shed, she finally spoke.

"So Beej, what comes next?"

K im was right.

With the exception of her belief that the Major League Baseball season is too long, she's been right so often throughout our marriage that it's annoying.

Talking openly with Mom, Joy, and Greg about my mental illness was as emancipating as she had said it would be, and I left Joy's home that evening feeling like I had reclaimed my role in our family, reconnected to our traditions and values. I was whole again.

Kim, too, benefitted from our family's long overdue conversation, although not in the way she had initially thought she would. She wanted to gain insights about what to look out for when bipolar mania is on the horizon. Joy and Greg and Mom couldn't provide her that because they weren't around to see my hypomanic behavior when it occurred. But as we talked through the emotional baggage we had been lugging around for a decade, Kim became closer to the Talarczyks than she ever would have at that point in our relationship had it not been for my illness. The same was true for Kim and me. Bipolar disorder had broadened the love we had for each other rather than divide us, forced us to have the harder conversations and steer clear of any passive-aggressiveness whatsoever – a purpose it still serves us today.

For Joy and Greg, my one-and-a-half co-parents, our discussion brought forth a level of catharsis they were not prepared for yet whole-heartedly welcomed. The sharp pain Joy had been carrying in her heart from the day we both screamed at each other in Salem Hospital didn't instantly deplete, but some redemption had been claimed. Joy was also pleased to learn the extent to which Kim and I had already discussed my illness and a few of the ways we were working together to manage it. She had already come to love Kim, but seeing how unfazed and practical and nurturing Kim was in the face of strenuous circumstances gave Joy a newfound respect for her – one that would continue to blossom as my relationship with Kim further developed.

As for Mom, while she kept to herself that evening, once she had time to process everything, she eventually shared her feelings with me.

"I'm sorry I kept the challenges Uncle Danny had with bipolar disorder from you, Beej," she said. "That was a mistake, and one I'd like to rectify. Please ask me anything about him that you'd like to know and I will gladly tell you what I remember."

I would take her up on that offer, and in the years that followed, I learned a lot, much of which I've already shared here. Mom, too, found comfort in talking openly about the bipolar struggles both her brother and me faced, and now that the mighty elephant was out of the closet, we both agreed to keep it there.

My dad wasn't physically sitting with us in Joy's living room that Christmas, but after our conversation, as I held Kim's hand and nestled beside the balmy fire, I certainly felt his presence. Amidst the tearful discourse and our collective vindication, his spirit was surely hovering, and it would continue to as my relationship with Kim expanded.

We miss you, Dad.

Shortly after our night of full disclosures I proposed to Kim. Happily she said yes, and on a crystal clear afternoon in the Spring of 2012 we got married in the historic Hawthorne Hotel surrounded by as many of our friends and family we could squeeze into the ballroom.

It was a fairy-tale wedding, and Kim and I were leading a blissful, fairy-tale life. But no marriage is free from disconnect and strife, especially one over which an acute mental illness perpetually looms. For us, the first significant blowout occurred as we prepared to usher our first child, my son, into the world.

As a one-year anniversary gift to ourselves, Kim and I took a trip to Ireland, leaving our work responsibilities behind us to traverse the southern half of the Emerald Isle. Somewhere along our peaceful travels, Kim got pregnant. Luck of the Irish, I guess. In 9 months, we would become parents. I would be a father.

We returned to Salem, and, as my son grew inside his mom, so did my anxiety over maintaining my mental equilibrium while meeting the demands of an infant. How would I manage the loss of sleep from late-night diaper changes, early morning feedings, and the endless worries I knew we'd encounter? What would happen if I couldn't make the time or didn't have the energy to go running or play music or participate in other activities that were critical to my health?

The requirements of parenthood were a credible threat, and I was concerned. Kim, however, remained unperturbed.

"You don't have to worry about that," she said. "I'll stay up with the baby while you get your regular sleep."

"That's unfair to you," I replied, upset. "I don't want my issues to be your burden."

"You're not a burden, Brian, and you don't have issues," she said. "You're my husband, and you have a mental illness. Your health, and mine, is as important as the baby's. You'll help in other ways."

We talked it out further. My fears and guilt looped around and around, filling me with dread. What kind of a husband am I to let his wife bear the full brunt of the exhaustion? But Kim's insistence that we would be fine never flagged. The conversations were stressful, and we argued ferociously, but I was eventually calmed by her reassurance and our continued dialogue.

And so it was, on a warm May evening in 2014, roughly a week past Kim's due date, our son was born. I knelt beside Kim and cried as the nurse placed him into her arms for the first time, his tiny fingers scratching against her bare neck as he nestled into her chest and drifted off to harmonious sleep.

Dear Kids,

My dad gave me every morsel of love that he had in his heart, and since the day you both were born, I've tried to give you the same.

I hope this recollection of my bipolar experiences extends the loving relationship that we have, and may you both know that Mom and me will always be here for you.

Love,

Dad

From the moment we brought our son home from the hospital, motherhood came naturally to Kim. She knew exactly what he needed, and whatever that was, it had been purchased months prior. Baby accessories I never knew existed came out of the hallway closet as if we owned an infant retail business and maintained an extensive inventory. I, on the other hand, felt awkward performing every parental task that was handed to me, including things as basic as preparing formula, which is difficult to screw up. But with Kim's patient guidance, I learned what I needed to do.

The three of us quickly settled into a comfortable routine, one that preserved my steady sleep pattern, just as Kim had said we would. She took the overnight shift so I could sleep undisturbed, and I spent the early morning with him while Kim rested. In the quietude of the pre-dawn hours, he and I cuddled on the couch to watch Yankees highlights from the previous day's game, or I'd strap him into our running stroller and we'd log several miles together before I got on the train to Boston. I cherished every second of my time alone with him as we got to know one another.

Once Kim and I got into the swing of things, settling into fatherhood ironically helped me manage my mental illness in ways I was not prepared for. The busy rhythm of changing my son's diaper, tracking his nap schedule, giving him a sponge bath, and the rest of our daily childcare activities kept me mentally focused. When outside stressors threatened my stability, I'd recognize them sooner and confront them more aggressively. There was no time for distractions, I decreed to myself. I had new responsibilities. My son had needs beyond my own, and he needed me to be healthy to take care of them.

As he grew older, I began to struggle with my career in ways I had not expected and couldn't readily dismiss.

After my contract with the technology company in Boston came to an end, I returned to working in the financial services industry, taking on several management roles, each coming with increased responsibilities further up the corporate leadership food chain. That trajectory culminated with an opportunity to be a Senior Vice President in one of the world's largest banks.

I was under-qualified for most aspects of the role, and I lacked the experience of managing the large, globally dispersed team that came with the position. But I was also confident in my abilities, intrigued by the substance of the regulatory work, and appreciative of the high executive salary that was an accelerated path to early retirement before I even turned 50. When they offered me the job, I took it without reservation.

I enjoyed the work and collaboration with my team, but over time the demands of my job increased, as did my need to be in the office. That, coupled with my long commute into Boston took me away from my son and Kim for much longer than I would have preferred. As the months passed, I felt like I was missing out on seeing him grow up, and that hurt. How much more of his childhood would I miss as he got older? What type of relationship could we have if I only saw him a handful of hours each day? Over time, that guilt began to weigh heavily on my heart and mind – a disconnect I could not internally reconcile.

I was standing at the crossroads. Down one path was financial bliss if I continued working at what I had once considered my "dream job." Down the other was *time*. More time to be with my son. More time to be with Kim. More time to take care of my mental health needs, my own essential restfulness, which is difficult to do when you're moving at the speed of high-finance and rarely resting.

My career was sucking time away, and in the process, creating an imbalanced mental health environment. Yes, my illness was in check at that moment. But as I became increasingly blinded by the empty promises of financial decadence, it was only a matter of time before a category 5 bipolar hurricane blew through, just like it had done twice before when I wasn't paying attention. Now, would Kim have helped me recognize the dangerous winds preceding that storm and steered me clear of trouble? In retrospect, probably. But that wasn't the plan. That wasn't the promise I had made to her, to Joy and Mom, to myself. The plan was to avoid any bipolar mania triggers before they occurred, to make my illness a top-most priority, to retain a healthy work/life balance and keep my mental health demons at a safe distance.

Eventually it became clear that my career was corroding the values that were instilled in me during my formative years by my father. Empathy. Selflessness. Above all, slowing down time, as best as you can. I realized that I needed to re-center my life on those values, and in the process, become the type of father that I had always envisioned myself being, to emulate my own dad. By choice, my father's career was a simple means to an end, far from what defined him. His identity evolved from the role he played best: the omnipresent parent – always accessible for whatever Joy and me needed, and whenever we needed it.

That clarity also helped me understand that there was no better place to become the father I had always aspired to be and maintain the stability my illness required than to return to Connecticut, to return home, settle down in a community that moved much more slowly than Boston, and give my son the privilege of growing up surrounded by our loving family. I had been grappling with that decision throughout my entire adult life – constrained by an illness that made me selfish, fearful, and ashamed. But with Kim by my side, and my son's needs now at the forefront of my decision-making, I was finally ready. It was time.

I shared my thoughts with Kim, and we talked extensively about the future of our family – how we wanted to raise our children, and where we wanted to live as we did. To my delight, over the previous few months, she had arrived at the same conclusion.

Kim's reasons for moving back to Connecticut were plentiful. More pragmatic than mine, but no less passionate. She missed being around her parents, the love they showered all of us with. She missed getting pedicures with her sister and playing golf with her brother. She wanted more of her mom's help taking care of our son – more than a two-hour drive to Salem could ever offer. She was not bothered by my longer commute to the city nor the additional parental responsibilities she took on because of it. She loved taking care of our son, and she wouldn't have traded it for anything. But after we talked further about it, she did have reservations about the stress of my executive career and its long-term threat to my overall health and stability.

"That is always on my mind, Brian," she said. "No matter where we live or how stable your life has become."

Together, Kim and I made the decision. We were moving home. We had no idea where we would live. I had no idea where I would work. But none of that mattered, Kim assured me. We would figure all that out in due time.

NAMI 24/7 Suicide
Prevention Crisis Hotline

Call 988

Or text HOME to 741741

Additional resources on bipolar disorder and other mental illnesses available at **BrianTalarcyzk.com**

A Note from the Author

A year after Kim and I returned home, the prophecy of that daguerreotype which fell from my chimney was fulfilled when our daughter was born. Along with the endearing dimple which adorns her left cheek, our daughter shares Kim's tenacious spirit, warm heart, and belief in herself to accomplish anything she sets her mind to. Our son was enthralled with his younger sister from the moment he held her in his arms for the first time, and Kim and I are elated to watch their love for each other grow stronger with each passing season.

My daughter's birth marked a critical turning point in my professional career. It was then that I returned to consulting, and committed to working remotely for every client I support. That decision has granted me the extra time I need to be a daily fixture in my children's lives. On my son's first day of kindergarten, as I watched him climb onto the bus and take off with his young school mates, I calculated just how much time I had recouped by removing my long commute to and from Boston. The magic number was 3,000 hours. In work terms, that's 375 additional days of PTO – time I spent playing Go Fish and checkers, cuddling while reading superhero books, and flipping pancakes high up in the air at breakfast for my children's amusement. Today I use that time to coach baseball and softball, to attend robotics tournaments, and to enjoy an occasional round of golf with Kim while both kids are in school.

My children are a source of great comfort in my life. Ironically, while I was once deathly afraid of having them because of my mental illness, they have become critical elements in regulating it. Parenting is a daily reminder of my need to maintain my equilibrium. In that balanced state, I derive the patience required to support them as they figure out their own young emotions. I try, as best I can, to listen to them before speaking, to learn from them before teaching, to love them before lashing out. I do not always have that patience, nor do I consistently maintain that balance. No parent can. My children's moods are perpetually changing, and it's difficult to ascertain what they need in every moment. But I strive for the emotional intelligence and self-control required to help them through. They deserve that, and my mental illness demands it.

The joys, and challenges, of parenthood have strengthened my partnership with Kim, who continues to support me in the day-to-day maintenance of my mental stability and overall health. She continues to ask, "How did you sleep last night?" as we sip our morning coffee, and I continue to answer with 100% honesty. Sometimes I don't sleep well. Sometimes my inadequacies as a parent, a husband, a work colleague, or a friend keep me awake at night thinking about how I might have screwed up. But Kim's pragmatism and benevolence keep me on track, and her willingness to take on any burden that may interfere with my biorhythmic repose is as obstinate today as it was when our son was first born.

For that, I am forever grateful.

When our daughter was finally out of diapers, and everyone was "peeing and pooping where they're supposed to," as Kim joyfully proclaimed, we added Sally, the final member of our family. Sally is our sweet and spunky goldendoodle, who swaggers about the house each day in search of crumbs to eat, socks to steal, and as many belly-rubs as we are willing to give her. I often find my children lying beside Sally in their bedrooms, using her back as a pillow and reading a book while she's taking a nap. In those moments, fond memories of Sammy, my beloved, floppy-eared healing companion, return. Just like Sammy did, Sally reminds us that a happy life can be as simple as chasing a ball across the yard, or taking a long walk in the woods with the people you love.

All our immediate relatives on both sides of our family still live within a short drive from us, and we see each other often. As our children grow up amongst their cousins, family traditions are being passed down, and new ones are forming. On Friday afternoons in the summer, I often leave work early and we take the kids to Joy's house for an impromptu pool party. After a cool, refreshing swim, we eat New Haven style pizza and drink birch beer and jam on acoustic guitars. Our regular pilgrimages to Yankee Stadium continue, as do our recurring wiffle ball games in the front yard. Each summer we cut the grass low, line the batter's box and base pads with spray paint, and invite as many of my son's and daughter's friends over as can fit on the field. We don't count balls or strikes, or even innings. We just play until the sun fades into the horizon and it's too dark to see the pitch coming in.

Joy and Greg remain two requisite and encouraging fixtures in my life. When I look back on all my time away from home, it's clear to me now that I had embarked on a quest to find two very specific things: the love that Joy and Greg have for one another, and the adoring community in which their love is nourished. The devoted relationship they have cultivated over the years is as compelling to others as the empathy they provided me in my time of need. While I do not share their Christian faith, I am thankful for the many virtues their beliefs have taught me. Without those virtues, and without Joy and Greg's unparalleled selflessness, I would never have found the courage to crawl out of the darkness.

After being diagnosed with stenosis in her lower back a few years ago, my mother was forced to stop driving, and in her older age now, she requires more attention and care, which Joy and I work together to provide her. As we shuffle her from one doctor's appointment to the next, we're reminded of all the support she has given both of us over the years, and the values she has instilled: kindness; humility; living simply, and never suffering under the weight of financial debt. She taught us the importance of not taking oneself too seriously, and of always giving others the benefit of the doubt, even if they don't deserve it. She never told us these things, never pulled any of us aside and preached to us. We learned them from what she did and did not do. We learned them from her silent serenity.

Though it's been nearly 25 years since my father died, he remains as prevalent in my life today as he was when he was alive. When I am struggling with important decisions, he still speaks to me through the lyrics of songs he plays on the radio at the precise time I need to hear them. When I start moving too fast and veering off a mentally healthy track, he drops cigarette butts on the ground beside my car to caution me. When I am sad that he isn't sitting on the sidelines beside Mom and me as we watch my son and daughter run around the ball field, he suddenly appears in the sky, his spirit taking the form of a lone eagle encircling us, looking down on his grandchildren, keeping us safe. I do not question these ethereal gestures nor do I dismiss their meaning. Doing so would refute two important lessons I have learned from my mental illness: death is as much a part of life as the air we breathe, and suppressing grief can have dangerous repercussions.

When Josh and Jason were in high school, Joy and Greg started another family tradition. They sat their boys down and talked to them at length about bipolar disorder. They shared how the illness has manifested itself in our family, and particularly how it affected Uncle Danny and me. They asked them to be mindful of what may be lurking inside their genetic makeup, and they offered a few ways the boys could be on the lookout. Kim and I will pass this tradition down to our children as well when they are old enough by sharing this book with them and other means. It's my hope that the mental health conversation in our family will never be concealed again. There is too much at stake if it is.

It's been fifteen years since my last battle with psychosis or depression or other bipolar turbulence. Time has altered my perception of my mental illness, and what scares me the most now is not what might happen in the future, but what could have happened in the past. Many factors contributed to my survival, but none have been more important than the love and compassion I received from the family who raised me. I had a father who instilled confidence in me, a mother who is the personification of grace and tranquility, and an older sister and brother-in-law who exemplify humility and resolve. What if that weren't the case? Where might my insanity have taken me if my childhood were afflicted by neglect, or intense pressure to achieve greatness against my desires, or far worse – by violent acts born of hatred? I am blessed it was not, and that is why I am alive.

My "journey" with bipolar disorder has been a long one, but it is one I have not travelled alone. The truth is, while I am the one who has a mental illness, I am far from the only member of my family who suffered from the anguish and uncertainty it once caused. We all survived together.

We continue to survive. Together.

Acknowledgments

This memoir would not have been possible without the literary talents and extensive support of Carla Stockton, prestigious author of many works, including *Too Much of Nothing: Notes on Feminism, Identity, and Womankood*. Thank you, Carla, for helping me breathe life into this story and encouraging me to continue challenging myself. I could not have done this without you.

Special thanks as well to Andi Cumbo and Caroline Topperman at Mountain Ash Press for their publishing acuity, editorial skills, and getting this book across the finish line.

More Thank Yous. . .

In addition to the people referenced in this memoir, there have been many others who helped me push through my mental health struggles through the years and I will forever be grateful to each of them:

To Chris, for your wisdom and encouragement that continues to help me put things in perspective and keep moving forward. My sincerest gratitude for our life-long friendship and everything you've done for me.

To my other "circle of trust" friends – Steve, Heather, Adam, Janice, Paula, Cousin Ricky, Niki, Katy, and Glenn – had it not been for your unmitigated love, selflessness, and all the laughter we shared, I am certain the demons would have won.

To Jack & Coryn, Greg & Tom, and all the other musicians I've had the pleasure of playing with throughout my life, thank you for keeping my spirit alive, one song at a time. Music will forever be my true north, and may we keep on following its promise together.

To Orus, the leader of the band and our guiding light, may you rest in eternal peace, brother. Thank you for encouraging me to complete this memoir, and for leaving all of us with an example of how to live our lives.

To my local friends, school teachers, neighbors, fellow youth sports coaches, and little league parents, may the mental health conversation in our community continue. Our children and their children and their children will be all the better for it.

Finally, to all the Scecinas & Talarczyks & Bartholomews & Shields & Walshes & Pantalones, local to New England and afar, thank you for instilling the importance of family in me, and accepting me for who I am, not what I have.

I love you all.